SÜSSKIND VON TRIMBERG
German-Jewish minnesinger of the thirteenth century
(*From a manuscript in the University Library, Heidelberg*)

THE JEWISH CONTRIBUTION
TO CIVILISATION

By the same Author

THE LAST FLORENTINE REPUBLIC
  (London 1925 : Italian translation,
  Florence 1929)

THE CASALE PILGRIM
  (London 1929)

L'APÔTRE DES MARRANES
  (Paris 1930)

HISTORY OF THE JEWS IN VENICE
  (Philadelphia 1930 : Italian translation,
  Rome 1933)

A JEWISH BOOK OF DAYS
  (London 1931)

HISTORY OF THE MARRANOS
  (Philadelphia 1932)

LETTERE DI DONATO GIANNOTTI A
    PIERO VETTORI
  (In collaboration with R. Ridolfi :
  Florence 1932)

THE NEPHEW OF THE ALMIGHTY
  (London 1933)

A LIFE OF MENASSEH BEN ISRAEL
  (Philadelphia 1934)

A SHORT HISTORY OF THE JEWISH
    PEOPLE
  (London 1936)

ETC.

THE
JEWISH CONTRIBUTION TO CIVILISATION

BY

CECIL ROTH

MACMILLAN AND CO., LIMITED
ST. MARTIN'S STREET. LONDON
1938

PRINTED IN GREAT BRITAIN

To

My Brother

LEON ROTH

'Tra cotanto senno'
(*Inferno*, iv. 102)

PREFACE

THIS work is intended as a contribution towards the settlement of a discussion of long standing, which is now once again to the fore. It is alleged by modern anti-Semites (in order to justify a prejudice which, in these ostensibly tolerant times, they hesitate to base on theological grounds) that the Jew is essentially a middleman, who has produced nothing: that he is an alien excrescence on European life: and that the influence which he has had on western culture, during the past two thousand years, has been entirely negative, if not deleterious. Such a criticism demands an analysis based not on theory but on fact: and this is what I have endeavoured to provide. I have set out to write this book as objectively as possible. I am making no attempt to evaluate the Jewish genius, or even to decide whether such a thing exists. Perhaps, on the basis of the material collected in this volume, it may be possible to come to some conclusion upon these problems in future. My task has been a comparatively simple, if laborious, one. I· have tried to assemble and set down in this volume a representative selection (at least) of the contributions made to the civilisation, the culture and the amenities of the western world by persons of Jewish lineage. The common qualities, and the philosophical implications, of those contributions, I leave others to investigate.

There has been in this no question of a theological test of any sort. To-day (as has been indicated), the assault upon the Jew is made on "racial", not religious grounds. Persons in whose veins there runs the blood[1] of a single Jew as far as three generations back—of one traceable Jewish great-grandparent, that is—are officially penalised on that account to-day in Nazi Germany, on the plea that their stock is alien, and *ipso facto* harmful to German, "Nordic", and European cultural life. The Jewish people, moreover, is consistently blamed for the actions of persons of Jewish origin, who not only have cut themselves off from Jewish life, but even have professed markedly anti-Jewish sentiments, which they have not scrupled to translate into action. Hence one is justified in attempting to evaluate the Jewish contribution in terms of Jews, and not of Judaism alone—by taking, that is, into account those contributions made by persons of traceable Jewish ancestry, whatever their religious affiliation or sympathies.

I must confess, however, that normally, in the absence of such a religious distinction, I would find it difficult to assess precisely what a Jew is. I have no intention to enter into any of the current controversies on "race" and "blood", nationality and religion. I can only state, as an historical fact, that however distinct the Jews may have been from their neighbours ethnologically at the beginning of their settlement in Europe, this distinction has been progressively modified. For countless generations, every European country (not excluding Germany) pursued as a point of principle the policy of encouraging conversions from Judaism to the dominant

[1] This term in the present connotation is of course based on an ancient and exploded embryological theory. To make use of it (as in the present instance) is sometimes convenient: to draw further implications (and still more to make it the basis of a political theory or policy) is absurd to a degree. So also the terms "Aryan" and "Non-Aryan", while occasionally convenient in use, are a scientific monstrosity. It is one of the most regrettable features in contemporary intellectual life that an imposing pseudo-scientific structure—sometimes dominating public affairs—can be erected on the basis of a linguistic misusage.

faith by every means which lay in its power, fair or foul. There were baptisms from conviction. There were baptisms from material interest. There were forced baptisms, on an enormous scale, in more countries than one. If this violent pressure has been relaxed during the last century and a half, the tendency has been maintained by the constant procession of those converted from conviction or from convenience, or who have drifted insensibly into the majority by the gradual process of assimilation.

On the other hand, even at the darkest hour of degradation, there were not lacking Christians who saw fresh spiritual potentialities in Judaism and became integrated in the Jewish community as "children of Abraham our Father". The numbers in question were never great: but a process of this sort, continuous during a period of two thousand years, necessarily modified whatever purity of stock may originally have existed. To this must be added the degree of illicit admixture which was inevitable on either side, the result of scenes of violence or interludes of romance, and the children of mixed birth who came into the world after every pogrom.

It is impossible to escape the conclusion that the much-discussed "racial" differentiation between the Jews and their neighbours—especially in those countries, like Germany, in which their settlement is of oldest date—is largely artificial. The amount of traceable Jewish blood among non-Jews is surprisingly great, even if one goes back for as little as a single century. *Vice versa*, few Jews can fail to have (whether they realise it or no) some tincture of non-Jewish blood in their veins. To quote the words of the late Lucien Wolf (which gather fresh point in the light of these facts): "the Jew who emerged from the ghetto was no longer a Palestinian

Semite, but an essentially modern European, who differed
from his Christian fellow-countrymen only in the circumstances that his religion was of the older Semitic form,
and that his physical type had become sharply defined
through a slightly more rigid exclusiveness in the matter
of marriages than that practised by Protestants and
Roman Catholics".

My use of the term "Jew" etc. in the following pages
hence denotes a person whose immediate ancestors
professed the Jewish religion.

The differentiation is clearly to some extent an
artificial one. The background and the upbringing of
the Jewish and non-Jewish elements are in many instances
identical. In the case of persons of mixed ancestry, the
fifty or twenty-five per cent. of Jewish blood cannot be
proved the decisive factor, in the determination of the
particular genius of a poet or playwright or philanthropist.
No more is it, of course, in the determination of the
character of a criminal, a decadentist, or a revolutionary.
If the Jewish people is to receive a full measure of blame
for the one category, it is justified in claiming some
measure of credit for the other.

It must be realised that the author has no intention
of giving here anything in the nature of a connected
account of those subjects on which he touches. Those
who may be interested in "Jewish art" or "Jewish
medicine" must be referred to the specialist works
devoted to those questions. It would have been beyond
the power of a single man to give a satisfactory survey
of the many fields of human activity on which this book
impinges; and the author will have served his purpose
if he has indicated, by mentioning some outstanding
names, how Jews have collaborated in each sphere.
The psychological and philosophical nature of the contribution he is not in a position to judge: nor can he agree

with what is generally so confidently asserted on these subjects. The Jew is distinguished, perhaps, by a slightly greater degree of intellectualisation: possibly by a freshness of outlook, natural in one whose approach tends to be external; and, in consequence, by a faculty for synthesis and for introducing new ideas. He is apt to shew, in fact, certain characteristics inevitable in persons who belong, through the circumstances of their history, to a single sociological group. To say more is hazardous.

The outcome of my enquiry has been more than a little surprising, even to myself. There is no branch of human culture or civilisation which Jews (I refrain from speaking of "the Jews") have not touched and enriched. In some branches, the contribution has been more significant than in others. But, whether we consider literature or medicine or science or exploration or humanitarianism or art, the Jew has been prominent. That he has not produced giants in all these branches is of course true; for the same is the case with every other fraction of humanity. England has produced only one Shakespeare, Germany only one Goethe: and who will say that they stand on a higher level, whether as thinkers or as masters of the written word, than the prophet Isaiah? England gave birth to no philosopher on the same plane as Spinoza: no musician who excels Mendelssohn: no contemporary painter, perhaps, of the calibre of Pissarro or Liebermann. In the fields of medicine and science, moreover, the Jewish contribution during the past century can well stand comparison with that of any country of the world, without exception—and that notwithstanding the fact that emancipated Jewry numbered, until a few years ago, far less than the population of one of the Balkan or Scandinavian States.

Certain assertions made in this volume may appear to some readers extravagant. I can only plead that I have taken the utmost pains to verify my statements, and have included nothing for which I was unable to find reliable authority. Many will doubtless be surprised, for example, to discover the extent of the participation of the Jews in the maritime discoveries of the fifteenth century. But the data are indubitably as I have stated them—my account cannot claim even the merit of originality. It must be borne in mind, after all, that general ignorance of a fact does not necessarily weaken its validity.

I am certain, moreover, that any baseless claims which may have been made, notwithstanding my caution, are far outnumbered by the omissions, whether due to ignorance or to the obvious impossibility of being able to ascertain the precise antecedents of every individual. Nothing has been further from my mind than any sort of Jewish chauvinism. A man or a group of men does not deserve particular merit for having performed his or their duty. Only when the fact is impugned does demonstration become necessary.

My indebtedness in the composition of a work of such complexity is too great to permit detailed acknowledgement to all who have assisted me. I must, however, express my deep gratitude at least to Dr. Charles Singer, who revised the chapters on the Jews in Medicine and kindred branches, in the light of his vast knowledge : to my brother, Professor Leon Roth, of the University of Jerusalem, for contributing the essential part of the section on Philosophy : and to my wife, who with heroic application compiled the Index.

CECIL ROTH

London, December, 1937.

CONTENTS

LIST OF ILLUSTRATIONS

CHAPTER I

THE HEBRAIC HERITAGE

§1

JEWISH History is approximately divided into two nearly equal stretches, the dividing line between them falling (whether one adopts the theological or the political standpoint) at the age of Jesus of Nazareth, or the destruction of Jerusalem by the Romans a generation after his death. During the early period, roughly coinciding with the nineteen centuries before the beginning of the Christian era, the Jews (or rather, as they are better termed over most of this period, the Israelites) constituted one of the many lesser nationalities of the Near East, distinguished from their neighbours principally by their religious beliefs and by the superior ethical code which resulted therefrom. During the latter, roughly coinciding with the nineteen centuries of the Christian era, they have been a people scattered throughout the world, in all continents and in almost every land, still adhering to their distinctive religious system but exercising their influence as individuals rather than as a collectivity.

It is with the latter period, best distinguished as the "Jewish", that this work will in the main deal. But it would be misleading to omit all reference to the Heritage of Israel, which, taken over by Christianity (in a somewhat modified or expanded form, as Jew and Christian respectively hold) has left an ineradicable influence upon the structure of the modern world.

B   1

It is a commonplace that modern civilisation is an amalgam of three elements. From Rome we have received our conceptions of law, and to some extent of politics. From Greece—operating sometimes through Rome—we have our philosophy, as well as our aesthetic standards, whether in literature or in the other arts. And to Israel, the western world owes its religion and its ethics.[1]

The basis of the Hebraic contribution to Western civilisation, and the Hebrew's greatest gift to humanity, is the ideal of the One God, Creator of Heaven and Earth. According to the Biblical account, this conception, familiar to the Patriarchs, was reaffirmed to their descendants at the foot of Mount Sinai; according to the critical view, it was a gradual discovery, fully realised only some centuries later. In any case, it is fundamental to a consideration of the Hebraic element in modern life. Greek and Indian thinkers may have had a glimmering of the same truth. Only the Hebrew proclaimed it aloud, adhered to it through persecution and vilification, yielded up his life for its sake, and made it central to his whole existence. The Jews of to-day, adhering to the monotheistic tradition of their fathers, number some sixteen million souls. But, through Jesus and Paul, the Hebraic teaching (in a modified form, yet basically identical) passed to Europe, and is now cherished by 650,000,000 Christians throughout the world. Six centuries later, it was reiterated in Arabia, with desert sternness, by Mohammed, and is now the creed of 220,000,000 Muslims. The kernel of both religions is the terse declaration which the Hebrews believed to be uttered by the Deity Himself

---

[1] To this conventional tripartite division may be added the modern contribution of technical efficiency, which constitutes the outward shell (too often confused with the substance) of present-day civilisation. In this, Jews as individuals have played a noteworthy part, which will be considered in detail in later chapters of this book.

from Sinai: *I am the Lord thy God. . . . Thou shalt have no other gods before Me.*

There is, of course, more in monotheism than this dogmatic self-affirmation of Deity. The most unfettered thinker of to-day, who steadfastly refuses to subscribe to any theological dictum, owes nevertheless to Hebraism the breaking of the shackles of polytheism—the worship of animals and images, of the stars and planets, of a plurality of deities such as those in the Hellenic pantheon, with their human appetites and lusts and failings. There was in this a degrading and demoralising effect, which cannot escape the notice of any student of ancient history. The commanding part taken by the moral code in the Biblical religious system is too familiar to require any amplification here. But the ideas of the value of human life, the sanctity of the home and the dignity of the marital relationship, which nominally prevail at the present time, are essentially a Biblical heritage. For the religion of the ancient Hebrews was not circumscribed in its application. As has been remarked by a modern thinker, the struggle for justice and the struggle against other gods in the Biblical age, instead of being two separate movements, are logically one and the same. Even at the present time, when the conception of mediation between man and his Creator and the cult of hagiology sometimes tend to obscure among the ignorant the monotheistic basis of European spiritual life, the clarion voice of the Hebrew prophets is an ever-present reminder of that underlying principle of Unity to which every Church adheres.

The monotheistic idea had moreover a far-reaching influence on European thought, even in its least theological aspects. We are used to connect Hebraism with morals, and we are apt to think that we have thereby exhausted its significance. But Hebraism has significance for science too. Science is the search for regularity. It is the attempt to find order and system. But regularity, order and system are only derivatives from the unity postulated in the Hebraic conception of God. The modern reaction against 'Laws of Nature' need blind us no more than the modern reaction against Puritanism to the immense significance, both historical[1] and actual, of monotheism. The triumphs of modern science have been made possible only by the 'superb and unshaken confidence in the rationality of the Universe', which is one of the ultimate heritages of the Hebrew prophets and the ethical monotheism that they taught. If Duty, with the capital D of traditional morality, is the 'stern daughter of the voice of God', the Law of Science is that Voice itself.

A necessary extension of the idea of the Divine Unity is that of the equality of *all* before this one God. Out of the same seed which gave birth to the conception of the Chosen People hence developed ultimately, in the Hebrew prophets and in the Talmud, the idea of the brotherhood of all peoples. The brotherhood of peoples makes abhorrent the idea of internecine war: and all the dreams of universal peace that have stirred mankind down to our own day are to be traced back to that Messianic vision of the prophet Isaiah, of an age when people shall not lift up its sword against people, nor shall they learn war any more. To us to-day, it may seem trite; but there was an epoch-making originality in it in an age when conquest was regarded as the natural right of the stronger, and a victorious war the ideal of every powerful state. Contemporary developments have given the Hebraic attitude a new force and value; and to-day it is no exaggeration to say that the future of civilisation depends upon the renewal of the Prophetic dream.

[1] The point is made by Whitehead, *Science and the Modern World*, Chapter I.

The God of Israel was, moreover, a God of Righteousness. This overwhelming passion for righteousness is insisted upon in the Bible hardly less than the monotheistic idea : for the one is the concrete expression of the other. Here was no impersonal deity, indifferent to men's affairs, nor yet a selfish one, swayed by flattery and bribes ; but a God Who loved goodness, Who abhorred oppression, Who laid down positive standards of conduct between man and his fellow, Who insisted on justice, truth and morality. The ideals of Social Justice, which Western reformers are endeavouring to carry into practice in our own day, are the ideals taught by Isaiah, Amos, and Micah, now become part of the common heritage of mankind. It would be absurd to claim that the affirmation of righteousness as a fundamental principle in the conduct of human affairs is peculiar to the Hebrew : it is to be found in the teachings of Buddha, of Confucius, of the Greek philosophers. These, however, made their protest against superstition and plea for righteousness, almost simultaneously, some two hundred years later than Amos and Hosea had sounded the call in Palestine, in the eighth century B.C.—and this, according to the traditional view, was nearly a thousand years after those same ideas had been proclaimed at Sinai. Moreover, the non-Hebrew thinkers in effect made ethics a substitute for religion. It is the enduring glory of the Hebrews that they made ethics central in religion—the ideal to which the western world pays at least lip-service. Nor is there any comparison between the academic reasoning of Plato and the burning hunger for righteousness which is characteristic of the Prophets.

In all this, the Old Testament is even now no less potent a force in the modern world than the New. But it is impossible to neglect in this connexion the essential Hebraic content of the Gospels. Jesus was a

Jew not only by birth, but also by upbringing: and some of the most striking of his sayings were part and parcel of the Rabbinic teaching of his day. The Lord's Prayer and the Sermon on the Mount have been paralleled from the Talmud, verse for verse and phrase for phrase. The Golden Rule—"Do unto thy neighbour as thou wouldst be done by"—is only a paraphrase of the recommendation of Jesus' older contemporary, Hillel, who died when the founder of Christianity was only ten years old: "What is distasteful to thee, do not to thy neighbour." The Rabbis of the age of Jesus joined with him, too, in averring that the Pentateuchal injunction, "Love thy neighbour as thyself" (Leviticus xix. 18) was a fundamental principle of religion. "This is the whole Law: the rest is but commentary", this same Hillel pronounced.

§II

When the Christian believer goes to Church to pray, he does not realise that he is making use of another Jewish innovation. In antiquity, the fundamental fact of public worship was animal—sometimes human—sacrifice. So, too, with the primitive Hebrews. But, from an early date, this method of worship was restricted by a prohibition to offer up sacrifice outside the Central Sanctuary which was ultimately situated in Jerusalem. Thus, even in remote times, pious believers in the more distant parts of the country had perforce dispensed with sacrifice when they poured out their hearts to God: and the Prophets, with their bitter denunciation of formalism without piety, strengthened this tendency. During the Babylonian Exile, when Jerusalem and its Temple lay in ashes, the nation dispensed altogether with sacrifice. To this period probably belongs the origin of the *Beth haKeneseth* or Synagogue—the "place of assembly", where the reading of God's law was accompanied by prayer. Hence, in the period of the Second Temple, a Synagogue was to be found in every city and township of Palestine, and the conception became familiar to the non-Jewish world by the erection of similar institutions in all the principal centres of the Diaspora.

Thus, after the destruction of Jerusalem in A.D. 70, when the Central Sanctuary ceased to exist, no irreparable blow was felt by Judaism as a religious system. Its spiritual potentialities, indeed, were strengthened. The Synagogues continued to function regularly, prayer taking permanently the place of sacrifice :[1] and this, at the time considered the most bitter element in the national disaster, subsequently came to be regarded by the Jew—earlier than any other branch of the human family—the natural mode of worship.

When Christianity began to expand through the world, under the aegis of Paul and his companions, the first centres of missionary activity were the Synagogues, to be found by now in all the most important cities of the Roman Empire. These, rather than the Pagan Temples, formed the model and the ideal of the new sect. First, the Christian missionaries attempted to convert the Jewish congregations to their own way of belief : in case of failure, they set up their own sectarian Synagogues. In either circumstances it was the Jewish, not Pagan, system which was followed. That which to us is so natural and so obvious must have appeared, to some contemporaries, a remarkable innovation ; but, in the long run, it carried the day. And, some six centuries later, when Islam began its triumphant course, the Mosque too, with its

---

[1] It is not generally realised how long the traces of animal sacrifice, on the pagan model, remained in the Church. Thus, for example, it was customary to slaughter a stag in St. Paul's Cathedral in London each Christmas until long after the Reformation—nearly fifteen centuries later than the Jews had abandoned such practises.

sternly Puritan procedure, was modelled upon the
spiritualised places of worship of the two Peoples of the
Book.[1]

The Church, of course, owes much more to the
Synagogue than this—though this is the essential. Its
structure and "orientation" copy the Synagogue, in
which worship was directed towards Jerusalem—that is,
in much of Europe, to the East. The stoup at the door,
for holy water, seems to reproduce the laver at the
entrance of the older (and, to this day, the Italian)
Synagogues, which enabled worshippers to precede their
Godliness by Cleanliness, as the Rabbis had prescribed.
The light before the High Altar was a reminiscence of
the Perpetual Lamp, which (following the example set
in the Temple) was maintained day and night in the
"lesser sanctuaries" which replaced it. Incense followed
Old Testament prescription, reverenced though not
practised by the Jews after the destruction of Jerusalem.
The separation of the sexes in public worship, which
Jewish reformers have tended to abolish in recent years,
was frequently practised by the Church, even after the
Reformation. And, when the ecstatic Christian revivalist
cries *Hallelujah*, or the devout worshipper pronounces
Amen, he is using a Hebrew term, familiar in synagogal
worship long before the Church came into being.

So, too, with ceremonial. Christian Baptism is to be
traced back to the symbolic bath which the proselyte
to Judaism had to undergo. The Communion Service
was modelled upon the *Seder* of Passover Eve. Though
theologians may dispute the exact degree of interdepend-
ence, it is clear that Jesus' last "Supper" with his
followers on this occasion constituted the prototype,
and his words the specific injunction, which lay at the

---

[1] The very term Mosque is apparently derived from the Judæo-Aramaic
masgeda.

bottom of this all-important Christian institution: while the elements recall the ceremonial breaking of bread and benediction of wine on the eve of Sabbaths and Festivals. The Lectionaries of the Church continue the tradition of the cycle of the public reading of the Law in the Synagogues. This, again, was not so obvious a procedure as centuries of usage have made it appear to us; but it was rendered essential in ancient Judaea in order to familiarise the people with the regulation of Jewish religious and social life which the Pentateuch embodied, and for that reason had been a regular practice ever since the fifth century B.C. As time went on, it became usual to read also a section from the Prophets, containing a passage reminiscent of the other: this has its echo in the Second Lesson of the Church. No small part of Christian worship is made up of the Psalms of David: while its original hymns are based upon these so closely as to be in certain cases (e.g. the English "O God, our Help in Ages Past") mere paraphrases.

§III

Though the influence of the Bible is greatest in the Western World on the theological and ethical side, it is discernible also in the field of politics. This does not imply that the Jews enjoyed a very high political development, in the sense that this is true of the Greek city-states and the Roman republic. Nevertheless, it has been suggested that the "people of the land" referred to at the time of the Hebrew monarchy constituted some sort of democratic assembly, and in the time of the Maccabees and the Last Commonwealth there certainly existed a popular Council, whose assent was considered necessary for any constitutional change.

The importance of Hebraism in the political heritage of modern Europe, however, does not lie in exterior details, but in the spirit. The Hebrew Monarchy came into existence under the influence of a conception, to be found nowhere else in antiquity, which regarded the constitution as the result of a tripartite agreement, or covenant, between the People, the Ruler, and the Deity. This may sound elementary. But, if the Deity is the embodiment of justice and righteousness, it follows that the monarchy is dependent on the maintenance, not only of certain religious, but also of human values. We see this conception in the story of the oldest Hebrew monarch, Saul: it reaches its highest development in the career of David. It underlies the outline of the ideal monarchy which is given in the Mosaic code. And, above all, it is implicit in the whole course of subsequent Hebrew history, when Prophet after Prophet dared to admonish the ruler for his breach of the fundamental laws, for his callousness to human misery, for his oppression of the poor. It is remarkable that in almost all cases (there are few exceptions) the Prophet's reproofs are listened to with forbearance, as though to acknowledge his right to criticise and the fundamental justice of his claim. A remarkable phrase occurs in the description of the king's prerogatives in the Pentateuch (Deuteronomy xvii. 20)—a phrase which sums up the Hebraic ideal of the monarchy: "that his heart be not lifted up *above his brethren.*"

In the course of the sixteenth and seventeenth centuries, when the study of the Bible in the vernacular acquired a new vogue in western Europe, these stories were revitalised. In every land—but especially in the English-speaking countries—pious Christians identified themselves with the Israelites of old, people with people and tyrant with tyrant. When a nation thinks in this way, Absolutism cannot be condoned. In just the same manner as the oppression of Israel by the Court of Samaria had been against God's expressed will, so (imagined the Puritans of the seventeenth century) they were fulfilling the desire of God when they fought against arbitrary government. Elijah's reproof of tyranny on the part of Ahab applied no less (they considered) to the unconstitutional attempts of Charles I. They read an indictment of the Star Chamber in the ratiocinations of Amos, and found that Ship Money was condemned implicitly in the episode of Naboth's vineyard. The Bible, moreover, was in diametrical opposition to the idea of the Divine descent of kings, which was one of the basic principles of primitive absolutism.

Hence the Hebraic conception of the tripartite agreement between God, His people, and the ruler, a breach of which might forfeit the latter's throne, lay at the basis of the reaffirmation of Constitutional Government in England, which was the final outcome of the great cataclysm of the seventeenth century. This, in turn, was taken over by the fathers of the American Revolution. It was Hebraic mortar (in Lecky's famous phrase) that cemented the foundations of the Republic; and not without reason did the first seal it adopted depict the overthrow of Pharaoh in the Red Sea, with the motto: "Rebellion to Tyrants is obedience to God." A few years later this same conception was adopted to some extent (though with a different philosophical background) in France. Imitated in the course of the nineteenth century in almost every other country of the western world, it is thus intimately connected with the conception of Constitutional Government such as we knew it until yesterday.

§IV

The literary influence of the Hebrew scriptures has been vast. In a score of European languages, the Bible was the first book to be translated: and among so many peoples it first set a literary tradition, establishing the standard of orthography, composition, and style. For the whole of Europe, but especially for the so-called "Nordic" peoples, the Scriptures continued to play an almost dominant literary role. This was not the case in the Dark Ages only, or with unimportant tribes. It was Luther's translation of the Bible into High German which rendered that particular dialect supreme, and first demonstrated the force and malleability of the German language. It hence marks the beginning of modern German literature. The greatest German orator of to-day, when he holds his thousands of hearers spell-bound by his command of language, apparently does not realise that he is making use of an instrument which became what it is to-day only through the force of the Hebrew scriptures.

In England the stimulus of the Biblical literature, in the incomparable version "authorised" by King James in 1611, has been incalculable. Generation after generation, the Englishman heard the Bible read in Church, and studied it at home. In many cases, it was the only Book: in all, it was the principal Book. At last its cadences, its music, its phraseology, sank into his mind and became part of his being. He quoted it, intentionally, more frequently than modern taste approves; more often still, he quoted it unwittingly. Hence by slow degrees his daily speech was not merely enriched, but to some extent moulded, by its influence. Phrase after phrase, figure after figure, became current in the English language, which would be a strangely denuded thing if all these Semitic influences were removed.

Few people can realise to-day to what an extent their ordinary conversation is coloured by the Hebrew scriptures. When a man escapes by the skin of his teeth, when he goes down to the sea in ships, when he enquires whether a leopard can change its spots, when he threatens to make his enemy lick the dust, he is not so much quoting the Bible, as using Biblical phrases which have become an inseparable part of his language. The way of a man with a maid, the tale that is told, the multitude of counsellors, the crown of her husband, the pride that goes before a fall, the bread of idleness, the way of an eagle, the apple of the eye, the wife of a man's bosom, the love that is strong as death, all became naturalised in English through familiarity with the Proverbs of Solomon. In chapters xxx and xxxi of that work alone, it is possible to enumerate no fewer than twenty-four passages which are familiar to every Englishman in his daily round. Even so un-ecclesiastical a conception as "a thirsty soul" (not necessarily used to-day in its original meaning) is based on Proverbs xxv. 25. "He who runs may read" is a mere mistranslation of Habakkuk ii. 2 (the correct rendering is "He who reads may run"). . . . The list could be protracted indefinitely. Similarly, we owe many phrases to the earlier Prayer-Book version of the Psalms, based upon Coverdale's rendering. There is only one work the influence of which on the English language is comparable to that of the Bible—the plays of William Shakespeare. But, as has recently been demonstrated, Shakespeare's use of the Bible was itself very considerable, and its stimulus may be traced throughout his writings.

This Biblical inspiration is not necessarily direct. English prose of the heroic period is soaked and soaked again in the Biblical atmosphere. Bunyan's *Pilgrim's Progress*, for example (which with the Bible itself and Foxe's *Book of Martyrs*, constituted the normal library of the average English yeoman for many generations) is so far imbued

with the Biblical atmosphere as to be both in conception
and in language a direct continuation of that tradition.
Through this and similar works, the Hebraic influence
was refracted, the original radiance appearing from a
dozen different directions and in as many different forms.
It is difficult in fact to imagine what the English language
and English literature and the English mind would now
be but for the influence of the Scriptures—the influence,
that is, of the ancestors of the Jewish people of
to-day, as expressed in and through their literary heritage.
Moreover, the Hebraic faculty for associating moral ideas
with the name of things (bread, wine and so on) and
sublimating them into a call to virtuous living, has contributed to the general background of the English mind
and the thought and style of generations of writers.

Apart from this literary influence, which English and
German illustrate to such a remarkable degree, every
language of Europe has been enriched by various Hebrew
words (not for the most part used to-day in their precise
original sense) which have now become wholly naturalised:
Jubilee, Satan, Paradise, Cherub, Armageddon, and many
others.　Moreover, all European languages contain words
which are now reserved for conveying certain specifically
Hebrew conceptions.　The Greek $\overset{\text{\'{}}}{\alpha}\gamma\gamma\epsilon\lambda o\varsigma$ means a mes-
senger—by no means the same thing as our "angel".
The Latin *benedicere*, to Commend, is far removed
from the conception now universally found in European
languages, to Bless—that is, to pronounce a formula
conveying spiritual beneficence. To adore is very
different from to pray—the meaning of the Latin *adorare*.
The case is identical with terms such as "The Lord",
"Prophet", etc.　The words may be derived from the
Greek or Latin, but their "semantic" meaning is essentially Hebraic.　This is not a point of mere philological
interest.　It must be realised that the reason why the

words in question had to be borrowed by the European tongues from the Hebrew, or else to have their original meanings modified, is because no conceptions of the sort, or words to express them, hitherto existed. They are therefore an index of how far the spiritual and ethical life of Europe has been enriched by the Hebraic heritage.

Even from the point of view of literary form, the Biblical influence has been a potent one. The Book of Ruth is as perfect an idyll as literature can provide, the Story of Susannah is an admirable detective tale, the Book of Tobit has provided the direct model for a novel of our own day. Moreover, the Old Testament may be said to have provided the world with the pattern of its present historiography. According to the Russian thinker Berdyaev, the Jews were the first people to contribute the concept of "historical" to world history, "thereby discharging the essence of their specific mission". The Chronicles of Kings and relations of individual episodes are a general phenomenon in ancient literature. But the grandiose Biblical conception, starting with the creation of the Universe and continuing through the centuries to almost contemporary events, was something different. The Hebrew was brought by it to a realisation of his own relative position in the scheme of things—as the heir to the ages but neither their author nor their causation. Particular significance from this point of view attaches to the Book of Daniel—perhaps the first expression of the true philosophy of history. "In it," writes Berdyaev, "we are made to feel dramatically that mankind is engaged in a process that tends towards a definite goal." And in Daniel's interpretation of Nebuchadnezzar's dream, this thinker sees the earliest attempt to attribute a design to history—an attempt which was later to be repeated and developed in Christian philosophy.

The Bible, moreover, was only incidentally interested in dynastic history. The People is central throughout: and the modern type of history which centres its attention upon the ordinary man, neglecting the Kings on the one side and the Captains on the other, found its prototype in Biblical narrative. It was not until after a lapse of many centuries that an audacious pioneer of our own day was able to revert more closely to the Biblical conception, attempting a universal history which should trace the record, not of a few centuries or groups only, but of the whole evolution of mankind.

§v

The outcome of what has been stated above may be summed up very briefly. The Jewish people is largely a product of the Bible, exerted however under the influence of some thirty-five centuries of history, seldom uneventful and frequently tragic. In the peoples of the western world, the Biblical influence has not been quite so direct or so protracted. Yet, for a period varying between ten and twenty centuries, it has been an integral part of their background, modifying their religion, their thought, their conceptions—to some extent, even their politics and their language. Deprive modern Europe and America of the Hebraic heritage, and the result would be barely recognisable. It would be a different, and it would be a poorer, thing. In Woodrow Wilson's expressive words, "if we could but have the eyes to see the subtle elements of thought which constitute the gross substance of our present habit, both as regards the sphere of private life, and as regards the action of the state, we should easily discover how very much besides religion we owe to the Jew".

CHAPTER II

§1

THE Jew's association with the European world began far back in Classical times. There are indications that even during the Biblical period he was known in the Greek isles. Aristotle encountered one, who is reported to have given him much information, during his travels in the company of Alexander the Great. They were very numerous in Alexandria—long the capital of Hellenic culture—from the moment of its foundation: and they were found in Greece itself at least from the third century B.C., when the classical glories had barely departed from Athens and from Thebes. In Rome and elsewhere in Italy, they were numerous from the second century B.C.; and Italian Jews may still be encountered whose families trace their descent, according to legend, from the nobles of Judaea, brought home by Titus after the fall of Jerusalem.

In Spain, Jews were present in some numbers at least as early as the beginning of the Christian era, centuries before the Visigoths had absorbed the Romans, or the Arabs had displaced the Visigoths, or the Christians had driven out the Arabs. They were to be found in France from the first century onwards, well before the Franks arrived from beyond the Rhine to give their name to the country. Inscriptions and literary evidence attest their presence in Hungary, in the Balkan States and in South Russia in the classical period, long anterior

c   17

to the Barbarian incursions and the arrival of the peoples
who were to give those regions their present ethnic
character.   Even in the remote border-province which
stretched along the Rhine, Jews were familiar in the
Roman period, as a number of venerable relics serve to
show.   By the beginning of the fourth century, a Jewish
community—fully-organised and with the customary
religious and lay leaders—flourished, for example, at
Cologne.   In 321, Constantine the Great issued an edict
curtailing certain privileges formerly enjoyed by the
Jews of this city, and ten years later he exempted the
"rabbis, heads of synagogues, elders, &c.," from various
onerous personal obligations.   It was 150 years after
this that the Germans first permanently crossed the Rhine
and established themselves in the Roman province.
The aliens to-day therefore are not the Jews, the only
representatives perhaps in the Rhineland of its inhabitants of sixteen centuries ago.   As a modern authority
has phrased it, "the Jews had settled in Western Europe
before many of its most typical inhabitants had emerged
from Asia, and before others had crossed the Central
European Plain or had traversed the North Sea to invade
the West."

There was still, indeed, a considerable Jewish nucleus
in the East; but it was henceforth a diminishing quantity.
From the late classical period onwards, Jewish history,
Jewish literature, Jewish thought, and the predominant
part of the Jewish people, have been inseparably associated
with Europe and the Western world.

Yet it was in Europe that the Jews' lot was hardest.
This is not the place to trace the progress and development of Jewish persecution, or to attempt to assess the
responsibility for it.   It is enough to sum up the result.
It took some time, of course, for the process to be completed.   There were isolated corners where something of

the spirit of freedom long persisted. Before the clouds gathered to their fullest extent over the old-established Jewish centres of the Mediterranean, they had begun to disperse in the new centres on the Atlantic seaboard. But, taking Europe as a whole, it may be said that, from the period of the Christianisation of the Roman Empire down to the French Revolution, the Jew was subject to a systematic degradation, an exclusion from opportunity, a warping of his natural bent, and a distortion of his normal functioning. The history of the Jews in the western world, during the last 150 years, is the record of their gradual recovery from the effects of all this, and their return to a more or less balanced existence, socially and economically—a process which began with prodigious rapidity but which, before it could be fully accomplished, was reversed in that country where it had achieved its most remarkable progress.

§II

During the first half of their history, the Jews had been a normally-constituted people, rooted on the soil and with a solid basis of peasant proprietors. Their economic development was retrograde, rather than advanced : and trade was in the hands of non-Israelitish traders— to such an extent indeed that the words "Canaanite" (that is, it is to be presumed, Phoenician) and "merchant" were used interchangeably. The mercantile colonies in the towns of Palestine, in the Biblical period, were largely composed of strangers : and the great commercial *entrepôts* lay on the coastal plain, in non-Israelitish hands. After the return from the Babylonian captivity, conditions were much the same. It was in the Greek cities, not in the strongly Jewish uplands, that trade was centred. It is not without its significance that no money was coined by any Jewish ruler until shortly before the beginning of the Christian era. "Ours is not a maritime country," wrote Josephus (*Contra Apionem*, I. xii) in the first century of the Christian era. "Neither commerce nor the intercourse which it promotes with the outside world has any attraction for us."

This natural balance was inevitably disturbed when, owing to the circumstances of their defeat by the Romans, the Jews were forced to leave their former country and were scattered throughout the Western world. Emigrants, even from an agricultural country, tend to abandon agricultural life (the United States to-day provides an illustration of this fact). Yet, for a long time after their Diaspora began, the Jews resisted this temptation. The great Jewish settlements in Mesopotamia, in which Jewish life flourished as it did nowhere else outside Palestine, were predominantly agricultural: to such an extent that the most detailed picture of the methods of farming which obtained here in the first centuries of the Christian era is preserved in the Babylonian Talmud. In other centres, perhaps, there was greater variety: but everywhere—in Egypt, Cyrenaica, Greece, Italy, Spain, even France and Germany—there was in early times a solid nucleus of Jews settled on the land, and earning their livelihood by tilling the soil.

It was first in Europe, and in Christian Europe especially, that the Jew was compelled to abandon his predominantly agricultural interests. Partly, this was the result of circumstances: for it is the trader rather than the farmer who travels, and (as has been pointed out above) the immigrant into a land already occupied must perforce congregate in towns and in urban occupations. But, in addition to this, the growing religious prejudice and the consequent insecurity made it unsafe for individuals who did not belong to the dominant faith to live in rural isolation. With the passage of years and the increase of fanaticism, the life of the isolated Jewish agriculturalist became more and more dangerous. The frequency of persecution uprooted him time after time from his previous home and drove him into a strange country where there was no room for him on the soil; and he was compelled to forgather with his brethren in the towns. Successive Church Councils forbade him to work in the fields on Sunday, notwithstanding the fact that he rested completely on Saturday. Finally, the Feudal idea made land-holding dependent upon military service, from which the Jew was generally excluded (the English *Assize of Arms* of 1181, for example, specifically forbade him to possess any weapons).[1] Thus, he was prevented both from holding land and tilling it, a Jewish farmer being almost as curious an anomaly, in northern Europe at least, as a Jewish monk would have been.

In the towns, the Jews were at the beginning mainly artisans, as they have remained to the present day in those countries where fewer restrictions have been placed upon their economic life. In Roman Egypt, the boatmen were predominantly Jews. In Sicily (as in Salonica, down to our own day) they were the porters and stevedores. In Germany and northern Italy, they were expert miners. In Imperial Rome they had been represented in all walks of life, from painters down to pedlars. Throughout the Middle Ages, we find Jewish craftsmen and Jewish trade-gilds—those of the weavers,

[1] Not that the Jews entirely lost their martial qualities, even under these circumstances. They frequently served, in Spain, both in the Christian and in the Moorish forces; they assisted in the defence of Naples in 537, of Worms in 1201, of Pernambuco in 1654, etc.

With the removal of mediaeval disabilities, professional Jewish soldiers began to be found. Fifteen Jewish officers served under Wellington at Waterloo; and many Jewish soldiers have since attained high rank (e.g. General Giuseppe Ottolenghi, Italian Minister of War in 1902-3, or General Sir John Monash, who commanded the Australian forces in France during their smashing victories in 1918).

carpenters, dyers, blacksmiths, and so on—sometimes maintaining their own gild-halls and even their own synagogues. Many, of course, were engaged in trade, selling above all imports adventurously brought from distant countries, as will be shown in another chapter.

With the process of time, this too was restricted. Gradually, religious disabilities extended until they excluded the Jew from almost every form of normal economic activity. The cities became organised on a new corporate basis, with civic control over manufacture and commerce; and the new prejudices prevented the Jew from being a citizen. The Craft Gilds claimed a monopoly in the various branches of manufacture: but these bodies were united in a quasi-religious brotherhood in which the unbeliever could generally find no place. The Gild Merchant, when it arose, extended the same idea to trade: and the Jew would normally have been excluded, even had he been able to pray or feast with the rest. The frequency of attack, massacre and pillage compelled him to discover a walk of life in which his property could be easily concealed and, above all, easily transferred. And, as chance would have it, just at this period a re-adjustment in the economic organisation of Europe provided such an opening, into which he was reluctantly forced.

In antiquity, the Jew had shewn no proclivity towards finance. Rather, indeed, the reverse, as the passage quoted above from Josephus clearly shews. In Egypt only, where Jews were actively engaged in every branch of commercial life, we meet with Jewish bankers and financiers from the beginning of the Christian era. With this exception, there is no mention until the sixth century, when they are encountered in France. This was, of course, not unnatural: for the Jews in France at this period played an important role in commercial life, and the transition from wholesale trade to finance is in most cases imperceptible. The impetus which ruined the Jewish economic and social balance came from without.

As the Middle Ages advanced, the Church had begun to set its face sternly against the lending of money at interest, on the ground that this was prohibited not only by the Old Testament (Deuteronomy xxiii. 19), but also by the Sermon on the Mount (Luke vi. 35, in its current mistranslation), and by nature itself, which did not make money breed by the ordinary processes of reproduction. The prohibition was an impracticable one (as was soon discovered): for in a money-economy any man may be reduced to momentary necessity, and thus have urgent need of a loan in order to carry on his business, to prepare for the harvest, sometimes even to live.

The situation would have been an impossible one but for the presence of the Jew, who, just as he found himself excluded from other manners of making a livelihood, was forced into this most unhonoured of professions. The non-Jewish capitalists lent to kings and magnates, under the cover of various devices (such as making out the bond for a larger amount than the sum lent, or euphemistically calling the interest by some other name); but the more open, least lucrative, and most unpopular branches of the profession—such as lending on pledge for a short period to the artisan and tradesman—were forced upon the Jew. Thus (to take only one example) in the heroic days of Florence, when a great part of the city ultimately depended for its livelihood upon large-scale financial operations abroad, the Jews were summoned to the city for the purpose of administering to the requirements of the populace, to save Christians from being contaminated by the sin of usury![1]

[1] For a fuller and consecutive account of the subject treated of in this chapter, reference may be made to the present author's *Short History of the Jewish People*, London, 1936. See also below, Chapter X.

In mediaeval England, as is familiar to all who have read the literature of the period, the Jews were invariably, or almost invariably, money-lenders. But why? Because they were not admitted for any other purpose. Why, therefore, did they not leave? The answer is, that they were not allowed to; that they applied for permission to do so on more than one occasion, but were refused. The Crown, in fact, insisted on retaining them, so as to fleece them at incredibly frequent intervals for the benefit of the Exchequer, thus becoming the sleeping partner, and ultimate beneficiary, of all their transactions. "No Jew may remain in England unless he do the King service," ran the opening words of a notorious Edict of Henry III of 1253, "and, from the hour of his birth, every Jew, whether male or female, shall serve Us in some way."

But the Jew (as has been indicated) was not the only usurer during the Middle Ages—though he was the only usurer of whom the Church did not ostensibly disapprove. Italians (known under the generic name of Lombards) and South French (generally called Cahorsins) had a particularly bad reputation for their remorseless activities in this direction: and, among the former, the Paduans were especially notorious, being singled out by Dante in his *Inferno* for condign punishment. The fact that the centre of the money market in London, to this day, is in "Lombard" Street, is an eloquent reminder of that period. Sometimes, pitiless usurious activities were carried on in the shadow of the Papal *curia* itself. So remorseless were the Christian usurers that St. Bernard of Clairvaux called attention to the fact that they far outstripped the Jews. Similarly, when the Jews were expelled from France in 1306, the chroniclers deplored their departure, as it left the people in the hands of much less reasonable Christian competitors—for example, the notorious Gianfigliazzi family, from Florence, who lent money in Languedoc at the preposterous rate of 266⅔ per cent.[1] In Italy, indeed, one reason why the Jews were often summoned to open a loan-bank was that the local money-lenders had become too extortionate. Thus the Jews were admitted to Todi, in Umbria, only when the normal rate of interest had reached a shattering figure. In Brindisi, the poor burghers had good reason to rejoice when the Jews were authorised to lend money at the rate of 40 per cent, as otherwise they "would have been forced to sell their belongings at vile price"; and after the latter's expulsion, the rate of interest charged by the Christian usurers rose to 240 per cent.

Sometimes, it was notorious that the Jews were mere decoys, acting for the Christian capitalists behind the scenes. Joseph Sessa, an anti-Semitic Italian jurist of the eighteenth century, gives reluctant testimony to this fact. He writes: "A majority of the sums lent by the Jews to Christians at an interest of 18 per cent, whether on security or otherwise, are advanced to the Jews themselves by Christians. The latter ordinarily retain the pledge, in order to safeguard themselves, sharing in the Jewish usury to the extent of eight, ten, or even twelve per cent. These facts have often been laid bare, and continue to be daily."[2] An even more astonishing commentary upon the state of affairs is provided by contemporary documents from Italy, from Poland and from the south of France, which demonstrate that the poverty-stricken Jewish communities were forced to have recourse for loans, at an

[1] The author may be excused for quoting once more the expressive words of Geoffrey of Paris:

"For the Jews were debonair,
Greatly more, in this affair,
Than now the Christians are."

[2] So too at Nuremberg, over the period 1304–7, we find the Christian firm of Holzschuher lending money to Jews at a virulent rate of interest, apparently going as high as 220 per cent.

extremely high rate of interest, to Christian religious houses.[1]

§III

Other than money-lending, there was one calling only, or at the most two, which the Jew was normally permitted to practise in Christian Europe. In order to prevent any competition with the non-Jewish merchants, closely organised in Gilds to which he was not admitted, he was in most cases rigorously excluded from ordinary trade—that is, purchasing from the manufacturer or producer, and selling to the consumer. But this restriction did not extend to second-hand commodities. Accordingly the Jew was the universal ragman and old-clothes dealer. Attempts were made to exclude him even from this unenviable walk of life (in Venice, for example, the gild of *strazzaiuoli* periodically voiced its indignation, and begged that this concession should be withdrawn), but generally speaking, no difficulties were raised. Finally, though prohibited from opening a shop, the Jew was normally allowed to hawk unimportant trifles (sometimes of home manufacture), in the countryside if not in the towns: and, throughout Western Europe, the "Jew Pedlar", pack on back, was a familiar figure in the seventeenth, eighteenth and early nineteenth centuries.

These three callings—money-lending, old-clothes dealing and peddling—were the only ones which were universally permitted in Europe down to the period of the French Revolution. Here and there were exceptions—more generous facilities, conceded either to individuals

---

[1] The story of Shylock, the prototype of the Jewish usurer of legend, is symptomatic of the manner in which fantasy has been allowed to travesty fact. The story of the pitiless creditor and the pound of flesh first appears in the sixteenth century, as sober history, with a Roman Jew, Samson Cesena, as victim and a Christian merchant, Paolo Secchi, as his persecutor. In *The Merchant of Venice*, the incident is reproduced, but the roles are reversed!

or to the whole body. But nowhere was there complete freedom of vocation and movement. In England, for example, it was not until 1831 that Jews were able to open shops for retail trade in the City of London; yet the English policy was particularly liberal, in comparison with that which prevailed on the Continent. These regulations, moreover, were enforced with the utmost ruthlessness. Thus, in the various German and Italian cities, the Jews were allowed to exist only for the purpose of money-lending. Once their utility in this direction had disappeared, they would be expelled: while any individual who attempted to gain his livelihood in a more dignified manner was debarred.

In Venice, for example, down to the close of the eighteenth century, the Jewish community was only tolerated on the express condition that it maintained in the Ghetto four loan-banks (a more polite designation of pawn-broking establishments) for the benefit of the poor. The only other professions legally permitted here were old-clothes dealing and the wholesale export trade to the Levant, which did not compete with Christian traders. The same was the case in the cities of the *terra firma*. And this ignominious condition of affairs was sternly enforced, any attempt on the part of the Jews to broaden their economic status, or to bring it on a slightly more dignified plane, being systematically blocked. Even as late as 1777, the Venetian government closed down all the factories owned by Jews throughout its possessions— including the silk-looms at Padua, where the industry had been established and developed by the Jews; and thousands of hands were thrown out of work. In this same place, the Jews were not even allowed to work as turners and carpenters and to sell the products of their industry to their fellow-townsmen. As late as the middle of the nineteenth century, the Roman Jews (still restricted almost completely to old-clothes dealing) were compelled to close down the shops opened outside the Ghetto. In Russia, similar regulations existed—at least, outside the rigorously-restricted Pale of Settlement—down to the War of 1914–18.

§IV

Though the channels of livelihood which were left open to the Jew were so few, and so ignoble, levies were made upon him as though he were the sole capitalist. He contributed to all the ordinary taxation, in full proportion. But, in addition to this, there were dozens of other imposts. The Jewish community, as such, had to pay heavily for the privilege of toleration—so heavily, indeed, that in the eighteenth century many ancient congregations were reduced to insolvency. Their ordinary tolls and market-dues were double what the Christian had to pay. There was a tax on Jewish weddings, a tax on the Sabbath candles, a tax on the citron used at the Feast of Tabernacles, a dice-tax which could be levied by every ruffian encountered on the high-road. A special poll-tax—similar to that levied on animals, and included in the same list of tolls—had to be paid in Germany at the entrance to every town and state. Even when dead, there was a special toll to be paid at the city boundary, as the body was escorted to its last home. In Frankfort, it was computed that no less than thirty-eight different imposts were levied upon the Jews, mostly additional to those incumbent on the ordinary townsfolk.

Much is sometimes said about the influence of the Jewish moneyed dynasties in the Middle Ages. This is generally pure invention, as there are very few cases in which the mediaeval Jew, however wealthy, was able to transmit his fortune to his heirs (see below, pp. 229–230).

Legally, indeed, his property escheated to the Crown: though the reality was seldom so severe, and in most cases (though not in all) the Treasury restricted its claims to one-half the dead man's property, handing the rest back to his legal heirs so that they might accumulate further profits for the royal benefit. Yet even after the Middle Ages were closed, and the former conception of royal rights was modified, the actual result was frequently identical. Thus Samuel Oppenheimer, the Court Factor at Vienna at the period of the War of Spanish Succession, was forced into bankruptcy in consequence of an unpaid debt from the Imperial Treasury amounting to 6,000,000 florins. A more astonishing case still was that of Mordecai Meisel, the Jewish philanthropist, the synagogue built by whom is still among the sights of Prague. The story is best related in the words of the writer of a Fugger News Letter—an observer who can hardly be described as pro-Jewish:

From Prague, the 5th day of April, 1601.

"A short time ago there died here the Jew Meisel. Notwithstanding that he had left His Imperial Majesty ten thousand florins, and much cash also to the Hospital for poor Christians and Jews, His Imperial Majesty on the following Saturday, viz. the Sabbath of the Jews, ordered Herr von Sternberg, at that time President of the Bohemian Chamber, to enter the Jew's house forcibly and to seize everything there was. The widow of Meisel handed this over willingly, for she had already set aside and hidden the best part of the treasure. That which was taken away came to forty-five thousand florins in cash, promissory notes, jewels, clothes and all kinds of coins. After this, however, the President, against whom the Jewess and the sons of the two brothers of Meisel had raised a strong protest to the privy councillors, was not

satisfied with all this money and booty, and, no doubt
at the command of His Majesty, once more broke into
the house at night. The son of one of the brothers
was taken prisoner, secretly led away and tortured."

Apart from such episodes, there was no limit to the
indignities, deprivations and restrictions from which the
Jews suffered in their long Middle Ages. They were compelled to live together in a separate quarter of the town,
known as the Ghetto; generally insalubrious, and rarely
large enough to accommodate them without the most
appalling overcrowding. The Ghetto gates were closed
every night, and, until they were opened again in the
morning, no Jew might show his face outside and no
Gentile might venture within. On the great solemnities
of the Christian Church, and over the whole of Easter-
tide, the entrances were barred and the Jews treated
virtually as prisoners. In the streets (sometimes in the
Ghetto, too) the Jew had to be distinguished by an ugly
badge of shame—a yellow circle worn on the outer gar-
ment above the heart in Germany; a yellow or crimson
hat, or kerchief, in Italy. The number of weddings was
restricted, in Germany at least, only one member of each
family being permitted to set up his own household, and
the remainder being compelled either to emigrate or to
remain unmarried; yet, at the same time, any association with non-Jewish women was punished by the most
drastic penalties, including even death.

In the courts of law, a special oath had to be taken
more judaico, to the accompaniment of a degrading ceremonial. Each Sabbath, the Jews were forced to attend
conversionist sermons, where they were compelled to hear
long tirades against Judaism. Their children might be
seized and forcibly baptized; after which, uncanonical
though it was, there was no redress, and they were brought
up in Christian surroundings, sedulously removed from

any possibility of contact with their parents. They were not allowed to have Christian servants in their employment, or even to enlist the service of Christian neighbours for the purpose of kindling their fires on the Sabbath-day. Christian midwives, and Christian wet-nurses, were not allowed to give them any assistance in their hour of need. They were not allowed to ride in coaches, or to be addressed with the customary courteous prefixes, or to be called by names which were not charac-teristically Jewish, or to wear ordinary clothing. On Good Friday, in many places, they were stoned by the rabble and buffeted by the authorities—sometimes with fatal results. They were not allowed to erect tombstones over their dead, or to escort them to their last resting-place with the prescribed religious dirges. They were harried with absurd accusations, such as that of the Ritual Murder of Christian children (repeatedly, indeed, con-demned by the Popes) and the even more absurd charge of Desecrating the Host, which caused the loss of thou-sands of lives from the thirteenth century onwards.[1]

So many restrictions, in fact, were placed upon the Jew that life would have been impossible for him had he obeyed them all. Evasion was necessary, if he were to continue to exist. Thus, for example, in places where the Jews were restricted to dealing in old clothes, tears were deliberately made sometimes in new articles, so as to render them technically second-hand. Where the Jew was excluded from manufacture, a fictitious Gentile partner was occasionally acquired, in whose name the business was carried on. If taxation became too crushing, it was not remarkable that the victim attempted to minimise his apparent profits. Restric-tions on residence and occupation might perhaps be over-

---

[1] It may be remarked that, in present-day Germany, a large number of these prohibitions are closely paralleled, some even excelled.

looked, if the police authorities received a douceur.
. . . There was, in fact, the same experience that
modern theorists accentuate: that laws, in order to be
obeyed, must be reasonable: that a ridiculous rigour
defeats its own object, penalising the law-abiding at the
expense of the less responsible elements: that the multi-
plicity of galling restrictions tends to bring the fundamental laws of security and government into disrepute.
This generalisation applies all the more when the restrictions are of a definitely unethical character, as were
so many of those from which the Jew suffered. The
result was what might have been expected—the growth
of evasion, of sharp practice, of petty deceit, a perpetual
state of suspicion and grievance against those responsible
for the hard lot of the victim, a feeling of contempt for
the laws which they enacted. This sentiment continued,
in some unhappy cases, after the justification had passed.
But the wonder is, that in the majority of instances it
should have disappeared so rapidly.[1]

§v

Yet the relations which prevailed between the Jews
and their neighbours were friendly enough, when no
outside pressure was brought to bear; and their services
were appreciated in the most unlikely quarters. Two
or three examples may be adduced. In the eleventh
century, Rüdiger, Bishop of Speyer, ambitious for the

---

[1] On the other side, it is possible to adduce instances of an exaggerated
scrupulosity. The story is told, for example, of a saintly Russian
rabbi of the last century, who made a practice of destroying a postage-
stamp every time he sent a note by hand, as the Post was a government monopoly! Such in fact was the general delicacy of feeling that
no man was admitted to pray with the congregation on the Day of
Atonement until he had been formally absolved from ill-considered
vows which he had hastily taken on himself during the year and
which were clearly impossible of fulfilment. (This is the origin of the
much-maligned *Kol Nidrei* formula.)

expansion of his episcopal seat, invited the Jews to the
town, endowed them with lavish privileges and provided
them with a special quarter within the walls. "Wishing
to make of Speyer a city," he boasted, "I thought to
increase its honour a thousandfold by bringing in the
Jews." He was by no means alone in holding such
ideas. At the other extreme of the Middle Ages, in 1569,
the city of Orange, in the south of France, was in the
depths of depression, its wealth dwindling and its commerce
languishing. There were at that time no Jews in the
city, and the Town Council recommended, as one of the
measures for restoring prosperity, that "two hundred
Jewish households" should be invited to settle. So also,
when the position of the Jews at Neustettin was menaced,
the gilds appealed almost unanimously to the King
of Poland to leave them undisturbed.[1]

Or take another scene—one of the most tragic of this
period. When the Jews were expelled from Spain, in
1492, the overseas possessions of the Crown of Aragon—
particularly Sardinia and Sicily—were included in the
edict. It was in vain that the Council of the latter
kingdom protested, pointing out the loss which the
people as a whole would (and indeed did) suffer in consequence of this measure. On January 12th, 1493, the
last Jews left Palermo. It is on record that, so long as

---

[1] It must not be imagined that these instances are isolated. In
Lindau, when the interest on loans made by Christian merchants rose
to 216 per cent, the citizens begged for the admission of the Jews
to the town as their only salvation. In 1544, and again in 1550, when
the Emperor Charles V issued a decree expelling the crypto-Jews from
Antwerp, the magistrates of the city protested, on the grounds that
such action would spell ruin to the city and the state. The new oppres-
sive legislation enacted by the Venetian Government at the close
of the eighteenth century elicited protests from the municipalities
of Verona and Ceneda. In 1781 the civic authorities at Avignon
testified that the Jewish community of that place contributed greatly
to its welfare, and gave no cause for complaint by their conduct as
regards morality, religion, or commercial life. Similar illustrations can
be multiplied.

D

the vessels which bore them were in sight, the inhabitants stood on the housetops, waving farewell to their old neighbours, who had lived in their midst, in peace and amity, almost as long as Sicilian history itself. They had, indeed, good cause. It was not long after, at the beginning of the sixteenth century, when Aragonese intolerance drove the Jews likewise from the neighbouring mainland. A recent learned work shows that Calabria has not yet recovered from the blow. Or, again, we have the delightful episode of the romantic lady in mediaeval Worms who was so impressed by the ceremony of the Rejoicing of the Law and the beauty of one of the male participants that she bequeathed a parcel of ground to the Jewish community for use as a public garden.

§VI

Notwithstanding his physical degradation, there were certain specific values which the Jew succeeded in keeping alive, even amid the squalor of the Ghetto. There was, in the first place, the idea of the family. His home life, in the Middle Ages, was generally on a plane distinctly higher than that of his neighbours. Marriage was regarded as a natural and praiseworthy state—not (as in the Church) a concession to human weakness. The monogamous ideal, though formally accepted by the Jews of Northern Europe only about the year 1000,[1] had already long been the general rule. It was, moreover, more seriously taken than among the European Christians: for concubinage, adultery, and prostitution were rare phenomena in the *Judengasse* (if only because the small society restricted opportunity) at a time when sexual life without was at its lowest

---

[1] It will be recalled that legalised bigamy was not unknown in Europe as late as the sixteenth century, this being one of the suggested solutions to the marital quandary of Henry VIII.

level.[1] In the twelfth and thirteenth centuries, when in the general world wife-beating was not only customary among all classes but expressly permitted by Canon Law and by the statutes of some small towns, Rabbis could declare: "This is a thing not done in Israel." The practice was, indeed, regarded in the Codes as justifiable ground for divorce.

As a corollary to the purity of the home, drunkenness was rare, instead of being considered a natural pastime. The warmth of domestic life extended till it embraced outsiders—even utter strangers. The visitor from a distant Ghetto could always count upon welcome, hospitality, and assistance: and there was a highly-developed system of charity, in advance of modern ideas in that it showed the utmost delicacy for the feelings of the recipient, besides trying to substitute self-support for pauperisation (see below, p. 287).

Furthermore, education was considered a religious duty. Illiteracy was almost unknown, and even the illiterate had the profoundest respect for learning. A universal system of education had existed in Palestine since the first or second century B.C. That early ideal was never lost sight of. Hence in the Ghetto period there existed, in the smallest Jewish community, an educational system of a breadth and universality which the most advanced state in modern Europe or America has even now barely equalled, and certainly not surpassed. Enrolment for either sex was free. The number of pupils in each class was regulated. The elements of the vernacular were taught, as well as of Hebrew. Meals were given to those who required them. Boots and clothing were distributed to the most needy in winter. A

[1] It may be observed that a certain contrast persists even at the present time. In 1933, there were in England 2,549 marriages according to Jewish law, but only 40 decrees *nisi* were pronounced between couples: in 1934, the corresponding figures were 2,600 and 46.

community of less than 1,000 souls, in eighteenth-century Italy, would maintain a school of this type, with no less than six teachers and assistants. Compare this with the provision which would have been made in a contemporary English or American village! Or one may take another criterion. In 1861, there were no less than 54·5 illiterates in each hundred Italians above the age of ten years : among their Jewish fellow-citizens, only 5·8!

Arrival at adolescence did not mark the end of education. Every synagogue had attached to it voluntary associations for the purpose of study, which would assemble after the morning and evening service. Wealthy enthusiasts would establish regular courses of instruction in their own houses. In Poland, in the seventeenth century, we are told, "there was hardly a single house in which they did not study. Either the householder himself was a scholar, or else his son or his son-in-law studied perpetually : or, at the very least, he gave hospitality to some young student." Adult education was thus taken as a matter of course among Jews, centuries before the conception had begun to penetrate the outside world.

The scheme of education was not restricted (as might be imagined) to quasi-theological studies, but, by reason of the wide humanity of Judaism, necessarily extended to every field of human interest. When Germany, for example, had hardly emerged from barbarism, there were in the Rhineland Jewish schools, to which students streamed from every part of the world, hardly distinguishable from the primitive universities which Christian Europe was beginning to develop at this period. It was not until these academies had already been in existence for centuries that the first German university— destined to have an ephemeral existence—was started, at Erfurt (1379). Not long after this, in 1466, the handful of Jews living in Sicily, numbering at the most not more than 100,000, received formal licence from the King to open their own properly-constituted University, with faculties of Medicine, Law, and presumably the Humanities. Twenty-four years later, the idea was revived in Northern Italy. These facts are in themselves sufficient to show the profound Jewish veneration for scholarship, quite apart from the Rabbinic disciplines, even at that unenlightened period.

As a natural consequence of all this, there was in the Ghetto and the Judengasse a spirit of free enquiry which was elsewhere rare, if not unknown. In this fact, perhaps, lay the greatest service of the mediaeval Jew to mankind. It was a period when Authority was triumphant in the intellectual sphere, when thought was circumscribed even more than practice, when uniformity had established itself, not as an accident but as a principle, throughout European life. Had this state of affairs continued unchallenged, progress—scientific as well as philosophical—would have been impossible. The mere fact that the Jew existed, and that he preserved the habit of independent thought, helped to save the world from this menace. It was impossible even for the least original mind to fail to realise that, in the Jewish quarter, there existed a class as intelligent at least as other men were, who yet did not believe as other men; who possessed literature and beliefs and practices which were not like those of the rest of the world, and who refused to pay even lip-service to the prevailing conceptions. This very fact saved the world from accepting uniformity finally as a natural thing. It stimulated students and thinkers to realise the existence of other spheres to conquer, over and above those which were delineated from the pulpit. And, if from time to time Europe shook off its lethargy, and began to re-examine for itself the wells of human thought, the propinquity of the Jew was in part responsible.

§VII

The Age of Degradation lasted, roughly speaking, up to the period of the French Revolution. In England, Holland and America, there had been a very considerable measure of social emancipation even before this time; in Central and Eastern Europe notable relics of the old system continued long after. But in general it may be said that it was the French Revolution which broke down the gates of the Ghetto and permitted its downtrodden denizens to enjoy for the first time the same rights and opportunities as their neighbours.

The consequences of this were remarkable. A section of the European population, of at least normal intelligence, with their wits sharpened by generations of intensive Talmudical study, were suddenly allowed after centuries of repression to emerge into the world, and given for the first time their natural outlet. Once the outside pressure was removed, the inevitable happened. These Jews began to find their own level. The grandchildren of the petty Ghetto traders and usurers became leaders of business, of thought, of society. Those whose brains and intelligences qualified them rose in a remarkable manner in the circles to which they were at last admitted. It was, of course, no more than what might have been expected. The Jew of the Ghetto period was not a usurer, a petty trader, and so on by choice. His intellectual interests were at least as wide and as varied as that of the patrician or citizen in the outside world. It was not therefore that his descendants rose above their level: it was that, after a lapse of centuries, they at last found their level.

In what direction could these newly-emerged scions of the Ghetto seek an outlet? The centuries of repression could not fail to leave their trace; and it was impossible for those who during long generations had been restricted to the more degraded forms of business life to become immediately farmers or artisans, simply because the statute-book no longer forbade it. It was inevitable that they found expression partly in the more dignified forms of business, and partly in the so-called "professions", for which their artificially-stimulated intellectuality perhaps gave them special qualifications. They could not fail to be attracted particularly by those callings where there were no vested interests, to discourage or exclude them. They tended therefore to congregate where personality and personal ability were of decisive importance, or in newly-opened fields of activity, where family connexion and tradition counted for little. In Central Europe, moreover, Jews were even now excluded, with considerable rigour, from the Civil Service and from commissioned rank in the Army and Navy—fields of activity in which elsewhere, too, much prejudice yet prevailed. This stimulated a disproportionate concentration in those professions still left open.

This is the reason why, in the nineteenth century, the forward progress of the Jews in certain spheres appeared to be so astonishingly rapid. Answering their natural bent for study, they seized the opportunity of entering the professions of Law, Medicine, Literature, Journalism, and quickly assumed their natural place. In the economic world, they were primarily attracted by the new businesses which the Industrial Revolution had called into existence, or those which were entering upon a fresh phase of their existence, and were calling for new blood, new ideas and new methods. We thus find them figuring, in more than their due proportion, in (for example) Banking in the nineteenth century, in the Entertainment Industry in the twentieth.

Like a cork released under water, they forced their way to the surface after having been artificially depressed for so long. Like water spilled on uneven ground, they followed the contours of the soil, took advantage of every opening, and flowed irresistibly into every gap. But the analogy may be pursued a little further. After a time, the water is absorbed by the soil. Its moisture has been drunk in, with beneficial results. The earth on which it fell has to some extent been fructified. Yet in the process the water has ceased to have an independent existence. So, too, in the phenomenon which we are attempting to examine. It was seldom long before these Jewish pioneers of the nineteenth and twentieth centuries lost their specific Jewish characteristics—in many cases, even their Jewish loyalties. The fertilising impetus and enthusiasms which they had brought became absorbed into the common store and enriched the common life : but the distinctiveness had passed away. On the other hand, the new ideas and methods were by now universal property. Hence in many callings in which the Jews were once imagined to have a dominant position, their influence dwindled progressively as the nineteenth century advanced and the twentieth began : though in many instances the legend outlived the actuality.[1]

It was natural that, the older established a Jewish centre was, the more rapid was the rise of its children :

[1] A fact which tended to obscure this phenomenon was that the emergence of the Jews from their repressed condition was not simultaneous. In some places, emancipation was retarded : in many families, the influence of conservatism was stronger : sometimes, the percolation took longer to achieve. The impression might thus be given of a continuous advance. Actually, this did not take place. In more than one generation, there was a fresh exodus (though on a scale which was in fact unimportant) : but by this time the earlier wave had reached its climax, or even begun to recede. The initial impetus, indeed, seldom lasted for more than one generation, or two at the most ; for the transmission of outstanding ability from generation to generation is at least as rare among Jews as among their neighbours. The children of the Ghetto prodigy, who dazzled the eyes of his neighbours, generally developed into Englishmen or Frenchmen or Germans of normal tastes, normal interests and normal ability, indistinguishable from their neighbours excepting by a diminishing family tradition.

for, on emergence from the Ghetto, they did not have the problem of acclimatisation added to that of emancipation. This is perhaps the explanation of the disproportionate distinction attained in so many fields by the Jews of Germany, with their tradition unbroken since the fourth century: or by those of Italy, who were already acclimatised in the country at the time of the birth of Jesus. In England and in France, where the settlements were less ancient, the number of names of first eminence is smaller by far: and it is noteworthy that in these countries a majority of instances probably belong to the oldest strata.

The following pages will assemble a number of examples from which these generalisations may be illustrated. The process is in most cases identical. There was consistent collaboration between the Jews and their neighbours, in every field of endeavour, from the beginning of their settlement in Europe and throughout the Middle Ages, so far as it was permitted. The long night of the Ghetto put an end to this tradition, save in a few exceptional instances. With the downfall of the system, the collaboration was resumed, with an intensity naturally heightened by reason of the previous unnatural repression. In new fields of endeavour especially, Jewish names begin to figure with a peculiar frequency. But in most cases the lessons which they taught, and the stimulus which they provided, were rapidly assimilated. Activities which owed their origin to Jews became part of the common stock. Before long, there is everywhere a tendency for this participation to recede to its natural proportion, modified perhaps only by an hereditary proclivity in favour of intellectual activities and an enforced tendency to urban life.

Even before the Ghetto walls were effectively established, however, Jews played a vital part in the intellectual process to which modern Europe owes its birth.

CHAPTER III

§1

FROM the point of view of intellectual history, the modern world began with the Renaissance, that rediscovery of the treasures of antiquity which deeply stirred the man of the Middle Ages and brought about a "new birth". The old conception, that this reawakening began with the rediscovery of Greek literature in the fifteenth century, is misleading. Well before that period, the classical heritage had begun to be available to western Europe—not, indeed, in the Greek originals (for few men could read or understand Greek), but in Latin versions. The texts in question were barbarous, inelegant, often inaccurate. But the conceptions of the originals were conveyed faithfully enough, and the result was sufficient to open up new horizons before the wondering eyes of students. It was of this revival—the "Latin" Renaissance—that Dante, Chaucer and Petrarch were born.

The part played by the Jews in this process was of the utmost importance. It may be said, indeed, that it could not have come about as it did but for their agency: and that without them, the revival of the fifteenth century would inevitably have been retarded or assumed a different form. The story is familiar how, in the Dark Ages and after, when the Hellenic tradition was entirely lost to Christian Europe, it was nurtured and yet further developed in Moslem Spain. It was here that the wisdom of Hippocrates, the astronomical records of Ptolemy, and above all the philosophy of Aristotle, continued to be revered, studied, commented. The original texts, indeed, were inaccessible; the studies centred around Arabic renderings, in many cases made from the Syriac versions which had been current in the Levant at the time of the Saracen invasions. The matter, however, was the same: and from the eleventh century onwards, when the breath of intellectual interest had begun to stir again in Europe, it was to the Mohammedan sages of Andalusia that eager Christian students looked for some notion of the wisdom of ancient Hellas. Of course, it was not the Greek authorities only who were thus revered and sought after. Their Arabic exponents—Averroes, Avicenna, and the rest—enjoyed a prestige which was barely less than theirs; and, if Christian Europe imagined that the former provided a gate to wisdom, it was no less convinced that the latter owned the key.

The Mediterranean world at this time was divided culturally and politically, it may be said, into three portions. There were the Greeks, possessing the treasures of antiquity, yet hardly aware of their value: the Arabs, studying them in vernacular versions in their schools, particularly in Southern Spain: and the Latins, painfully conscious of their inferiority yet for linguistic reasons unable to obtain access to the sources for which they thirsted. All these three sections were cut off from one another by differences of language, religion, and tradition. The gulf would have been unbridgeable, but for one element which was to be found in all. From the truly catholic point of view, the Jews were the only real Europeans, whose purview extended beyond the boundaries of the Latin world to the Greek on the one hand and the Arab on the other; who possessed a common language—Hebrew—which was understood, in certain circles at least, the whole world over, and could thus form a medium of intercourse; who were so endowed with linguistic knowledge that they could travel from land to land without great difficulty, and could generally find some co-religionist who could read and speak the most recondite foreign tongue.

The Jews were hence peculiarly qualified to serve as a bridge between these mutually exclusive and mutually intolerant worlds. The Jews of Spain shared the intellectual heritage of their Moslem neighbours—some of them, indeed (such as Maimonides or Israeli[1]), were reckoned among its greatest adornments. But the Hebraic heritage was available to Jews throughout the world. The humblest Jewish scholar, in Italy or Provence, thus had access to intellectual resources of which the most erudite of his Christian neighbours was ignorant. It was hence to the Jews (in most instances) that Christian students had recourse for some inkling of the intellectual achievements of the Arabs, and even the ideas of the sages of ancient Greece.[2]

There have survived many hundreds of translations carried out by Jews in the mediaeval period, illustrating their intense interest and their fruitful participation in every branch of intellectual activity of the age. It was the resultant Latin versions of the Greek classics and of their Moslem exponents (whether made directly from the Arabic, or through the medium of Hebrew versions prepared by Jews for their own use) which penetrated Europe from the eleventh century onwards with such far-reaching results.

[1] See *infra*, pp. 160–2, 193, 195–7.
[2] The best account of this available in English is to be found in Joseph Jacobs' *Jewish Contributions to Civilisation*—a work of studied moderation—and in the chapters by Charles and Dorothea Singer in *The Legacy of Israel*, on both of which I have drawn lavishly in this and the following chapters.

This intellectual, scientific and philosophical system, based upon the encyclopaedic teachings of Aristotle as preserved and developed by the Moors and Jews in Spain, was accepted unquestioningly throughout Europe, and was embodied by Dante almost in its entirety in that greatest literary monument of the Middle Ages, his *Divine Comedy*. Thus Dante's entire cosmogonic system, enveloped within the *Primum Mobile*, is in fact an adaptation of the Hebrew-Arabic conception of the world. It is symptomatic that Aristotle ("The Master of those who know" as Dante calls him) has in his train in the Inferno Averroes "who made the Great Commentary". In the famous pictorial representation of the Middle Ages which is to be seen in the Spanish Chapel in Florence, vanquished philosophy is represented by turbaned figures—typifying its legendary association with the Moslem world. But though the system was expounded by Mohammedan thinkers (with the aid, indeed, of Jews and persons of Jewish origin), it was mainly through the agency of Jews that it was transmitted from the Moslem to the Christian world.[1]

The importance of this process in European thought, science and civilisation was incalculable. To it is to be traced the origin of mathematical study in Europe—the ultimate basis of all technical progress. It was the foundation of mediaeval medicine, which, though long superseded, is nevertheless the basis of our own. It enriched mediaeval Europe with fresh conceptions in literature and fresh literary forms, to be traced

[1] Joseph Jacobs, in his *Jewish Contributions to Civilisation*, draws a distinction between the philosophical texts, which according to him were for the most part derived by the Latin world direct from the Arabic, and the scientific, which in many cases were transmitted *via* Hebrew. The opposite thesis is maintained most brilliantly by Renan in *Averroès et l'Averroïsme*. But in any case the indubitable collaboration of Jews with Christian translators (e.g. Michael the Scot) must be taken into account.

in every country. It formed the basis of astronomical investigation, which in its turn was all-important at the period of the great discoveries. Arabic, and indeed mediaeval science in general, is to-day no longer of more than academic importance. But it is upon it that our modern thought and science in the last instance depend.

Before we leave this subject, a point referred to cursorily above must be accentuated. Just as the Jews played a part of vast significance as intermediaries in the transmission of Islamic culture to the Latin world, so they contributed in no small measure to the evolution of that culture. To an anonymous Jew is due for example (below, p. 169) the translation into Arabic of the Indian work, *Kalilah and Dimnah*, to which at least one-tenth of the fairy-tale store of modern Europe is to be traced. Again, in 680, a Basran Jew named Masurjuwaik translated a handbook of medicine from Syriac to Arabic, and wrote original treatises on the benefits and evils of foodstuffs and drugs. The Jewish scientist, Mashaala (pp. 97, 279), was a figure of great significance in the intellectual life of the Moslem world in the eighth century. Other names of considerable importance will be mentioned elsewhere in these pages from time to time. Bertrand, the French historian, goes so far as to suggest that the greatest of the philosophers and physicians for whom Moslem Spain was famous were without exception of Jewish, when they were not of Christian, extraction. This, though clearly an exaggerated claim, contains in it the germ at least of a truth which should not be overlooked.

§II

There were three main centres for this fruitful activity of the Jews, as interpreters to Europe of Graeco-Arab science. One was Toledo, at the court of the kings of Castile. Another was Naples, under the auspices of the House of Anjou. The third was Provence, the bridge between France and Spain, where the local Jewish scholars (particularly of the family of Ibn Tibbon) translated large numbers of texts from the Arabic of their native Spain into Hebrew, for the benefit of their co-religionists north of the Pyrenees. These were frequently rendered subsequently into Latin at the request of Christian savants. Here, too, worked Jacob ben Makhir[1], a prolific translator in all branches of knowledge, whose original contributions to science (as will be seen) were also of the utmost importance. But even in Northern Europe the process was repeated. Thus, in 1273–4 a Jew named Vives translated into French in the house of Henri Bate, at Malines, several books by the Spanish Jewish globe-trotter, exegete and philosopher, Abraham ibn Ezra. These works were subsequently used by Bate to good effect in his own writings.

The contemporary appreciation of this activity may be conveyed by an enumeration of the patrons under whom these Jewish translators worked, many of whom were normally far from friendly towards the Jews—men like Raymund, Archbishop of Toledo in the twelfth century, the Emperor Frederick II, Manfred of Sicily, Charles of Naples and Alfonso the Wise of Castile in the thirteenth, Robert of Naples and Pedro III of Aragon in the fourteenth.

The case of Alfonso the Wise was particularly interesting. He was not himself conspicuously pro-Jewish; indeed, the legislation contained in his famous code, the *Siete Partidas*, was notably intolerant. But he realised painfully how backward his kingdom was in

---

[1] [The vital dates of persons mentioned in this work will be given in the text only when it is necessary for understanding the chronological setting. In other cases reference should be made to the Index.]

intellectual matters, as compared with the high standard
of civilisation which still prevailed in the remnants of
the Moorish principalities of the South. Accordingly, he
deliberately set himself to adapt the masterpieces of
Arabic science and literature into Spanish—incidentally
creating, thereby, the Spanish language as we know it
to-day. And naturally, and inevitably, it was to the
Jews that he had recourse for the purpose—the Jews,
who alone of his subjects were at home both under
Moslem and Christian rule, and piously retained some
knowledge of the Arabic language even in northern Spain
and beyond. The first task undertaken was the translation of a curious work known as the *Lapidario*—a discourse
upon the property of metals and precious stones, the
part author of which, incidentally, had himself been a
Jew, one Abolays. This version was completed in 1256
by the royal physician, Rabbi Judah ben Moses. Then
followed a long series of similar translations—works
astronomical, philosophical, and scientific; treatises on
the quadrant, the candle-clock, and quick-silver; literary
exercises and philosophical disquisitions. Much of this
literature was subsequently translated into Latin; all of
it formed henceforth part of the general European heritage.

There was similar activity, if not quite so systematic,
under the auspices of the Holy Roman Emperor, Frederick
II. Of the Jewish savants under his patronage the most
important was Rabbi Jacob Anatoli, whom he invited
to Naples, where he had not long before established a
University. Anatoli was the first to translate the
philosophy of Averroes from the original Arabic. His
version was in Hebrew: but the Latin texts of the great
Cordovan philosopher which were current in the Middle
Ages (and as late as the seventeenth century in some
important European centres) were based upon this. In
his original work, which was of portentous bulk, he

FARAJ BEN SALIM OF GIRGENTI

Right: Receiving the Liber Continens. Left: Delivering the translation to Charles of Anjou

(From a manuscript in the Bibliothèque Nationale, Paris)

mentions with respect various suggestions which emanated from the Emperor himself.

When the Hohenstaufen were ejected from southern Italy, their intellectual interests were maintained by their successors of the House of Anjou. Charles of Anjou in particular turned to Jews to assist him in acclimatising in the Christian portion of his dominions the lore of the Arabs, still numerous in Sicily. For this purpose, he employed Faraj ben Salim of Girgenti, the first of the professional translators of the Middle Ages, whose *magnum opus* was a version of the enormous medical compendium of Rhazes, the *Liber continens*. Another translator who worked under the same auspices was Moses of Palermo, specially instructed in Latin by the king's order, to whom we owe a Latin version of a work on the diseases of horses ascribed to Hippocrates—one of the earliest veterinary treatises to become current in Europe.

Not that the Jews were always solely responsible, or that when they were their names were always associated with the work. In many cases, no doubt, one has to imagine them reading from the Semitic original, which they would translate extemporaneously into the vernacular—Castilian or Italian—which some eager Christian student sitting by their side would write down in execrable Latin. In addition, there were a number of converted Jews who played a prominent role in this activity. Such were Petrus Alphonsi, an important figure in the history of literature, who brought an echo of the revival into England; or Constantine the African, one of the earliest of them all (a convert either from Islam or from Judaism), who translated many works of Jewish origin in southern Italy, and was greatly utilised by the English thinker Adelard of Bath; or Jacob of Capua, who worked at Padua. Most important of all was John of Seville (Avendeath), a baptised member of the Ibn Daud family,

E

who took a particularly prominent part in this activity, working in collaboration with such men as Plato of Tivoli. No mediaeval translator, with the exception of the indefatigable Gerard of Cremona, produced a greater bulk of work. He translated Avicenna, al-Gazali and 'Avicebron' among the philosophers, as well as many works in all branches of science. He was responsible for the introduction to Europe of the *Secretum Secretorum* ascribed to Aristotle—one of the most popular works of the Middle Ages, which has not entirely lost its vogue even to-day. He may be said, indeed, to have provided a large proportion of the scientific equipment of the average mediaeval library.

Similarly, in astronomy, the Jews played a most important role in transferring the Arabic knowledge of the stars, and Graeco-Arabic astronomy in general, from Islam to Christendom: and all the more important astronomical tables of the Middle Ages were either translated or compiled with Jewish aid. This, as we shall see, was to be of the utmost importance for its bearing upon the progress of maritime exploration. It was John of Seville who translated into Latin the works of al-Battani and al-Farghani, the two chief Arabic writers on astronomy. The latter, under the name Alfergano, is cited by Dante: various passages in the *Convito* and the *Vita Nuova* are based upon his theories. Al-Kindi's treatise of the Stations of the Moon was translated for Robert of Anjou by Kalonymus ben Kalonymus ("Maestro Calo"). Al-Heitham's astronomical compendium was translated from Arabic into Spanish by a Jew named Abraham at the request of Alfonso X; Jacob ben Makhir translated al-Hazen's *Astronomy*, and the works of Autolycus and Menelaus on the Sphere.

While working at the court of Frederick II, Jacob Anatoli (who has been mentioned above), came into contact with the great Michael Scot, one of the outstanding figures in the intellectual life of the Middle Ages, whose name is still a byword for supernatural knowledge. It was he who was sent by the Emperor on a mission to the Universities of Europe to communicate to them versions of Aristotle which he and others had made, and this mission makes him one of the most important figures in the Latin Renaissance. It is highly probable that he is to be identified with a certain remarkable Christian sage, whom Anatoli often cites cryptically though with the utmost respect. Whether this is so or no, it is certain that Jews were very closely associated in his work. For this, we have for instance the evidence of Roger Bacon, who informs us categorically that a Jew named Andrew was principally responsible for those translations from the Arabic which are bound up with the name of Michael the Scot, as well as with those ascribed to Herman the German, Alfred the Englishman, and William the Fleming. These translations included works no less important than the *Metaphysics* of Aristotle and his *On the Secrets of Nature*—two compositions fundamental for mediaeval philosophic thought.

Bacon infers that Michael was ignorant of Arabic; in which case the share of this Andrew (who has been conjecturally identified with Anatoli himself) must have been all-important. This evidence confirms and illustrates in a remarkable fashion the fact that the Jewish share in the early revival of learning was of the utmost significance.

§III

The participation of the Jews in European intellectual currents knew no intermission, continuing—though with abated force, owing to the growth of persecution—through the period of the Italian Renaissance. Down to the middle of the sixteenth century, Jewish savants (such as Jacob Mantino, one-time physician to the Pope at Rome and to the Doge at Venice: or Abraham de Balmes, medical attendant on the Cardinal Grimaldi) continued to carry on the work of translation—now, indeed, into an elegant Latin, and not, as hitherto, into the "barbarous" mediaeval scholastic dialect. By this time, the original Greek sources were being opened to the world with increasing rapidity, and the work of translation became less important. The Jew, excluded with growing rigour from academic life, henceforth played a part less fundamental than he had in the earliest stage of the Renaissance. Yet it was far from a negligible one; for, notwithstanding all the difficulties in his way, his intellectual interests could not be suppressed, and his collaboration is to be traced in almost every facet of the Renewal of Learning. It is thus no coincidence that the countries which led in the revival of the fifteenth century were those which still contained considerable Jewish settlements. A King of Portugal, successor and namesake of the ruler who was responsible for the peculiarly brutal Expulsion from that country in 1497, has left on record his own conviction that "the Renaissance found Portugal ready to receive its impetus because the way had already been prepared partly by the learned Portuguese Jews."

It was symptomatic that one of the flood of Greek scholars who streamed westwards after the Fall of Constantinople in 1453, and brought the Revival of Letters to flower, was himself a Jew—Elijah del Medigo, of Crete. This savant was regarded in his day as one of the foremost, if not the foremost, exponent of Aristotelian philosophy, as distinct from the fashionable Platonism then gaining ground. In 1480, he was summoned to Padua as referee in a dispute in University circles. Here he made the acquaintance of Giovanni Pico della Mirandola, who invited him to Florence to act as his tutor. Pico, that knight-errant of the Renaissance, was himself deeply interested in Hebrew studies and particularly in the Cabbala, which he first introduced to the Christian world; but it was in philosophy that he desired Del Medigo's guidance. The latter thus became a familiar figure in humanistic circles in Florence. He was depicted in Gozzoli's famous fresco in the Medici Palace in the Via Larga; and there can be little doubt that he was to be met among the brilliant company which assembled to discuss philosophical problems in the Orti Oricellai. Nor was he the only Jewish savant who figured in the cosmopolitan body of scholars which the Medici attracted to Florence. There was (for example) Johanan Alemanno, an expert in the Greek and Arabic philosophies as well as Hebrew literature, in whose writings there is a penetrating delineation of Lorenzo the Magnificent and his surroundings: or again Abraham Farisol, the cosmographer, who informs us how he saw at the court of the Medici a giraffe sent by the Sultan of Egypt. The influence of these Jewish savants on the Florentine thinkers, such as Marsilio Ficino as well as Pico himself, cannot be overlooked.

Other Jewish participants in the New Birth in Italy illustrate the great breadth of their interests, co-extensive with that of the Renaissance as a whole. Among those who enjoyed Lorenzo the Magnificent's patronage in Florence was Guglielmo da Pesaro, author of one of the earliest extant treatises on the art of dancing, which had a considerable vogue in Italian society during the fifteenth and sixteenth centuries: Giovanni Maria, the musician, who subsequently apostasised and was raised by Leo X to the dignity of Count of Verocchio: and more than one other. This activity was not, of course, restricted to Florence. Benvenuto Cellini had as one of his masters

Graziadio the Jew, of Bologna: and the metal-worker
Salamone da Sessa (subsequently converted, as Ercole
de' Fedeli) worked at the Courts of Mantua and Ferrara,
as well as for that most discriminating patron, Cesare
Borgia. There were lesser artists all over Italy, of whom
Moses da Castellazzo is best remembered in Jewish
annals. In the seventeenth century, Joseph Levi and
Angelo de' Rossi of Verona (whose names would appear
significant) enjoyed a high reputation, and their productions are still sought after by collectors. And, at the
Court of Mantua, when it was one of the centres of Italian
intellectual life, the Jews played a part of real importance,
in their corporate capacity, in the development of the
nascent drama.

Much of the activity of the Italian Jews at the period
of the Renaissance will be dealt with below in different
connexions. As an illustration however of the extent
of their interests, one may take a single humble instance
—the handkerchief. Further research is still required
on the early history of this indispensable article. In
England, it does not appear to be a very ancient institution: for the Oxford English Dictionary does not furnish
any instance of the use of the word previous to 1530.
But Italian Jews were familiar with the institution long
before then. In the writings of a certain Rabbi named
Isaiah of Trani, who died in the first half of the fourteenth
century, we find a detailed description of "the piece of
cloth used for cleansing the nose" which he called by
its Italian name, *fazzoletto*. This is certainly one of the
earliest mentions of the object. To assume on the basis
of this that the Jews invented it would be too much.
But we are justified in deducing that they soon adopted
it, and used it widely before it was in general employment in any but the highest circles, and certainly before
it was familiar in England.

As it happens, this record may be carried on a little further. At the beginning of the sixteenth century, a French student who visited Italy, named François Tissard, took the opportunity to study local Jewish life. His observations are embodied in the prefatory matter to his Hebrew and Greek Grammar which he published shortly after his return home, *Grammatica Hebraica et Graeca* (Paris 1508: this is the earliest surviving work printed in France, in which Hebrew type was used). Among other matters, he calls particular attention to what he considered the disgusting habit of one of his Jewish teachers at Ferrara, who used to carry a piece of cloth about with him and would put it to his mouth to remove his spittle, instead of expectorating on the ground like a decent Christian! "I began to abhor this fellow for this to such an extent," observes Tissard, naïvely, "that I may take him as my example."

This Jewish anticipation of what is now regarded as an elementary piece of hygiene, ridiculed by non-Jewish observers, has its parallel in a practice to which attention was drawn by Rammazzini, the great Italian physician of the seventeenth century and originator of the study of occupational diseases. He mentions, among the outstandingly insanitary habits of the Jews of Venice, their practice of keeping the windows open, day and night! The Italian physician's attitude is in striking contrast to the prescriptions of Moses Maimonides, who, five centuries before, had recommended air and sunlight as being among the most important safeguards of health.[1]

---

[1] A modern parallel may be adduced. In the lavatories in New York restaurants, a card is prominently displayed requesting employees to wash their hands after using the toilet, in accordance with a recent municipal regulation. This hygienic practice has been universal among Jews (not only for restaurant employees) for twenty centuries, as a quasi-religious prescription.

Or, to take a final instance; a public bath was regarded as an essential institution of the Jewish quarter (it was better for a Jew to live in a town without a synagogue than in one which lacked a public bath, the Rabbis had taught), and systematic ablutions were part of the recognised system of religious hygiene. Hence John Locke, in urging the benefits of cold water on his fellow-countrymen, appealed to the example of the Jews:—

"If the rivers of Italy are warmer, those of Germany and Poland are much colder than any in this our country; and yet in these the Jews, both men and women, bathe all over, at all seasons of the year, without any prejudice to their health."

(Some Thoughts concerning
Education. (1690) §7)

§iv

The revival of learning would have remained the prerogative of a comparatively small class had it not been for the invention of printing. The Jews were quick to realise the potentialities of this new art. As early as 1444—six years, that is, before the date generally assigned to the beginning of Gutenberg's activity—an agreement for the cutting of a Hebrew fount "according to the art of writing artificially", was entered into at Avignon between a wandering German craftsman and a member of the local community. No specimens of this earliest Hebrew press, unfortunately, have survived: a fact for which the persecution of Hebrew literature (hardly less ruthless in its day than the persecution of the Jews themselves) may well be held responsible. But before long Hebrew presses were active in more than one part of the Jewish world: and in several places the Jews were pioneers, anticipating the other local craftsmen by some years. Thus, in Portugal, Hebrew printing began in 1478, but non-Hebrew only seven years later, when the first Latin book appeared (no work in the Portuguese language earlier than 1495 is known)[1]. Indeed, of the twenty-four known books printed in Portugal before 1500, the first eleven are in Hebrew.

When the Jews were driven out of this country in 1497, they took their skill and their equipment with them : and various Hebrew works are extant printed at Fez shortly after—notably an edition of the liturgical guide, *Abudrahim*. This is the earliest book printed in the whole of the African continent. Similarly, the first book printed in the Balkans was the Hebrew Code of Rabbi Jacob ben Asher (Constantinople 1493); and the earliest work printed by the European method in Asia is a commentary on the Book of Esther, published at Safed, in Palestine, in 1577. At Cairo, where a European press was started only in 1798, during Napoleon's expedition, a Hebrew press had been active as early as 1557.

It was not only in Hebrew printing that Jews were active. Notwithstanding the efforts made to exclude them from honourable walks of life, a few managed to become engaged in secular work. Thus, Abraham Zacuto's Almanac and astronomical tables were published by Abraham d'Orta at Leiria in 1496, in two editions —Latin and Spanish. The latter is noteworthy, as it is the only incunable printed in Portugal with the text neither Latin, nor Portuguese, nor Hebrew. At the beginning of the following century, Girolamo Soncino was active as a publisher in Northern Italy, mainly in Latin and Italian. He was at pains to search out manuscripts in order to establish the best texts, his edition

---

[1] There is, indeed, a vague and probably inaccurate reference to a book of 1490, but even this is some time after the initiative had come from the Jews.

of Petrarch being particularly noteworthy. Moreover, he contests with the great Aldo the credit for first realising the potentialities of the so-called Italic type.[1] Similarly the most famous Portuguese romance of the sixteenth century, Ribeiro's *Menina e Moca*, was first published by the Jew Usque at Ferrara in 1554.

Perhaps the most important factor in the popularisation of learning, without which the newly-invented printing-press would have remained little more than a toy, was the substitution of parchment—always expensive, and necessarily restricted in quantity—by an unlimited supply of paper. The Chinese had long ago made paper from silk and other materials. The Arabs had learned to manufacture it from cotton: but it was not until a late date that Western Europe mastered the art, beginning to make linen paper. The Jews once again were among the pioneers: and the earliest known paper factory in Europe was that which they now established in Jativa, near Valencia.

§v

The Renaissance, when it crossed the Alps from Italy to Germany, took on a different complexion. The serious, introspective Germanic spirit found itself compelled to take into consideration various questions which the light-hearted Italians had preferred not to raise, or the answers to which they had taken for granted. The spirit of enquiry, which had been fostered by a re-examination

---

[1] It is not uninteresting to note that bilingual typographic activity was not confined to western Europe. The first Turkish press, founded at Constantinople in 1729 (over two hundred years after the first Hebrew press in that city, set up in 1503) was carried on with the help of a Jew named Jonas.

It may be mentioned at this point that the greatest step forward in printing after the days of Gutenberg, the invention of the composing machine at the close of the nineteenth century, was due to Otmar Bergenthal, a German of Jewish origin.

of mediaeval science, was now applied to mediaeval religion. Literary criticism, developed in order to cope with the texts of classical literature, was applied to that of the Latin Bible. The new-found passion for going back to the sources was applied to the Catholic tradition : and the same spirit which had questioned authority in philosophy began to question it in matters of faith. The Renaissance, in fact, developed in its Northern form into the Reformation. This in turn had its repercussions south of the Alps in the Catholic Reaction, or Counter-Reformation. In the end, the religious life of Europe, whether it titularly retained the old faith or embraced the new form, was revolutionised.

The share of the Jews in bringing about the Reformation is frequently exaggerated, and generally misunderstood. The Reformation (like all Christian Reform Movements before and after) implied a return to the Scriptures. All agitators for Reform necessarily applied to the Bible for support, and occasionally approximated to Biblical practice in one matter or the other. It was hence natural that one of the commonest terms of ecclesiastical vituperation in the Middle Ages was "Judaiser"—an epithet which recurs in the controversial works of the period with wearisome frequency.

But in fact it was very seldom justified. The Jew, as such, had no interest in the dispute, one way or the other. There was little for him to choose, theologically speaking, between the Reformed and Catholic forms of Christianity. Nor was there any material reason why he should prefer the one to the other. It was true that Martin Luther at the outset of his career had referred to its atrocious treatment of the Jews as an additional argument against the Church of Rome. Yet later he had reversed his opinions, and inveighed against them with a virulence which surpassed the worst precedent that the Middle

Ages could provide. For many years to come, there was very little to differentiate Catholic from Protestant Europe, so far as their treatment of the Jews was concerned; and, if the latter subsequently changed its policy, originally the reason lay in considerations of economics and expedience rather than in abstract, disinterested toleration.

It is thus misleading to speak of a direct Jewish influence upon the Reformation.[1] Yet the influence upon it of Jewish scholarship, and hence of individual Jewish scholars, was far from negligible. As has been pointed out, the Reformation was based upon the rejection of Catholic tradition in favour of the authority of the Bible and the removal from the latter of the glosses by means of which (as the Reformers claimed) the Church of the Middle Ages had attempted to maintain its ascendancy over religious thought. But the Bible was available to the western world only in its official Catholic version, the Vulgate; it was the Jews alone who possessed the Hebrew original and the key to its interpretation. Hence, just as Italian savants applied to Greek scholars for guidance in their researches into Plato, so German theologians applied to Jewish Rabbis for assistance in understanding the Hebrew Scriptures. It was only a coincidence, perhaps, that the intellectual clash in Germany began with an attempt on the part of the Dominicans to suppress the Talmud, which was doughtily championed by Johannes von Reuchlin; yet it was

[1] An exception is to be made only as regards the Marranos, or crypto-Jews of Spain and Portugal. Compulsorily converted to Catholicism, they could not be expected to appreciate its spirituality; yet in many cases they entirely lacked Jewish knowledge and loyalties. They were hence a particularly favourable soil for the Reformed doctrine, and played an important part in its propagation in Flanders. Thus Marc Perez, the Calvinist leader at Antwerp in the middle of the sixteenth century, was of Jewish extraction, as were many of his coadjutors.

symptomatic in its way of the trend of events. All the great leaders of Reform—Luther, Zwingli, Melanchthon, Tyndale, Servetus, and so on—studied Hebrew. Many of them, too, had Jewish scholars to teach them. Reuchlin, for example, had been instructed by Jacob Loans (physician to the Emperor Frederick III) in Germany, and by Obadiah Sforno in Italy; and these two savants have been reckoned for that reason among the fathers of the Protestant Reformation.

The newly-aroused interest could not be confined to the Hebrew text of the Bible. In order to understand the Scriptures, it was necessary to have recourse to Rabbinical literature, so as to discover what was the Jewish tradition on the subject. From this period dates the real beginning of Christian Hebrew scholarship, the establishment of effective Chairs of Hebrew at the principal European universities, and the emergence of a class of Christian Hebraists of real ability, whose contributions to Jewish scholarship have sometimes been of the utmost value.

The recourse to Jewish tradition was fruitful, and left a permanent mark. In particular, the writings of the great mediaeval Franco-Jewish Biblical commentators —Solomon ben Isaac of Troyes ('Rashi') and David Kimhi of Narbonne—were of the highest importance: for it was upon them that the new translations of the Bible, the bedrock of the Reformation, in the last instance depended. Luther, indeed, relied principally upon Nicholas de Lyra, the fourteenth century Franciscan exegete (himself said to have been a Jew by birth). His critics indeed sneered at him on that account: had Lyra not lyred, they said, Luther could never have danced. But Lyra himself was dependent to an overwhelming extent on the writings of Rashi, whose interpretations in many instances he simply adapted, giving them a

Christian tinge. Subsequently, Lyra's writings were
furnished with an important supplement (likewise used
by Luther) by Paul de Santa Maria, Bishop of Burgos,
who had formerly been Rabbi Solomon Levi and naturally
derived to a large extent from Jewish sources. Kimhi's
commentary was similarly used in a large degree by
successive generations of Christian exegetes—particularly
in the preparation of the English "Authorised Version"
of 1611. To such an extent was this so, indeed, that (as
has been aptly said) though no Jews were tolerated in
England at the time when this magnificent achievement
was being produced, Rabbi David Kimhi was present
at Westminster in spirit.

Hence, just as Jewish collaborators assisted in the
labour of translation of secular and scientific texts into
Latin which marked the beginning of the revival of
learning, so the Hebraic spirit, Jewish learning, and
individual Jewish scholars, participated to a marked
extent in its latest phase—the Biblical research and
re-examination of doctrine which accompanied the revival of religion.

CHAPTER IV

THE GREAT VOYAGES OF DISCOVERY

§1

"THE greatest event which has happened since the creation of the world (leaving aside the incarnation and death of Him who made it) is the discovery of the Indies" wrote a sixteenth-century Spaniard, Francisco Lopez de Gomara, dedicating his *Hispania Felix* to the Emperor Charles V. There was less exaggeration in this statement than was customary in such effusions; for the disclosure of the sea-route to India in the one direction, and of the existence of the vast American Continent in the other, was among the most epoch-making occurrences in all recorded history. The succession of maritime discoveries, at the close of the fifteenth century, suddenly enlarged men's horizons, shewing them the existence of a new world, other than that known to their fathers and fathers' fathers before them. It provided humanity with a new universe to conquer. It shifted the balance of power from the Mediterranean to the countries of the Atlantic coast. It laid the foundation of Europe and of the world as we know them to-day.

The discovery of America and of the Indies was not, to be sure, a sudden stroke of genius or of luck, but the culmination of a gradual movement spread over many generations. The earth had, from antiquity, been regarded as a sphere of which only a small part was known. Already in the thirteenth century, the English friar, Roger Bacon, had adduced the authority of Hebrew

63

writers to shew that Asia could be reached by sailing west from Europe. Indeed, the Rabbis had made some astonishing guesses about the structure of the universe, which by coincidence were near enough to the truth. The so-called "Jerusalem" Talmud (*Aboda Zara*, 42c.) boldly states that the world is in the form of a globe. The *Zohar* (Leviticus i. 3.) goes even further, asserting that the earth rotates on its axis like a ball; thus, when it is day in one half of the globe, the other half is plunged in darkness, and those living below have their heads in the opposite direction to those above. This statement —which was accepted by mediaeval scholars, like the thirteenth-century author of the *Mashal haKadmoni*, Isaac Sahulla—familiarised in wide circles among the Jews the conjecture of antipodean conditions which, from the days of Cosmas Indicopleustes, had been treated with general derision.

The progress of maritime discovery at the close of the Middle Ages was bound up with certain technical improvements. Ships were small: knowledge was limited: mechanical aids almost non-existent. Even after the introduction of the compass, it remained impossible to estimate the position of a ship at sea. The starting-point in the history of modern exploration was hence when navigation became oceanic—that is to say, when ships could sail out boldly into uncharted seas instead of hugging the coast or steering in a direction which would bring them in sight of known land within a few hours.

In the development and perfection of the instruments and tables by means of which this became possible, Jewish savants—who were deeply interested in astronomy —played a part of the utmost importance, which associates their names inseparably with the whole story of the maritime discoveries.

The most important nautical instrument in the early days was the quadrant, for the determination of the Right Ascension of the sun and stars, and hence the relative position of the vessel at any given moment. For a long time, the quadrant in general use was one devised by that twelfth-century genius known as Robert the Englishman, first translator of the Koran into any European language. His invention held the field for many generations, until it was superseded by an improved instrument introduced by Rabbi Jacob ben Makhir ibn Tibbon—compiler, incidentally, of the Calendar used by Dante. This was known after him as the *Quadrans Judaicus*. The importance of Jacob ben Makhir's work was universally recognised; for he was read, and quoted with respect, by the founders of modern astronomy—Copernicus and Kepler—long after his day. More than a dozen works from his pen are recorded: and he is said to have acted as Regent of the faculty of Medicine at Montpellier.

A more important invention was due to Rabbi Levi ben Gershom of Bagnols, in South France, the most eminent Jewish philosopher and exegete of the fourteenth century. His *magnum opus* was a philosophical work, *The Wars of the Lord*, which covered also a considerable part of the field of natural science. An entire section, comprising no less than 136 chapters out of a total of 237, is devoted to astronomy. Such was the reputation which the author enjoyed that, almost as soon as the book was put into circulation, Pope Clement VI had the astronomical portion translated into Latin: a fortunate occurrence, as, when the original Hebrew was ultimately published, that part was not considered to be of sufficient theological importance to warrant inclusion. In this treatise, the author described an improved quadrant which he had invented, more easily handled than the

F

cumbrous old affair. The great Regiomontanus, reading this account, was so impressed that he constructed an instrument according to the Rabbi's recommendations, which he named *Jacob's Staff*. This was the instrument which accompanied all the great explorers of the age of the Renaissance on their travels, and was principally relied upon by them for their calculations—Vasco da Gama, Magellan, even Christopher Columbus himself. It remained in use for approximately three centuries; its general employment among mariners was not given up until John Hadley's reflecting quadrant was adopted by the British Admiralty in 1734; and even after that date it long continued to be used by surveyors for land-measurements.[1]

The quadrant, used alone, was inadequate as an aid in navigation; and, in the heyday of the Portuguese maritime activity, at the close of the fifteenth century, the scientists at the Court of King João II of Portugal advised him to find out whether it was possible to extend the scope of the mechanical devices hitherto employed by adapting to nautical use the old planispheric astrolabe known to the Greeks. The King entrusted this task to a commission of three scientists. One of them was Martin Behaim (that is "the Bohemian"), said by some

[1] The 'Jacob's Staff' consisted of a long central bar marked with a scale and provided with a movable cross-bar (or four of varying sizes, used alternatively). One end was placed to the eye and the traversal was adjusted until one end was in line with the sun and the other with the horizon. By calculating the length of the cross-piece and its distance from the eye, the angle between the sun and the horizon could easily be calculated. With the aid of this instrument, it was thus possible to prick the chart while at sea, instead of landing (as had hitherto been necessary) each time the position was to be determined. A remarkable representation of the instrument is constantly before our eyes in the picture of the Knave of Diamonds, as it is to be found in any ordinary pack of playing-cards. Under the name 'sun-glass', it continued to be used by Suffolk sailors within living memory. From Marlowe's *Tamburlaine the Great*, II. iii. 3, it seems that, besides being used for navigation, Jacob's Staff was the earliest form of range-finder.

authorities to have been a Jew. With him were associated the King's two Jewish physicians, Master Rodrigo and Master Joseph Vecinho. The three savants set to work methodically; and the result of their labours was the manufacture of an improved astrolabe which, used in conjunction with tables of the solar declination which they prepared, rendered it possible to navigate by observation of the sun. Portuguese historians record this discovery with unalloyed pride: for it was from now only that oceanic navigation in its complete sense became possible.

Navigation necessarily required one other aid, without which the instruments were useless—reliable astronomical tables, essential in all work based on solar or sidereal observation.[1] It happens that all the more important astronomical tables of the Middle Ages, without exception, were at least translated or compiled with the help of Jews: in the most important cases they were entirely of Jewish authorship.

Shortly before the capture of Toledo by the Christian forces in 1085, a series of astronomical tables had been drawn up in that city—the swan-song, as it were, of Arab science in the old capital. In the compilation of these (the Toledo Tables, as they are termed) a number of Jewish astronomers had assisted. Some time later, in the thirteenth century, Alfonso the Wise, King of Castile, in his endeavour to naturalise Moslem science in his dominions, set about having these adapted for the use of non-Moslem scholars and brought up to date. Among those to whom he applied with this object in view were Judah ben Moses Cohen, a Jewish physician, and Isaac

---

[1] What follows is based upon, and in part quoted from, Joseph Jacob's admirable summary in his *Jewish Contributions to Civilisation* —a superb achievement which, had he been spared to complete it, would have rendered a great part of the present work unnecessary. Much use has been made in this section also of the chapter in *The Legacy of Israel* on "The Jewish Factor in Mediaeval Thought."

ben Sid, *hazan* or Reader in a Toledo Synagogue. These two, in collaboration with other Jewish savants, were the authors of the famous "Alfonsine Tables," which they themselves translated into Spanish and which continued in great repute for centuries. They are found in innumerable manuscripts and were published time after time long after the invention of printing (the last edition which appeared for practical use was that of Madrid of 1641). As late as the seventeenth century, they were still being consulted by Kepler and even Galileo.

The Alfonsine Tables in their turn were adapted for his contemporaries in 1310 by Isaac Israeli of Toledo, and in his rescension became classical throughout Europe, being utilised by Scaliger, the sixteenth-century founder of the modern science of chronology, and by Petavius. Further astronomical tables formerly in general use were compiled by Joseph ibn Wakkar at Toledo in 1396, and in Aragon by various Jewish savants for Pedro III (IV). Other calculations were made by Emanuel ben Jacob, known to the outside world as Bonfils de Tarascon. These were shortly afterwards translated into Latin from the original Hebrew, and were extensively used by many European scholars of the age of the Renaissance —pre-eminently by Pico della Mirandola and Peiresc.[1]

§II

One of the principal centres of activity in the period of preparation which led up to the great maritime discoveries of the late Middle Ages was Majorca. The

---

[1] It is interesting to note that even the points of the compass, as they were known to mariners of old, owed their nomenclature to Jews. It is in the *Sepher Asaph* of the ninth (?) century that we first find these mentioned by the names current in the Middle Ages— *Graecum, Scirrocum, Garbinum, Magistrum.* These terms were taken over by the Latin world, and were crystallised by mention in the *Treasure* composed by Brunetto Latini between 1260 and 1269.

island lies midway between Europe and Africa. It inherited the traditions of Islamic civilisation—of which it was one of the last European refuges—as well as of Latin culture; its inhabitants—many of whom were Jews— were from necessity skilled navigators, as much at home on the high seas as in their own sea-girt birthplace. In consequence, they were considered to be familiar in an unrivalled degree with the art of navigation, the configura- tion of the coasts, and geographical knowledge in general as it then existed. By degrees, their reputation extended. In the end, they came to be the cartographers *par excellence* of Christendom, application being made to them on all occasions when new maps were required— more especially, of course, by the princes and rulers of the Spanish mainland. Their productions may be said to sum up geographical science so far as it was known in the later Middle Ages, and to have served as the point of departure for subsequent extensions of knowledge.

So much is more or less familiar. But what is not so generally realised is the fact that these Majorcan carto- graphers, upon whom Europe relied for its geographical knowledge, were for the most part Jews. At their head was the Crescas family. Abraham Crescas was so highly esteemed that he was appointed by the Infant Juan of Aragon as "Master of Maps and Compasses", a dignity for which he was paid, apparently, by an authorisation to establish a public bath for his co-religionists at Palma. On one occasion the Infant Juan of Aragon wrote to the authorities on the island stating that he wanted a chart which would represent the Straits of Gibraltar, the Atlantic coasts and the mysterious ocean beyond, in the most complete manner possible. It was natural that the task was entrusted to Abraham Crescas and his son Jahuda. They worked on it for two years (1376–7): and the result was their famous *mapamundi*—"that is to say, an image of the world and of the various states of the world and of the regions which are on the earth and of the divers manners of people which inhabit it." This, now famous as the Catalan Atlas, is one of the most remarkable monuments of mediaeval science that have come down to us. "Never have we seen so fair a map", cried Don Juan when he saw it. The sources from which Crescas obtained his information cannot be ascertained; but it is certain that he must have made use of the experiences of Yuceff Faquin, a Barcelona Jew who had settled in Majorca and who was reported to have navigated the entire known world.

The sequel was remarkable. In 1381, Charles VI of France (who was responsible for the expulsion of the Jews from that country thirteen years later) in a communication to the Infant Juan, informed him of his desire to possess an atlas of the world executed by the cartographers of Majorca, who enjoyed so high a reputation for their care and precision. The other replied that he knew of no "mapamundi" better than that recently executed by his Jewish subjects. This he generously despatched with his letter, with careful instructions as to its transport. It remained a prized possession of the Royal Library in Paris and is now among the treasures of the Bibliothèque Nationale. Much has been written about it and in recent times it has twice been reproduced in facsimile. This work marks a real epoch in European map-making, inasmuch as it added for the first time the discoveries of Marco Polo to the conventional map-drawing which had continued almost unchanged for centuries.[1]

[1] The most recent work which describes the activities of these Jewish cartographers is Lionel Isaacs' *The Jews of Majorca*, London, 1936. But it is more suggestive to refer to Charles de la Roncière's *La Découverte de l'Afrique au Moyen Age* (vol. I, Cairo, 1925; published by the Royal Geographical Society of Egypt) which devotes an entire chapter to this subject.

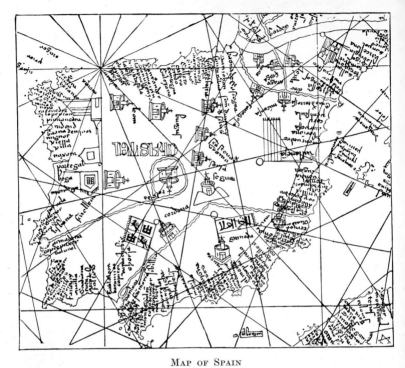

MAP OF SPAIN

From the Catalan Atlas by Abraham and Jahuda Crescas, 1376–7,
in the Bibliothèque Nationale, Paris

Abraham Crescas continued to work unremittingly under the patronage of the Aragonese Court until 1387. On his death in that year, his son, Jahuda (the Compass or Map Jew, as he was popularly called), who had long been associated with him, inherited his reputation and his clientèle, and we find his former patron, now King of Aragon, commissioning a new "mapamundi" from him to replace that sent to France.

In the wave of forced baptisms which swept through Spain in 1391, Jahuda Crescas was compelled to change his religion. Henceforth he was called Jayme Ribes. But he was too useful to be allowed to change his occupation, and he was summoned to Barcelona to conduct his work in the immediate neighbourhood of the Court. On the death of his patron and of the latter's successor, Martin I, who had continued his scientific interests, Jayme Ribes was invited by Prince Henry the Navigator to Portugal; and here, where he was known as **Maestre Jacomo de Majorca**, he was the first director of the famous nautical observatory at Sagres, cradle of the Portuguese discoveries, where the expeditions were prepared which resulted in the rounding of the Cape of Good Hope and the discovery of the sea-route to India.

Another Jewish cartographer of Majorca (who is conjectured to have belonged to Abraham Crescas' family) was Haym ibn Risch. He, too, became converted at the time of the persecutions in 1391, adopting the name of Juan de Vallsecha. He was probably the father of the Gabriel de Vallsecha who executed in 1439 another famous "mapamundi"—now one of the treasures of the Institute of Catalan Studies in Barcelona, for it belonged to Amerigo Vespucci—in which the meridian of the Azores is used for the first time in the history of cartography. Yet another Majorcan cartographer of Jewish birth was Mecia de Viladestes, a map by whom, dated 1413, is preserved in the Bibliothèque Nationale in Paris.

It is significant that the anti-Jewish persecutions marked the end of the glories of the Majorcan school of cartography. The little group of *conversos* continued the Jewish tradition for another generation; thereafter, there was a phenomenally rapid decadence. A single point illustrates this in a highly impressive fashion. The Jewish map-makers with their wide-spread connexions had known and indicated all that was possible about the cities, the trade-routes, and the oases of the Sahara. Their successors forgot it all. Pedro Roselli, in his planisphere of 1465, seventy-five years after the outbreak of persecution, marked only four localities to the south of the Atlas range; his successors knew only one.[1]

§III

With regard to the antecedents of Christopher Columbus, a certain degree of mystery, largely of his own making, still prevails. This is chiefly due, apparently, to the fact that, in his anxiety to claim a noble origin, he spoke as little and as confusedly as possible about his parentage. There are certain obvious discrepancies, moreover, between his own account of his career and

[1] It was not only by their provision of maps that the Jewish scientists of Majorca contributed to geographical discovery. They also excelled as manufacturers of nautical instruments. Two were especially famous. The physician Isaac Nafuci was a favourite of Pedro IV of Aragon, who called him "the celebrated Jew of Majorca" and never tired of singing his praises. In 1359, the King chose him "to make the clocks and quadrants that we desire", and in 1365, at a critical moment of the war with Castile, he ordered payment to be made to him for a silver quadrant which he had provided. Nafuci worked in conjunction with the Majorcan Jewish scientist Ephraim Bellshom (to whom, incidentally, a contemporary Rabbi turned to discover the area of a globe, in connexion with the construction of a ritual bath). The two collaborated in the manufacture of an astrolabe for the use of the Infant Juan, together with a translation into Catalan of an astronomical work of the famous al-Farghani.

what we know from documentary sources of that of Cristofer Colombo, son of the Genoese weaver, with whom he is generally identified.

Spanish scholars (such as Jose M. Erugo, C. Garcia de la Riega, Otero Sanchez, Nicholas Diaz Perez, etc.), in order to vindicate him for their own country, have put forward the hypothesis that he was of Marrano, or crypto-Jewish, extraction, obliged on that account to be secretive as to his origin. Certain it is that the name of Colombo, or Colon, is by no means unknown among Jews; that Christopher left a small legacy to a Jew living by the gate of the Jews' Street in Lisbon; that he shews a particularly strong Biblical influence in his writings; that his somewhat mysterious signature is capable of Hebraic interpretations only slightly more unsatisfactory than those generally current; and that his son states categorically that his father's progenitors were of the royal blood of Jerusalem—*a phraseology consistently used by Spanish Jews of the period when they desired to boast their aristocratic origin.* "The theory that Columbus was born at Pontevedra . . . cannot lightly be brushed aside," asserts André, in his biography. "On the other hand, there is perhaps equal reason for believing him born in Aragon, *the son of converted Jews.*"

Whatever the truth of this may be, it is incontestable that the great explorer had a penchant for Jewish society, and that Jews were intimately associated with his enterprise from the beginning.

Discouraged by his failure in Portugal, where he had first applied for assistance, Columbus had made his way to Spain. Here, too, he met with rebuff after rebuff. The only persons who took him seriously were a little group, all or nearly all of whom were either Jews or else of Jewish descent—belonging to the group of the so-called

Marranos who, converted to Christianity by force during the persecutions at the close of the fourteenth century and in the following three decades, still remained at heart, in most instances, faithful to the religion of their fathers. The most prominent of them was the learned Diego de Deza, later Inquisitor General, who, notwithstanding his Christian zeal, belonged to a family which originated in the *juderia ;* the latter introduced him to Abraham Zacuto, the astronomer (below, pp. 76-9), whose discoveries were utilised to such good effect by the explorer later on. A striking contrast to Deza was Don Isaac Abrabanel, the last scholar-statesman of Spanish Jewry, who occupied an important position in the financial administration of the country, yet devoted all his leisure to Jewish studies. His associate, Abraham Senior, last Crown Rabbi of Castile, was likewise a staunch supporter of the explorer. More influential still was Luis de Santangel, Chancellor and Comptroller of the Royal Household, a great-grandson of the Jew Noah Chinillo of Calatayud. Gabriel Sanchez, another of the most fervent supporters of the expedition, was similarly of full Jewish origin, being son of a *converso* couple and nephew of Alazar Ussuf, of Saragossa. Among Columbus' other patrons were Alfonso de la Caballeria, member of a famous Marrano family and Vice-Chancellor of Aragon, and Juan Cabrero, the Royal Chamberlain. Indeed, the only one of the high officials intimately concerned with the genesis of the expedition belonging to an "Old Christian" house was the royal secretary, Juan de Coloma, whose wife was, however, descended from the Jewish clan of De la Caballeria.

It was this group which rallied round Columbus when he seemed faced with failure and was preparing to leave Spain for good. Santangel secured him an audience with the Queen and, representing to her the advantages which would accrue to the Crown and to Spain from the discovery of the sea-route to the Indies, persuaded her to neglect the adverse views of the pedants upon whom she had previously relied. When at last she had acquiesced, the question of finance remained. Once more, Santangel came forward, advancing without interest no less than 1,140,000 maravedis towards the expenses of the expedition. A certain amount was still requisite; this was found by Don Isaac Abrabanel. (The story that the Queen pawned her Crown jewels for the purpose of financing the expedition is a pious invention.)

Preparations for the expedition were now pushed forward. Columbus' crew consisted of some ninety men all told. Among the few of these whose names have been preserved, persons of known Jewish origin are prominent. One was Alonso de la Calle, whose very name indicated that he had been born in the Jewish quarter. Roderigo Sanches, a relative of the High Treasurer, joined the expedition at the personal request of the Queen. A New Christian named Marco was ship's surgeon; while Mestre Bernal, the ship's physician, had been punished a couple of years previously by the Inquisition as a Judaiser. Land was first sighted by the Marrano sailor, Rodrigo de Triana; and Luis de Torres, the interpreter, who had been baptised only a few days before the expedition sailed, was the first European to set foot in the New World. The expedition, moreover, was equipped with the astronomical tables and instruments of Abraham Zacuto and other Jewish scientists. On his return to Europe, the famous letters in which Columbus first announced the news of his discoveries were addressed to his Marrano patrons, Luis de Santangel and Gabriel Sanches. In view of all this evidence, it may be stated without exaggeration that the discovery of the New World as early as 1492 would have been unlikely but for the assistance of persons of Jewish origin.[1]

§IV

The Jewish scientific activity of the later Middle Ages culminated in the work of Abraham Zacuto, one of the most remarkable savants of the fifteenth century, whose work was of the utmost importance in the period of the great maritime discoveries. The most capable astronomer, perhaps, of his day, he had taught that subject (informally, as appears from the latest researches on the subject) at the University of Salamanca, where he met, and was consulted by, Columbus. On the expulsion of the Jews from Spain in 1492, he made his way to Portugal, where he received appointment almost immediately as Astronomer-Royal; and, when persecutions followed in that country in 1497, he managed to escape to North Africa, where he compiled the well-known chronicle, *Sepher Juhasin*, which made his name memorable in the annals of Jewish literature.

While at Salamanca, he compiled a series of astronomical tables, based on the work of his predecessors but considerably improved, which immediately obtained general recognition. His pupil, Joseph Vecinho (pp. 79-80), translated them into Latin and Spanish, and had them published at the press of the Jewish printer, Abraham d'Orta, at Leiria, in 1496. So highly esteemed was this work that, before the century was out, it was twice

[1] It is an ironic consideration that, notwithstanding the assistance which the Marranos had given in the discovery of the New World, they were not safe from persecution even here. As early as 1515, the Inquisition started its operations, bringing persons suspected of Judaising back to Europe for trial; and before the end of the century *autos de fé* were familiar spectacles in every part of the Spanish dominions overseas. Among the earliest victims of the Inquisition in the New World was Hernando Alonso, who had followed Cortes to Mexico, as one of the *conquistadores*; he was burned at the stake, with another Judaiser, in 1528.

re-published at Venice, the classical centre of the maritime art.[1] This compilation continued to be cited in Portugal long after the author had been driven out: thus, in the *Reportorio dos Tempos* (Lisbon, 1518) there are to be found tables of the declination of the sun, "punctually taken from Zacuto by the honest Gaspar Nicolas".

The tables of Zacuto were carried in the fleets of Vasco da Gama, Cabral, João da Nova and Albuquerque; but are most important for the use made of them by Christopher Columbus. In his writings, the latter mentions how he consulted the "Almanack" on his voyages and how, on one occasion, he saved himself and his companions from a difficult position by predicting an eclipse with its aid. It is pretty obvious that it is Zacuto's tables to which he here refers. In any case, it is indubitable that he took them with him on his later voyages: for there is preserved at Seville a copy of the Leiria edition which belonged to the great explorer. It has been conjectured that it was presented to him by the author or translator, and bears manuscript annotations from Columbus' own pen.

It was in Portugal that Zacuto's personal activity reached its zenith. Here he devised a new astrolabe, which he manufactured for the first time of iron, instead of wood (as had previously been customary), thus rendering that hitherto cumbrous instrument available for ordinary use. The assistance which he gave to Vasco da Gama, before he set out on the voyage which resulted in the discovery of the sea-route to India, was of the utmost importance. His opinion was asked by the Court before the expedition was authorised. The ships were provided with his improved astrolabe, and in

[1]There were other editions here in 1500, 1502, 1525 and 1528, and the work has been reproduced more than once in facsimile. See, most recently, A. Fontoura da Costa, *L' Almanach Perpetuum de Abraham Zacut* (1934, 1935).

contemporary records we catch a glimpse of lessons in its use being given to the navigators before they put out to sea. Such, indeed, was the impression that this new experiment created that it is referred to by Camoens in his *Lusiads*, the greatest Portuguese epic poem, in flowing verse.

The ultimate object of the great mediaeval voyages of discovery was to find a more convenient route to India. While Bartholomew Diaz with his two tiny caravels was ploughing his way south by sea towards the Cape of Good Hope, two other audacious pioneers, João Perez of Covilhã and Alfonso de Paiva, were despatched eastward to investigate the overland route; with them, they took among their equipment maps made by Behaim's two Jewish collaborators. Subsequently, two Jews were despatched in their wake—Joseph Çapateiro of Lamego, who had great experience of Eastern travel and had presented the King a report on Ormuz, the emporium of the Indian spice-trade, and Rabbi Abraham of Beja, whose knowledge of languages was considered remarkable. At Cairo, they met João Perez, now on his way back from India: his companion had died meanwhile, leaving his last instructions to a faithful Jew who had accompanied him in his travels.

Rabbi Abraham remained with Perez, going as far as Ormuz and then returning by the caravan route *via* Damascus and Aleppo. Joseph, on the other hand, was despatched hotfoot back to Lisbon. With him he brought all the information amassed from Arabian and Indian pilots which pointed to the existence of a sea-route to the Far East. Armed with this information, with the Majorcan maps, with Vecinho's tables and with Zacuto's improved astrolabe, Vasco da Gama set out on the epoch-making voyage which was to result in the discovery of the sea-route to India.

Before sailing from Lisbon on July 8th, 1497, Da Gama conferred publicly with Zacuto and took affectionate leave of him in the presence of the whole crew. And, on his arrival at Anchediva, not far from Goa, the explorer was greeted by a tall European with a flowing white beard—a Jew from Posen, who had found his way to India after incredible adventures, and had risen to the rank of Admiral to the Viceroy of Goa, whom he had persuaded to treat the strangers kindly. Da Gama's conduct towards the old man was incredibly ungrateful, even according to the brutal fifteenth-century standards. He had him seized and tortured until he consented to be baptised and to pilot the Portuguese flotilla in Indian waters. Gaspard da Gama (as he was henceforth known) subsequently accompanied Cabral on his voyage to the East in 1502, the latter being instructed to follow his advice in all matters. At Cape Verde, on the return voyage, he met and was consulted by Amerigo Vespucci, then setting out to explore the eastern coast of South America; and the Tuscan explorer (who gave America her name) referred to him in his writings in terms of the highest esteem and admiration.

Joseph Vecinho himself (to whom reference has been made above) played a role in the age of the maritime discoveries no less important and barely less prominent than that of his master, Zacuto. He held the rank of physician-in-ordinary to João II of Portugal, and hence enjoyed great influence at the Portuguese Court. His opinion was regularly asked on all questions relating to science. When, in 1484, Columbus laid before the Portuguese ruler his plan for exploring the western route to the Indies, it was submitted to a *junta* of five experts, who included Joseph Vecinho and a Jewish mathematician named Moses. Vecinho, as we have seen, was also one of the Commission which adopted the astrolabe for ordinary nautical use. It was by the means of this instrument that he ascertained the latitude by solar observation on the Coast of Guinea, whither he was sent on a scientific mission by the King. On his return he reported the results of his observations at Court, on March 11th, 1495. Among those present on this occasion was Christopher Columbus, who did not fail to take careful note and to record the event in one of his characteristic observations.

The Forced Conversion of the Jews in Portugal in 1497—one of the most shameful episodes in the history of the Middle Ages—could not, of course, affect their scientific interests. Abraham Zacuto (as we have seen) went into exile. Joseph Vecinho was compelled to submit to baptism, and, under the name Diego Mendes Vecinho, was prominent in scientific work at the Court of King Manoel the Fortunate. None the less, Jewish loyalty remained strong in his descendants, and a century later one finds them settled in Italy as professing Jews, still maintaining, however, their ancestor's scientific bent.

Another victim of the forced conversions was Pedro Nuñes, who, a mere child at the time, subsequently became Professor of Mathematics at Coimbra and chief cosmographer to the Crown of Portugal. He, too, remained closely attached to Judaism in secret; so much so, that at the beginning of the seventeenth century (as we are informed in a document recently discovered) his grandsons were tried by the Inquisition for "Judaising". His *magnum opus* was the Treatise on the Sphere (first published at Lisbon in 1537), described as "one of the scientific glories of Portugal", which opened the way for Mercator's work and thus for the whole system of modern cartography. The late King Manoel of Portugal, in his *Early Portuguese Books*, had no hesitation in calling this Marrano scientist (whose Jewish origin he barely suspected) "the most distinguished Portuguese nautical astronomer".

§v

The Jews—particularly those of Spain and Portugal— thus provided no small part of the technical equipment of those voyages of exploration which suddenly widened the horizons of Europe at the close of the Middle Ages. But their work as actual explorers was by no means insignificant. It was the Radanite Jewish merchants of the ninth century who, according to Ibn Khurdadbih, Postmaster-General of the Caliphate of Bagdad, opened up the trade-routes between Europe and the Far East, either *via* Egypt and the Dead Sea, or along the courses of the Tigris and Euphrates, or else overland—by the southern route through Northern Africa, or by the northern across Central Europe (see below, pp. 217–8). When Germany was an outpost of barbarism, and all the culture of Europe was concentrated in Moslem Spain, an enterprising Jew, Abraham ibn Jacob, was among the mission which the Caliph of Cordova sent to the northern country, bringing back with him one of the most informative accounts now extant.

But the greatest of mediaeval Jewish travellers was Benjamin of Tudela, who in 1160 left his native city in Navarre, traversing in the course of the next thirteen years the whole of southern Europe, northern Africa, Byzantium, and much of Asia. His *Itinerary*, a classic of Jewish literature, is replete with information concerning not only the various Jewish communities which he encountered, but also the whole of the social and economic structure of those places through which he passed. For this reason he is still universally consulted and quoted by every writer on twelfth-century history—all the more

G

readily since, by universal assent, he was the first mediaeval traveller who generally told the truth. Another adventurous mediaeval Jewish explorer, whose account is still classical, was Benjamin's contemporary, Petahia of Regensburg.

But there must have been many more, mute and unrecorded, whose identity has not been preserved for posterity. When the great Arabic traveller, Ibn Battuta, arrived in the Turkish city of Majar about 1332, he was amazed to find there a Spanish Jew who had preceded him, making his way overland through Constantinople, Anatolia, and Transcaucasia—a four months' journey in all. The experiences of later Jewish travellers form an integral part of the history of European exploration. Thus, the venturesome sixteenth-century pioneer, Pedro Texeira, of Lisbon, who explored the overland route between Italy and the Far East with a degree of detail hitherto unexampled, and wrote an account of his travels which was translated into many languages, was a Marrano—by no means the only one of his kind who blazed out a way in regions as yet unknown.

Even in the heroic period of English exploration, Jews played a not insignificant part. When England first entered into the race, in the spacious days of Elizabeth, Jews were little known in this country. Nevertheless, the English pioneers did not scruple to take Jews into their service as interpreters, when they had the good fortune to find them. Thus one accompanied Sir James Lancaster, when he sailed to the Pacific in command of the first fleet of the East India Company in 1601; he was, indeed, the intermediary in the negotiation of the treaty with the Sultan of Achin which (it may be said) was the ultimate basis of British expansion in the Far East.

In the second great period of British exploration, which began in the eighteenth century, the Jews were

established in England, and played their part. Israel
Lyons the Younger, son of the Instructor in Hebrew at
the University of Cambridge, and a well-known botanist
in his day, accompanied Captain Phipps (subsequently
Lord Mulgrave) as principal astronomer, in his Arctic
Expedition in 1773. Among the other members was a
diminutive midshipman named Horatio Nelson, who had
on that occasion his classical encounter with a polar bear.

It was not long after that Captain Moses Ximenes
(subsequently Sir Maurice Ximenes, and father of
Lieutenant General Sir David Ximenes) led a band of
adventurers who proposed to establish a colony in West
Africa. One of his principal lieutenants was Joshua
Montefiore (subsequently the first Jew to hold a commission in the British army, who distinguished himself
in the West Indian campaign in 1809). The latter not
only took charge of the military side of the enterprise,
but also published a lively account of it. The party
occupied the island of Bulama and raised the British flag;
but after several conflicts with the natives they were
compelled to withdraw. It was characteristic that one of
Montefiore's first cares, immediately after landing, had
been to organise an educational system for the children
of his companions.

The next generation provides us with the adventurous
figure of Nathaniel Isaacs, born in Canterbury in 1808.
In 1822, he left England for St. Helena, where his uncle,
Saul Solomon (one of Napoleon's few intimates on the
island) was Consul for France and Holland. Here he
struck up a great friendship with Lieutenant King, R.N.,
whom he accompanied on an expedition to the Cape of
Good Hope in 1825 to trace Lieutenant Farewell. They
were shipwrecked off the coast of Natal, and before long
Isaacs was engrossed in a career of exploration and adventure. For seven years he travelled through the Zulu

and Fumos countries, in addition to visiting the Comoro islands. The party found Farewell; had interviews with Chaka, the great Zulu king; and took the coast lands under their protection. After King's death from fever, Isaacs continued his activities alone, fighting for Chaka with his European weapons and being severely wounded. In return for his services, he was created Principal Chief of Natal; and the claim of Great Britain to this province was partly dependent upon the formal charter which he obtained from the Zulu monarch in 1828. Not least of Isaacs' services was his work, *Travels and Adventures in Eastern Africa*, which gives the first reliable account of the topography and ethnology of the country, and which was republished by the Riebeck Society in a centenary re-issue in 1937.

Another intrepid Jewish explorer of the nineteenth century was Eduard Karl Oscar Theodor Schnitzer. A native of Oppeln, in Silesia, he was baptised in childhood (as so many other Germans were at that period, in order to assist their careers) and, after graduating as doctor of medicine, found the call of the Near East irresistible. In 1875 he joined General Gordon at Khartoum, assuming the less specifically Teutonic name of Emin. When Gordon became Governor General of the Sudan three years later, he appointed Emin Governor of the Equatorial provinces. Here he served with considerable distinction for some years. After the fall of Khartoum, he was entirely isolated. Nevertheless, he held out for a further two years, now becoming one of the centres of European interest in Africa in place of his dead leader. Stanley made his way to relieve him. At first he refused to desert his post, but at last was persuaded to accompany his rescuer back to civilisation. Inactivity was however impossible for a man of his nature, and he undertook a semi-political voyage of exploration into Central Africa in the German interest in 1890. Though disowned and recalled, he persisted. Arabs ultimately brought to the coast the news that Emin Pasha had been assassinated, in the autumn of 1892.[1]

Thus we are brought to our own days, when the Arctic only has retained its secret and its glamour. The part played by Jews in contemporary Arctic exploration has been outstanding. Greely had a young Jew, Sergeant Edward Israel, with him as astronomer on his Arctic expedition of 1881–4. He was the youngest of the party, yet, even when he was suffering from sickness, he refused to accept more than his usual ration of food, with the result that he died before the expedition returned. In 1882 he had rendered especially important services in determining the possibility of an overland route to Hazen Land in Greenland through the Bellows Valley. In reading the burial service, it is said, General Greely remembered the dead man's faith, and modified the ritual accordingly.

In General Nobile's ill-fated aerial Arctic expedition of 1928, he was accompanied by Aldo Pontremoli, a nephew of Luigi Luzzatti, the former Italian Prime Minister, who died under circumstances of particular gallantry. By a coincidence, the Russian expedition of relief—but for whose aid the whole party would have perished—was under the direction of Rudolf Samoilowitsch, who in 1931 conducted a Zeppelin flight over the Pole.

As with the frozen north, so with the parched deserts of Central Asia. From 1899 to 1926, Sir Aurel (Mark)

---

[1] It is worth while to recall, in this connexion, that Professor Palmer, Captain Gill and Lieutenant Charrington, who were murdered treacherously by Arabs while travelling in the Sinai Desert in 1882, were accompanied by a Jew, Bakhor Hassun, whose remains lie with theirs in St. Paul's Cathedral. Another associate of General Gordon's was Louis Arthur Lucas, the explorer of Lake Albert Nyanza, whose premature death alone probably prevented him from attaining a very high reputation.

Stein, by his repeated expeditions in Chinese Turkestan, Central Asia and Western China, has not only widened geographical knowledge but also revealed the treasures and the records of a lost civilisation. He has only one rival—Sven Hedin, the Swedish explorer of the Gobi Desert and discoverer of the Hedin Mountains; the latter is, as it happens, a descendant of Aaron Isak, the founder of the Jewish community in Sweden.

Other great Jewish explorers of the nineteenth century include Arminius Vambéry (Bamberger), a phenomenal linguist, who was the first European to traverse the heart of unknown Persia, living there for over two years disguised as a native Muslim; Nathaniel Wallich, Asiatic botanist and explorer of Assam; the converts Joseph Wolff and Henry Aaron Stern, who, as missionaries among the Jews, explored Bokhara and Abyssinia respectively; Samuel Sandberg, pioneer traveller in Thibet; Angelo Castelbolognesi, who explored the Sudan; Eduard Foa, who discovered the sources of the Zambesi; Louis Binger, the first white man to cross the watershed between Senegal and Timbuctoo; Hermann Burchardt, who perished in the Arabian desert in 1909; Siegfried Langer, murdered in the Yemen in 1882; Vladimir Jochelson and L. Sternberg, who explored northern Siberia; Isaac Israel Heyes, who led an expedition to Greenland in 1860, where it joined up with another under the direction of August Sonntag; and many subordinate members of enterprises of the same nature in every quarter of the globe.

The same spirit which impelled Jews towards new spheres of economic activity gave them in fact the urge to act as pioneers of European enquiry in unexplored regions of the world; for even the Ghetto was unable to quench that spirit of adventure which is to be found in all men alike.

CHAPTER V

§1

FROM the beginning of their association with Europe—
long before the present national languages and literatures
were known—Jews played a prominent share in
European cultural life. In Alexandria, when it was the
intellectual capital of the Hellenic world, there were
Jewish poets, Jewish playwrights, Jewish philosophers,
Jewish historians, all writing in Greek and with an eye
upon the plaudits of the non-Jewish public. One of the
first European Jews known to us by name is Caecilius
of Calacte, in Sicily, who flourished in the first century
B.C. at Rome. Characteristically enough, he was the
representative in his day of the Attic style of oratory,
in contradistinction to the verbose Asiatic style which
had begun to gain ground. Similarly, he and his Greek
friend Dionysius of Halicarnassus were the only appreciative students of Latin literature at a time when it
was the fashion to sneer at it in literary circles. The
body of his work must have been considerable, though
not much has survived. However, there can be little
doubt that there is due to him the famous passage in
the classic treatise on *The Sublime*, ascribed to Longinus,
which dominated English thought in the eighteenth
century: "Sublimity is the echo of greatness of soul.
This is illustrated . . . from the legislator of the
Jews, no ordinary man, . . . who wrote in the
opening words of his Laws: 'God said, Let there be light,

and there was light; let there be land, and there was land.'"

From the period of this pioneer of twenty centuries ago, the participation of the Jews in the cultural life of Europe, though at some times less marked than at others, has been almost continuous. For ever since then (as, indeed, for some time previous) Jews have not only lived in Europe but also have spoken European tongues and written them. Indeed, the tradition which they preserved was in some ways purer than that of their neighbours. A brilliant American scholar, by a detailed analysis of the various Judaeo-Romance dialects which were formerly spoken and written by the Jews of Spain, Portugal, France, Provence, Italy, etc., has traced them back to a prototype used by their ancestors throughout Europe before the downfall of the Roman Empire. What the educated Italian or Frenchman of a generation ago considered peculiarities of Jewish speech are thus in many cases relics of an earlier age, before modern Italian or French was dreamed of, but when the Jews were already familiar figures throughout the Latin world.

Everywhere, moreover, they translated their liturgies and their Biblical texts into the language of the country, which was their own natural native speech. The importance of these relics for the study of modern European languages is considerable, and scholars are becoming more and more appreciative of the fact. The eleventh-century Franco-Jewish commentator, Solomon ben Isaac of Troyes, or Rashi (consulted so much by Christian exegetes of the late Middle Ages) was in the habit of translating difficult words and expressions into the vernacular. These glosses, embodied in his various commentaries, are among the oldest specimens of the Langue d'Oïl vocabulary; they are eagerly consulted and collected by philologists, and a small library has by now been written about them. In 1290 (and again, finally, in 1540) the Jews were expelled from Apulia, in south Italy. Many of them ultimately found refuge in Corfu, where an independent Apulian Synagogue existed until our own day. With them they brought, not only their dialect, but also some of their religious poetry, written in Apulian though in Hebrew characters. These are among the oldest specimens of Apulian literature now extant.

The Jews were expelled from Spain and Portugal with a refinement of cruelty at the close of the fifteenth century. Their descendants in the Balkans and North Africa still speak the Castilian of their fathers; and students of Spanish dialects and folk-lore find them a happy hunting-ground for a reconstruction of various facets of the life and literature of mediaeval Spain. Similarly, one might have imagined that Germany would have been proud of the tenacity of her Jewish children who, migrating East-wards at the close of the Middle Ages, preserved in an alien land the German which their fathers had spoken in the Rhineland when the great Cathedral of Cologne was still building. Even the Arthurian romances and the Tales of the Round Table—which did not lack Jewish affinities—were familiar in the mediaeval Jewries and are extant in old Hebraic versions; while Sir Bevis of Hampton actually gave his name to a whole Ghetto cycle.

For the larger part of their literature, to be sure, the Jews used Hebrew, just as Christians used Latin; and for the same reasons. It was a semi-sacred tongue; it was universally read and understood, irrespective of national and linguistic boundaries; it was of proper scholastic status. But what they wrote in it was to a very considerable extent European in conception. Hence it happened that Jewish writers of the period—Moses Maimonides, Levi of Bagnols, Abraham ibn Ezra—could be translated into Latin and take their place, easily and naturally, as the mental pabulum of the schoolmen. The canonists' *jurisconsulta* were closely paralleled by the Rabbinical *Sheëlot uTeshubot*. The mediaeval moralists of the Rhineland had their counterparts in the *Judengasse*. Thus, there is little essential difference between the writings of Berthold of Regensburg and those of his Jewish contemporary and fellow-townsman Judah, compiler of the collection of godly anecdotes known as *The Book of the Pious*; and, when the German moralists turned to mysticism, their Jewish neighbours accompanied them, so that the flights of Master Eckhart (now considered the incarnation of the "Aryan" spirit, though influenced by the *Fons Vitae* and, in our own day, edited by a Jew) have their parallels in (for example) those of Eleazar of Worms, author of the Hebrew ethical classic, the *Rokeach*.

But the most remarkable instance is that classic of mediaeval Churchmen, the *Fons Vitae*, which was ascribed to the authorship of a Spanish Christian named Avicebron, and studied with religious reverence by successive generations of mediaeval theologians. It was only in the course of the last century that it was discovered that the author was identical with the Synagogal poet, Rabbi Solomon ibn Gabirol, called "the nightingale of piety". Nothing could illustrate more forcibly the essential unity of European culture, whether Gentile or Jewish, in the Middle Ages.

§II

It frequently happened that the parallels converged, so that we find Jewish writers contributing actively, even in the age of degradation, to the literary store of their environment. Thus, in Italy, one of the members of the poetical school, of whom Dante was the greatest, was Immanuel of Rome, who, besides being a physician, Hebrew poet and exegete, was a familiar member of the circle of the *dolce stil nuovo*. He exchanged sonnets in Italian with the litterateurs of the time, and was patronised by Can Grande della Scala of Verona, to whom he dedicated a *bisbiglio* describing his busy court. Here he may have met Dante, with whom he appears to have been on terms of some intimacy, to judge from the fact that Busone da Gubbio sent him a sonnet of condolence on the greater poet's death. The volume of his Italian work which has survived shews the promise, if not the final fulfilment, of a genius no less than that displayed in his Hebrew writings. It may be added that Immanuel of Rome has been conjectured to be the medium through which Dante received his knowledge of the Muslim cosmogony, of which such important influences have been found in his work.

Symptomatic of the Italian outlook of Immanuel of Rome, in whatever language he wrote, was his collection of Hebrew poems, known as the Compositions of Immanuel. In this work—one of the first to introduce to non-Moslem Europe the loosely-woven narrative framework perfected by Boccaccio in his *Decameron*— we find a picture of a completely Italian environment, European literary forms such as the sonnet, a good measure of the licentious spirit of Italian poetry of the time, and, above all, an imitation (or perhaps it is more correct to say, parody) of the *Divine Comedy*.

This work deserves closer examination, for it follows Dante's model from beginning to end. It commences, like the *Inferno*, with an allusion to the age of the author at the time of composition; it finishes, like the *Paradiso*, with a glimpse of the stars. The text is closely modelled on the Italian original—without, indeed, its profundity, its polish or its clarity, for this was a parergon appended by the author to a miscellaneous collection of his poems. The outstanding point of difference lies in the fact that, in *Tophet and Eden*, there is no Purgatory, in conformity with Jewish theological ideas. One other minor feature, however, calls for attention, for it illustrates strikingly the difference between the Jewish and Christian outlook at the period. Dante places in his Inferno all who did not believe in Jesus and in Christianity—including even those who flourished before the beginning of the Christian era, and so could neither have known nor believed. In striking contrast to this, Immanuel reserves a place of honour in his Paradise for non-Jews—"the righteous of the Nations of the world"; elaborating, subsequently, his ideal of an eclectic religion, embodying the best in all faiths.[1] This tolerance contrasts strangely with the contemporary Catholic doctrine, which put the proportion of "saved" to the "damned" at one to a thousand, or even one to a hundred thousand.

In Germany, similarly, the Jews participated in literary activity in the vernacular from a very early date. The thirteenth century provides us with a Jewish *minnesinger* in Süsskind von Trimberg, who sang of the virtue of woman and the nobility of man, and took high rank among the itinerant poets of his day. In the next century, one Samson Pine collaborated (1336) with Claus Wysse and Philipp Kolin of Strassburg, in adapting into German a French version of the *Parsifal* (of all romances!). In the preface, he is referred to repeatedly as a Jew and is thanked both for translating the poem into German and finding rhymes for it: certainly, it would appear, the lion's share of the work. Another name that may be mentioned in this connexion is that

---

[1] Another significant innovation of Immanuel's is his placing in the Inferno of a certain person "because he was miserly with his knowledge"—a failing for which perhaps only a mediaeval Jew could condemn a man to punishment in the hereafter!

of Johannes Pauli, a converted Jew of the age of Luther who became a Franciscan friar, and was a popular preacher in his day. He is better remembered, however, for his famous collection of jests, *Schimpf und Ernst* which, first published in 1519, ran through innumerable editions, imitations and amplifications, and may be described as the classical German "Joe Miller". Some of the stories were taken over in the *Hundred Merry Tales*, a favourite work of Elizabethan England, used lavishly by Shakespeare himself.

Most marked of all was the participation of the Jews in the literary life of Spain, which had a pronounced effect upon European literature as a whole. Here such activity began at least as early as the thirteenth century, Jews beginning to write in Spanish before this was either fashionable or common. Indeed, modern Spanish is in great measure the creation of the Jewish translators at the court of Alfonso the Wise, who moulded the despised Mozarabic dialect into a literary medium of considerable richness and force. A corpus of Spanish Jewish literature of the Middle Ages would fill many volumes : and a good deal of it is of really high quality. Thus the Catalan "Aphorisms" of Judah Bonsenior of Barcelona (fl. 1287-1305), and the "Moral Proverbs" of Rabbi Santob of Carrion, dedicated to Pedro IV of Castile (1357–1360) are considered classical by students of Spanish literature and are read even to-day.

Spain expelled her Jews in 1492 ; yet, because of the Forced Baptisms which had been common for a century before that date, Jewish blood permeated the whole Peninsula. Sancho Panza could perhaps (and did) pride himself that his blood was free from any admixture of Jew or Moor, but it is not so certain that his master would have been in the same fortunate position. It is possible that Jewish blood was to be found in the veins of some of the greatest Spaniards of the fifteenth, six-teenth, seventeenth and eighteenth centuries. In many cases, it is provable. The group of poets at the court of Henry IV of Castile, whose writings throw so much light upon the social history of the time, were to a large extent of Jewish birth. Foremost among them was the impudent Antón de Montoro, "the ragman of Cordova", who has been called "the most sympathetic and attrac-tive poet in the entire Castilian Parnassus of the fifteenth century", and who went out of his way to call attention to his origin in his audacious satires. Others were Juan de España, Juan de Valladolid, Rodrigo Cota de Maguaque, and the rest. Conditions were very much the same in Aragon, where the revival of vernacular literature under Juan II was due in considerable measure to the genius of persons of Jewish blood, being largely inspired by the *converso*, Alfonso de Santa Maria. Similarly the eminent physician, Francisco Lopez de Villalobos, a classical Spanish stylist, was of Jewish extraction, as was also Pedro Guttierez de Santa Clara, historian of the conquest of Peru. And even in our own time, the famous historical novelist, Camilo Castelo Branco, who may be described without any exaggeration as the Portuguese Walter Scott, descended from a Jewish family.

Two Marrano contributions to Spanish literature deserve more detailed consideration, because of their influence on European letters as a whole.

Luis Ponce de Leon was perhaps the greatest lyric poet that Spain has produced. Going back to the Bible for his inspiration (possibly this is not entirely a coin-cidence) he introduced a fresh naturalism into Spanish poetry, which lived on in the poets and romancers who came after him. To-day, he is remembered for a few odes and hymns which are said to reveal a majestic and serene simplicity not found again till Wordsworth. In his age, however, he was best known as a theologian, and in his lectures was considered to have shewn a sympathy for the Reform movement. When he was arrested by the Inquisition in March, 1572, it was discovered in the course of his examination that he was of Jewish blood, a great-grandmother having been "reconciled" by the Inquisition in 1512. This added to the gravamen of the charge against him. He remained in prison for over four years. It was only in the autumn of 1576 that he was able to resume his lectures at Salamanca, with the classical remark: "As we were saying the other day."[1]

A final illustration may be adduced. Spain's most important contribution to European literature before Don Quixote was *Calisto and Meliboea*, better known as *Celestina*, first printed in 1499. It is a tragi-comedy in prose of two lovers, and was marvellously popular in its day, being published time after time and translated into many European languages. In the judgment of the great critic, Menendez y Pelayo, the work would have deserved

---

[1] There is some echo of Ponce de Leon in the writings of two other Spanish poets of New Christian descent—Felipe Godinez, reconciled by the Inquisition at Seville in 1624, who wrote plays on Biblical subjects: and Juan Pinto Delgado, whom Menendez y Pelayo considered to be among the most inspired Spanish poets of the seventeenth century, and who ended his life as a professing Jew. Juan Perez de Montalvan—the friend, confidant and publisher of Lope de Vega, and the most prominent Spanish playwright between the latter and Calderon, whom he inspired—was similarly of New Christian extraction. A contemporary of Calderon's, and his rival for the favours of the theatre-going public of Madrid, was the Marrano Antonio Enriquez Gomez, or Enrique Enriquez de Paz, condemned *in absentia* by the Spanish Inquisition in 1660. In the following century, Antonio da Silva was a (perhaps the) foremost Portuguese playwright, one of his comedies being performed at Lisbon on the evening of the day when he was burned at the stake.

The name of one more Portuguese man of letters, out of many, may be added to this list—Didaco Pyrrho, of Evora, one of the foremost neo-Latin poets of the sixteenth century, who ended his days as a Jew at Ragusa.

the first place in Spanish literature, had Cervantes not written his masterpiece. Its name became a byword, its passages were universally quoted, and its characters and action long served as model in an age when plagiarism was not yet a vice. In the words of the *Encyclopaedia Britannica* it "caused the new theatre to make a gigantic step onwards. This astonishing novel taught the Spaniards the art of dialogue, and for the first time exhibited persons of all classes of Society speaking in harmony with their natural surroundings, thinking and acting in accordance with their condition of life".

Little was known about Fernando de Rojas, the author of this work, until the recent discovery of an Inquisitional record, which made it clear that he was a *converso*, *i.e.*, a baptised Jew, hampered for that reason in the exercise of his profession and, to boot, married to the daughter of another *converso* who had been put on trial for Judaising.

The importance of *Celestina* in European literature, as has been indicated, was vast. But for our purpose it is enough to point out its influence on William Shakespeare. Above all, it had a distinct share in the ancestry of *Romeo and Juliet*, who were, as a modern critic has put it, "own children" to Rojas' tragic lovers. Similarly, the "old bawd" who sustains the comic part foreshadows that most perfect of Shakespearian characters, Juliet's nurse.

§III

The extent of the interaction of Jewish and other elements in European culture may be illustrated most conveniently from England; all the more strikingly if we go back to the period of that astonishing renascence of letters under the Tudors, when Jews were virtually absent from the country.[1] Yet English literature of that glorious period was profoundly imbued with the influence of individual Jews, or persons of Jewish blood.

It is, of course, absurd to overlook the Bible in this connexion. Shakespeare did not read and speak, as does the Englishman of to-day, an English saturated with Biblical language: he belonged to only the second generation to whom the Bible in English was readily accessible. But, nevertheless, a recent enquiry has demonstrated the great use which he made of the Scriptures. His Biblical knowledge was, moreover, the fruit of deep love and study, growing more and more with the passage of years. He had his favourite books—Genesis, Job, Proverbs, Isaiah, in the Old Testament, as well as Ecclesiasticus in the Apocrypha and St. Matthew in the New— echoes of which may be discovered in his own magnificent lines. Deprive him of his Biblical—*i.e.*, his Semitic— background, and the Shakespeare we know would not be quite the same.

But it is more significant to discover in Shakespeare Hebraic influences nearer by far to his own day. Mention has been made above (p. 49) of the eleventh-century Spanish convert Petrus Alphonsi of Toledo, whose *Training School for the Clergy* contains all manner of entertaining fables for homiletic use. These passed into the common heritage of all Europe, a number being incorporated in the famous mediaeval collection, *Gesta Romanorum*. Some are printed at the end of Caxton's English *Aesop* of 1483, being thus among the earliest products of the English printing press. More noteworthy still, the collection was the source of many of Chaucer's stories. It was first printed in English by Wynkyn de Worde,

[1] It is possible to go back even further: Geoffrey Chaucer's Treatise on the Astrolabe (one of the earliest uses of English for scientific purposes) is based upon a Latin version of the Arabic treatise on that instrument, written by the Jewish scholar Mashaala about the year 800.

H

and republished in 1577. This latter edition was familiar to Shakespeare and greatly used by him. Similarly, the *Hundred Merry Tales*, another Elizabethan classic which Shakespeare read to good purpose, was based in part (as we have seen) on the *Schimpf und Ernst* of Johannes Pauli, a German friar of Jewish birth. Add to this the influence of Fernando de Rojas' *Celestina* (referred to above) and of Leone Ebreo's *Dialogues of Love* (exerted through the medium of Castiglione's famous treatise on "The Courtier," which taught Europe the ideal of the gentleman) and it will be realised that the "Semitic" influence on Elizabethan literature was far from negligible.

A good deal of Shakespeare's knowledge of things Italian—one of the most characteristic features and the most favoured sources of his plays—derives from John Florio, the translator-in-ordinary to Elizabethan England. The latter's great Italian-English dictionary was probably one of the most influential works of the century. Shakespeare without Florio would certainly have been different. The genius would have been there, and the humour, and the language; but the atmosphere of many of the plays would have been strangely unfamiliar. It is remarkable to find, then, that Florio was of Jewish extraction. His father was Michelangelo Florio, preacher to the Italian Protestant congregation in London and biographer of the ill-fated Lady Jane Grey. In his *Apologia* (Chamogasco, 1557) Michelangelo Florio states: "I was never a Jew nor son of a Jew, but born of a father and mother baptised as papists like yourself; *but if you should say that my progenitors were Hebrews before baptism, this I will not deny.*"

John Florio is best remembered to-day for his translation of the Essays of Michel de Montaigne, which is still classical. The latter was, of course, one of the great figures in sixteenth-century letters. It was he who for

En virtute suâ contentus, nobilis arte,
Italus ore, Anglus pectore, vterqͥ opere
Floret adhuc, et adhuc florebit; floreat vltra
FLORIVS, hâc specie floridus, optat amans.

Gul: Hole scuip: Tam fælix vtinam.

JOHN FLORIO
From a contemporary engraving

the first time raised French prose into a literary medium of the highest order; elevated everyday life and personal happenings into a subject-matter for great literature; and invented the essay form, in which the French were afterwards to excel. But what were the elements that went to make up this great Frenchman of letters, Michel Eyquem de Montaigne? His father's name, *Eyquem*, he claimed to be of English origin, deriving perhaps from the village of Ockham. His mother, on the other hand, was Antoinette Louppes, or Lopez, and was one of a Spanish family established at Bordeaux. A recent discovery has proved that her progenitors belonged to a New Christian family of Calatayud; that more than one of them had suffered at the hands of the Inquisition; and that they descended ultimately from the Jewish clan of Pazagón. It is, possibly, to this admixture of blood that the great essayist owed that slightly sceptical tone which seems to us to-day the most French of his qualities.[1]

Montaigne's influence in letters was, of course, immense. The new spirit which he introduced into European literature gave an impetus which is not perhaps exhausted even to-day. A license for an English translation of the *Essais* was issued in London by the Stationers' Company in the very year of their publication in Paris. Shakespeare was acquainted with them, echoing the language sometimes, the thought more frequently.[2] Francis Bacon's elder brother knew the author personally; and the indebtedness of Bacon's Essays to Montaigne's is constant throughout. It is a coincidence only that the classical English translation of Montaigne's Essays was due to

---

[1] Of modern writers, Anatole France perhaps inherited this quality to the fullest extent, and possessed most marked similarity to Montaigne; but France, too, is said to have had a Jewish grandmother.

[2] See especially Gonzalo's description of the ideal commonwealth in *The Tempest* I. i. 147, which is nearer a paraphrase than a reminiscence of Florio's version of Montaigne.

John Florio, who was similarly of Jewish extraction;
but the two facts, taken in conjunction, illustrate how
potent was the influence of Jews on English letters even
when religious intolerance excluded them rigidly from
the country.

It was with the seventeenth century and the publication of the Authorised Version of the Bible that Hebraic
influence in English literature rose to its highest point. It
reached its climax in John Milton, who might almost be
said to have thought in Hebrew, though he expressed
himself in English. This was not entirely dependent
(as was probably the case with the majority of his
contemporaries) upon acquaintance with the English
Bible. He was a competent Hebrew scholar, with a fair
knowledge of Rabbinical lore, which manifests itself
time after time in *Paradise Lost*. To what agency was
this due? The authority who has made the most detailed
enquiries into the subject speaks only of his University
studies at the feet of the erudite Hoseah Meade at Cambridge. But it may be conjectured that, during his
travels in Italy in 1637-9, he encountered some learned
Jews—possibly even in the company of Galileo, who is
known not to have been averse from their society. There
is evidence, moreover, that the blind poet made the
acquaintance of Menasseh ben Israel during the latter's
mission to Oliver Cromwell in 1655-7 to secure permission
for his co-religionists to resettle in England; and it is by no
means improbable that erudite conversations between the
two men, who had so much in common, may have ensued.

But Milton was only one out of many. George Herbert
and John Donne echoed the Psalmist: Herrick quoted
the "Ethics of the Fathers": and even so spontaneous
a production as Walton's *Compleat Angler* is filled with
Hebraic lore, obtained partly from literary sources and
partly through the medium of the learned globe-trotter,

Sir Henry Wotton, while he was "lying abroad" for his sovereign. It goes without saying that such influences were not confined to England. The Biblical inspiration of many of the dramas of Racine in France, and of Metastasio in Italy, is too obvious to require elaboration : and this spiritual atmosphere is known to have been reinforced, in some instances at least, by contemporary influences and personal association.

§IV

Direct Jewish participation in English literary and intellectual life began in the generation which followed the Re-admission. In the group of poets of the mid-eighteenth century (not, it must be admitted, a very inspired period) Moses Mendes, a grandson of one of the pioneer settlers, was an interesting figure. His works were produced at Covent Garden and Drury Lane : he wrote dramatic pieces, which were set to music by Boyce and Burney, and poems and songs which echoed Spenser piously, if without inspiration. He was famous in his day as *bon viveur* and wit : and he was celebrated as one of the few English poets to leave a fortune—not, however, gained at that profession. He wrote sometimes in collaboration with another poet of Jewish birth—Dr. Isaac Schomberg, who attended Garrick in his last illness, and whose brother Ralph was one of the most prolific and most uniformly unsuccessful writers of the generation. A kinsman of Moses Mendes, Solomon Mendes of Clapton, was also to be met with in literary circles, and was in regular correspondence with James Thomson and Richard Savage.[1]

[1] Moses Mendes, whose sons adopted their mother's name, was grandfather of Sir Francis Bond Head, Lieutenant Governor of Upper Canada, 1835–37 (who suppressed the 1837 rising), and of Sir George Head, Assistant Commissary General to the Forces in 1814, both also prolific writers.

The last years of the century produced, together with numerous writers of less ability, two at least whose rôle in English letters was far from negligible. Isaac D'Israeli would probably be better remembered to-day were his reputation not overshadowed by that of his son. His novels are, indeed, as dead as most novels of that period; his *Commentaries on the Life and Reign of Charles I* have outlived their usefulness. But, on the other hand, his series of literary anecdotes (beginning with *Curiosities of Literature*, published in modest anonymity in 1791, and ending with *Amenities of Literature*, completed when he was old and blind, in 1840) still retain their interest and were favourite works with more than one generation. But his literary ability was far excelled by his son's. If Benjamin Disraeli had not attained an abiding place in English history by his qualities as a statesman, it would be better realised that he was the most scintillating political novelist that England, and perhaps the world, has ever known.

Just after Isaac D'Israeli began the publication of his gravely mature works, an infant prodigy named Francis Cohen, son of Meyer Cohen, of Kentish Town, aged eight years, translated Homer's *Battle of the Frogs* from the Latin into French. The resultant work was published in 1797 by his proud father, Meyer Cohen, a stockbroker. Later, Francis Cohen changed his faith and adopted his wife's name, Palgrave, under which he became famous. He was Deputy Keeper of the Public Records, 1838-61; wrote, among other works, *The Rise and Progress of the English Commonwealth*—the earliest important study of English constitutional history based upon the records—and *The History of Normandy and England;* drew up the scheme for the work of the Historical Manuscripts Commission, for which he edited many volumes : and may be regarded as perhaps the first English scientific historian.

Sir Francis Palgrave founded a dynasty almost unique in the history of English letters. His eldest son was Francis Turner Palgrave, Professor of Poetry at Oxford and compiler of that classical anthology, *The Golden Treasury;* the second was William Gifford Palgrave, missionary, Oriental traveller and diplomat, author of *A Year's Journey through Central and Eastern Arabia:* the third was Robert Harry Inglis Palgrave, editor of *The Dictionary of Political Economy:* the fourth, Sir Reginald Francis Douce Palgrave, Clerk of the House of Commons from 1886 to 1900, was the editor of *Rules of Procedure of the House of Commons* and author of various works on constitutional practise, as well as a proficient water-colour artist.

A few other names belonging to this period deserve mention: John Adolphus, barrister (a converted member of the family which founded the Great Synagogue in London in 1690) who defended the Cato Street conspirators in 1820 and published, among other historical works, a *History of England* from 1760 to 1883, and *Biographical Memoirs of the French Revolution:* his son, John Leycester Adolphus, a well-known critic in his day, who was the first person to argue methodically in favour of Scott's authorship of the Waverley Novels: Lewis Goldsmith, a master of journalistic propaganda and an unrelenting opponent of Napoleon: and Grace Aguilar, whose historical writings and novels still retain their charm.

The second half of the nineteenth century naturally saw, with increase in numbers and growing acclimatisation, an extension of the Jewish participation in English literary life. Sir Arthur Wing Pinero summed up the tendencies of the age in his plays, such as *The Second Mrs. Tanqueray* and *Trelawney of the Wells*, and gave English drama a new heart. It was he who with Henry

Arthur Jones, rescued the English stage from artificiality, thus paving the way for Shaw, Galsworthy, and the other playwrights who were not afraid of ideas in the theatre. A little later was Alfred Sutro who, best remembered as a dramatist, best deserves remembrance for his translation of Maeterlinck's *Life of the Bee*, which he rewrote seven times before venturing upon publication. Israel Zangwill's genius would perhaps have received even wider recognition had he not been so intimately associated with the Children of the Ghetto; yet the new style of genre-fiction which he introduced had a considerable influence on English letters. Max Beerbohm, though best known as a caricaturist, is perhaps the finest living English prose-writer. . . . But the list may be extended to irksome length.

Two more figures at least of the first importance in this generation were of Jewish blood. Bret Harte, the first American imaginative writer to speak to England in its own idiom, was a grandson of Bernard Hart, a London Jew who had migrated to the New World; while Sir Henry Newbolt, chronicler and poet of the English navy, is descended from Dr. Samuel Solomon of Liverpool (as is also his brother Sir Francis Newbolt, Official Referee and, in his spare time, art historian).

In our own day, the list becomes more crowded, and only a few names out of many can be mentioned here. It is the considered opinion of many critics that the greatest loss inflicted by the War of 1914-18 on English letters was the death in action of Isaac Rosenberg, a young East End Jew, whose slender volume of surviving verse suffices to place him in the very front rank of contemporary poets. Another poet who made his niche in war-time was Siegfried Sassoon, who subsequently achieved fame—perhaps immortality—for his pictures of the atmosphere of the Shires. Other living poets include

Humbert Wolfe, L. Aaronson and E. W. Meyerstein. Leonard Merrick was one of the most brilliant English writers of the short story, almost worthy to be ranked with Maupassant. There is no space to do more than mention W. L. George, Stephen Hudson, Arthur Waley, Louis Golding, Gilbert Frankau, Naomi Jacob, G. B. Stern, S. L. Bensusan, and so on.

In another sphere, Philip Guedalla is one of the few contemporary historians who have learned to combine brilliance with research; L. B. Namier has set the study of English political history of the mid-eighteenth century on a new basis; and Gertrude Millin, besides being a novelist of distinction, may be said to have brought South African historical literature to maturity. In America, the number of prominent contemporary Jewish writers is too long even to catalogue; but Elmer Rice, Fannie Hurst, Ludwig Lewisohn, John Cournos, Gertrude Stein, George and Robert Nathan, Edna Ferber, Louis Untermeyer, Waldo Frank, deserve at least passing mention.

Shakespearean research should be considered the quintessence of English studies, and the contribution of Jews in this sphere has been particularly high. It was in the eighteen-eighties that Sir Sidney Lee began his series of Shakespearean studies, which culminated in his monumental *Life of Shakespeare*—rapturously greeted at the time of its appearance, and still a standard work, having passed through many editions. Yet perhaps Lee's most important contribution to English cultural life was in the capacity of Editor (previously Assistant Editor) of the *Dictionary of National Biography*, to which he contributed over 600 biographies from his own pen, and which might not have been completed but for his systematic persistence. Israel Gollancz approached English studies in the first instance rather from the philological side, and did much work for the Early

English Texts Society. His edition of Shakespeare is still a model of its kind and set an example for the popularisation of the classics : and he left a permanent mark by his many years of work as Professor of English at King's College, London. His most enduring influence, however, was probably exercised as organiser and first Secretary of the British Academy, which he raised to a level of dignity and scholarship proper to the Academy of a great Empire. The trio of eminent Jewish Shakespearean scholars is completed by Marion Spielmann, art critic and historian, who made an intensive study of the portraiture of William Shakespeare, as a result of which it is possible to have a much more accurate idea of the poet's actual appearance and to clear up a number of incidental points connected with his biography and bibliography. In Germany, the most recent of a long line of scholarly interpreters of Shakespeare was Professor Friedrich Gundolf, whose rendering of the English poet in German is one of the most superb achievements in the history of translation. If the sages of Heidelberg are to-day able to claim Shakespeare as a kindred Nordic spirit, it is partly because he found in Germany so gifted a "Semitic" interpreter.[1]

It is perhaps arguable, that something in the background of the Jew accustoms him from childhood to a realisation of the existence of countries beyond his own, and hence provides him with what may be termed (in order to eschew that decried word "international") a "European" outlook. He seems to have, accordingly, a certain faculty for entering into the spirit of countries other than that in which he was born, and to make contributions to their cultural heritage seldom paralleled by foreigners of other antecedents. To take the field of

[1] It may be added that Shakespeare's interpreter to Denmark was the Jew, Georg Brandes.

English history alone, the greatest authority on the laws of the Anglo-Saxons was a German professor, Felix Liebermann, whose writings in this field are still unsuperseded. In our own generation, the keenest survey of English history in the early part of the nineteenth century is that of Elie Halévy, which has received the compliment of translation into the language in which it might rationally have been expected to be written. There is not quite the same solidity, though far more brilliance, in the studies of André Maurois, which, written in the first instance as an interpretation of England to the French, have in a way served to interpret the English to themselves. And, in the days of bitterness which followed upon the War of 1914-18, it was Paul Cohen-Portheim who, unembittered by years of unnecessary suffering in an internment camp, set about interpreting the English character to England's erstwhile enemies, and thus laying the basis for a better understanding.

The most remarkable fact about the group of English litterateurs whose names have been mentioned in the foregoing pages is perhaps its lack of homogeneity. It is remarkable, not so much for its distinction, as for its comprehensiveness. For the past two centuries, Jewish writers, of various degrees of eminence, have contributed to English literature in every sphere, and from every angle. It is impossible to trace in them any common factor; they are as motley, as varied, and as inchoate as English literature itself. This may be illustrated amusingly from the following instances, which shew how far the process of intellectual assimilation has proceeded. That somewhat absurd composition, "Home, sweet Home," is one of the songs in the opera *Clari* (first produced at Covent Garden Theatre in 1823) the author of which was John Howard Payne, a son of one Sarah Isaacs and a grandson of a converted Jew. At the time when it first became known, perhaps the most popular English song was "The Death of Nelson": this was the production of John Braham, formerly a choir-boy in the Great Synagogue. In the same tradition was "A Life on the Ocean Wave", composed (with "Cheer, boys, cheer", and hundreds of less-known songs) by Henry Russell, a professing Jew. It is not suggested for one moment that these productions are to be numbered among the masterpieces of modern literature: but they demonstrate in a remarkable fashion the manner in which the Jew has identified himself with the literary heritage of the country, at its most typical as well as at its best.

§v

The German Jewish literary tradition, as has been indicated, dates back to the Middle Ages, to Süsskind von Trimberg and Samson Pine and Johannes Pauli. How far this literature might have developed but for the virulent persecution which raged at the close of the Middle Ages, it is impossible to say. The improvement in German Jewish conditions in the middle of the eighteenth century witnessed, however, a revival, associated with the name of Moses Mendelssohn—a yet more important figure in German than in Jewish literary life, though the fact is often overlooked: for it was by his contributions to German letters generally that he first came to the fore and achieved a reputation in intellectual circles, subsequently to be echoed in his own community.

His first important independent work, *Letters on Sentiment* (1755), virtually founded modern German philosophic-aesthetic criticism. His *Phaedon*—one of the most important contributions to pre-Kantian ethics—was the most widely read book of its time in Germany, no less for the subject-matter than for the limpid style, unknown hitherto in philosophical discussion. It was reprinted time after time, translated into almost every European language, and did more than any other work of the age to enhance the reputation of the German philosophical genius abroad. There was one possible exception only—Lessing's famous *Laokoon*, inspired largely by Mendelssohn's *Briefe über die Empfindungen*, buttressed by his correspondence with Nicolai. This work diffused the Mendelssohnian point of view in a yet wider circle. Moreover, Mendelssohn's writings first re-aroused German interest in their native philosophers, in particular Leibniz: and, in the formation of the Romantic Tradition which dominated Europe (including England) for the following generation, his influence was really profound. It is something more than a literary curiosity that Samuel Taylor Coleridge (whose greatest friend at Highgate was the Jewish writer, Hyman Hurwitz) was a devoted student of Mendelssohn's philosophical works, and that his copies of *Jerusalem* and *Morgenstunden*, preserved in the British Museum, are enriched with manuscript annotations.

Mendelssohn's intellectual interests were inherited by his brilliant daughters, and their associates, whose *salons* were the centres of intellectual (it would not be too much to say, intelligent) life in Berlin over some decades. Dorothea married, as her second husband, Friedrich von Schlegel; her novel, *Florentine*, published in 1801, was one of the finest specimens of romantic fiction of the generation; and it was she who introduced Mme. de Stael on the one hand, and Victor Hugo on the other, to the German-reading public. Her friend, Rahel Levin, who married Karl August Varnhagen, was another leader of Berlin intellectual life. "The little woman with the great soul," Goethe called her.... "She was the first to understand and recognise me." Rahel's brother was Ludwig Robert, poet and dramatist, whose *Die Macht der Verhältnisse* was the first play by a Jew to be presented on the German stage. But the most remarkable and most beautiful of the group was Henrietta Herz, who knew a dozen languages—English so well that she taught it in the household of the Duchess of Courland —and was a brilliant conversationalist.

When the intellectual life of Germany was beginning to stir, the houses of this group of cultured Jewish forerunners of the Feminist movement—whose sense of Jewish loyalty, incidentally, was non-existent—formed the principal centre. They knew everybody and had met everybody; they were the first to discern the genius in promising young men of letters and to give them their initial encouragement. In their houses, Fichte, Schiller, Niebuhr, Humboldt, Schlegel and Schleiermacher could meet illustrious foreigners like Mme. de Stael, the Prince de Ligne, Mirabeau and Lamotte-Fouqué. It was in this melting-pot, presided over by Jewish hostesses, that the German literature of the early nineteenth century was re-moulded and re-invigorated.

The tradition, it must be admitted, was a ponderous one. From this it was saved by Heinrich Heine—"a German Parisian, a Jewish German, a hated political exile who yearns for a dear, old, homely Germany, a sceptical sufferer with a Christian patience, a romantic poet expressing in classic form the modern spirit, a Jew and poor", as Israel Zangwill characterised him. He and his fellow-Jew, Ludwig Börne, that brilliant stylist and mordant critic, were associated in founding the liberal party, *Young Germany*. More enduring, perhaps (or so it seemed until a couple of years ago) was their work in creating a new standard for German journalism, which they saved from the overwhelming portentousness of the eighteenth century and imbued with a new spirit and technique. This amazing couple indeed invented the *feuilleton*, without which the press of Central Europe would now be unthinkable.[1]

Heine's own countrymen never forgave him his French sympathies. Yet he was, in spite of all, one of the very foremost European poets of his age, and one of the greatest German poets of all time. Though his native country has done its best to obliterate his memory, half a dozen at least of his lyrics remain among the most popular in the German language: and his *Lorelei* and his *Grenadiers* can hardly be driven out of the recollection of the German child even by anti-Semitic reaction.

At one time, Berthold Auerbach rivalled Heine, in popularity at least, and seemed likely to play the same rôle in fiction which the former had done in poetry. Time has brought a truer perspective: yet Auerbach remains one of the great names in German literature of the middle of the nineteenth century. But there was one profound difference between the two men. Heine's taste, and his wit, and his verve, were French—or at all events, non-Teutonic. Auerbach, on the other hand, represented the quintessence of German sentimentality and *Gemütlichkeit*. As was the case in art, a certain objective externality was necessary for the aesthetic appreciation of the slow-moving folk-life of the country-side: and, just as Liebermann enshrined the life of the German people in his canvases, so Auerbach achieved fame through his wonderfully intimate pictures of the life of the peasantry of the Black Forest, the heart of unspoiled Germany. Though in his student days he had suffered imprisonment for his democratic views, he became later a staunch advocate of German Nationalism, and distinguished himself for his patriotic effusions during

[1] The art was brought to its highest pitch of perfection by another Jew, Daniel Spitzer, of Vienna.

the Franco-Prussian War. Yet the fact that he had done so little for his own kindred did not save him from attack on the score of his origin, when the anti-Semitic movement raised its poisonous head a little while later; and this in the end drove him to his death.[1]

Imaginative literature could hardly be said to flourish in late nineteenth-century Germany, after the death of Heine. It is significant, nevertheless, that the most gifted German novelist of the time, Paul Heyse, who received the Nobel Prize for literature in 1910, as representative of German letters, was a half-Jew. He typified the heavy Augustan tradition, to-day barely readable, though at the time considered the height of good taste. On the other hand, the naturalistic and expressionistic schools, which have revived German literature in our own day and given it a European significance which it never previously enjoyed, provide a disproportionate number of Jewish names. Indeed, among those through whom German imaginative writing of to-day is best known to the outside world, Jews perhaps predominate: Jacob Wassermann, Franz Kafka, Stefan Zweig, Arnold Zweig, Lion Feuchtwanger, Emil Ludwig, Ernst Toller, Alfred Neumann, Franz Werfel, Max Brod and very many others of less calibre. Ernst Lissauer, lyricist and dramatist, entered into history when he wrote the famous war-time patriotic song, "Hassgesang gegen England". (It is not quite correct to translate it "The hymn of hate".) And one of the great losses suffered by German letters in the war was the death of that most promising poet,

---

[1] Auerbach is best remembered outside Germany for his novel, *On the Heights*.

Mention is deserved also in this connexion of Emil Franzos and Georg Hermann, well-known novelists in their day, who, though they devoted their talents in part to the Jewish scene, were much appreciated by the general world of letters. The latter in particular was an imaginative writer of the first rank.

Walter Heymann, who fell in action near Soissons at the beginning of 1915.

Special attention may be directed to Ludwig Fulda. His first story appeared when he was 22 years of age, in 1884, and for a generation he remained one of the most popular, as well as the most prolific, German writers. Many of his books were published in edition after edition: while one, *Die Zwillingsschwester*, which appeared in 1901, was dramatised and ran on the stage throughout Germany for years. As playwright he is noteworthy for his social dramas, in which, in advance of his age, he used the theatre as a medium for directing public attention to problems of the moment. An even more important place in contemporary letters is that of the Viennese Jew, Arthur Schnitzler,[1] one of the foremost dramatists of our generation. His plays are familiar in the repertoire of many countries. Apart from this, his influence has been a particularly potent one in modern German literature, for to him is due in no small measure the credit for making that naturally ponderous language more human and the subject-matter for imaginative treatment more real. Moreover, it was he who introduced for the first time the medico-scientific approach which is associated with the term Psycho-analysis.[2]

In the field of history, no German Jew has risen to the eminence of Ranke, Mommsen or Gregorovius: but many have attained a considerable reputation. Thus the German banker-critic turned historian, whose researches have placed the early history of Florence on an entirely new basis, Robert Davidsohn, was a Jew, as was also Ludo Hartmann, historian of Italy in the Middle Ages.

[1] The political boundary between Germany and Austria has, of course, been neglected in these pages.

[2] Three other outstanding modern German playwrights, Rainer Maria Rilke, Hugo von Hoffmansthal and Franz Wedekind, are half-Jewish by birth.

I

So was, by birth, Heinrich Friedjung, the greatest, perhaps, of Austrian historians, whose writings range from *A Life of the Emperor Charles V* to *A History of the Struggle for Supremacy in Germany* (1859–1866)—still the best historical introduction to the "Austrian Question", and recently translated into English. Martin Philippson, son of one of the religious paladins of German Jewry, was forced to leave Germany owing to anti-Semitism, and Brussels (where he then settled) owing to anti-Teutonism: yet the greater part of his considerable historical output was devoted to strictly non-Jewish subjects. One should mention also the great classical historian Ludwig Friedländer and the mediaevalists Harry Bresslau and Philipp Jaffé—foremost among the six Jews who collaborated in the *Monumenta Germaniae Historica*.

In connexion with historical study, a further point may be accentuated. It is to a German of Jewish stock that Clio owes the popularisation of the materialistic interpretation of history, which looks primarily to economic forces and factors for the elucidation of historic phenomena. It is not necessary to follow this school in its wilder extravagances or to its political deductions to realise the solid substratum of truth on which it rests. There can be no doubt, moreover, as to the profound influence which it has exercised on contemporary historiography, or the manner in which it has infused past movements and causes and leaders with the breath of life.

As is the case with Shakespeare studies in England, German literary criticism and research may be assessed by the study of Goethe. All his most scholarly biographers and interpreters, as it happens, have been Jews. The pioneer of Goethe studies in Germany was Theodor Creizenach: later experts have included Morris, Geiger, Meyer, Bielschowski, Simmel, and Gundolf. For many years, the Goethe Archive in Weimar was under the direction of Julius Wahle, co-editor of the standard "Sophien Ausgabe" of the poet's works. Similarly, it was Edward von Simson, a very considerable figure also in German politics and law, who founded the Goethe Gesellschaft.

A final illustration may be adduced. When, in 1876, the German Ministry of Education decided to eliminate foreign terms and expressions from the German language, one of the commission assembled for that purpose was the Jewish lexicographer, Daniel Sanders, whose researches on his native language have never been surpassed either in quality or in bulk. Logic should force present-day purists to believe that the tongue formed as a literary vehicle by Luther's Bible translation, made malleable by Mendelssohn and human by Heine, and purified with the aid of Sanders, is no longer a proper vehicle for expressing the thoughts of "Nordic" man.

§VI

The Jew had been acclimatised in European intellectual life for a generation or more (as is apparent from the foregoing pages) when the impact of modernism on letters began. In view of the impression which is widely held, it is necessary to accentuate the fact that the part played by Jews in the origins of this movement was negligible. Of the degenerate leaders of the *fin du siècle*, one only was a Jew—the poor, demented Otto Weininger, who committed suicide at the age of 25 and was, incidentally, one of the originators of modern anti-Semitism. None of the other fathers of modernism was a Jew—unless we are to include Anatole France, who, like the great Montaigne, might boast some Jewish blood. On the other hand, the sternest opponent of the modernistic school was Max Nordau, who thundered against these unhealthy tendencies in his *Degeneration,* and whose Jewish allegiance (for he was one of the founders of modern Zionism) was positive.

In France, indeed, the Jewish element in letters tended to the side of convention, or rather conventional unconventionality, typified if one assumes the truth of the report which makes Alexandre Dumas the younger of partially Jewish blood. There was no truer boulevardier than Philippe Auguste d'Ennery, author of *Michael Strogoff* and part-author of *The Two Orphans* (and some hundreds of other plays besides), whose name was seldom absent from the Parisian playbills for nearly half a century (his *Ambigu* alone was performed 1,000 times). Catulle Mendès, novelist, poet and dramatist, was one of the most faithful portrayers of Parisian life under the Third Republic. Georges de Porto-Riche, after a succession of failures, opened a new era in the history of the French stage by his *La Chance de Françoise*, presented at the Théâtre Libre in 1888, and henceforth ranked as the leader of a school. Tristan Bernard rivalled this success, and enriched the French vocabulary with a few immortal characters and phrases; his son, Jacques Bernard, is among the leading dramatists of the younger school in France. There was no suspicion of Jewish colouring in any of these; though Henri Bernstein, one of their rivals for the favours of the theatre-going Parisians in the early years of the twentieth century, turned his attention to Jewish problems in a couple of his plays, perhaps with more enthusiasm than understanding. Similarly, Baron Henri de Rothschild, besides his achievements in medicine and philanthropy, has made himself a reputation as a dramatist under the pen-name of André Pascal.

A very potent influence was that of Gustave Kahn, one of the leaders of the symbolist school, who introduced into French literature the *vers libre*, "strophes of psychical rather than syllabic unity, variable in number and duration in accordance with musical necessity." Though this new versification has not achieved the sweeping triumph that was at one time expected, it revivified the fatigued classical tradition which was still dominating French poetry, and for that reason alone (quite apart from his far-reaching work as editor and critic) Kahn deserves to be remembered as one of the important figures in Parisian letters of the close of the nineteenth century. The *vers libre* was perfected by André Spire, another figure of considerable moment in contemporary French literature. It is noteworthy that both these writers (unlike most of their contemporaries) show particular interest in Jewish subjects and affairs, the latter's enthusiasm having been first aroused at the time of the Dreyfus affair, when he was serving as Captain in a cavalry regiment. Among essayists, Julien Benda the philosopher, and André Suarès the poet, deserve at least cursory mention[1].

The literary significance of Marcel Proust, whose mother was Jewish, is particularly great. In his hands, the novel assumed a new form. Introspective analysis began to be used as a medium in fiction for interpreting human emotions. Whether there is anything Jewish in his uncanny faculty is still a matter for enquiry: but it may not be a mere coincidence that Italo Svevo, called by his admirers the Italian Proust, was of Jewish birth. (His original name was Ettore Schmitz.) Of Jewish origin, too, is André Maurois, who, in conjunction with Emil Ludwig in Germany (though with a more solid foundation) has created a new school of biography,

---

[1] The late Juliette Adam (d. 1936), whose salon was the focus of intellectual life over a long period and who was founder of the Revue Littéraire, was asserted to be of Jewish birth (her maiden name was Lambert), and was married to a Jew.

assisting to displace the former ungainly monuments of departed heroes, frequently forbidding and generally unapproachable, in favour of the breathing, plastic miniatures which hold the field to-day.

§VII

In other countries, too, Jews have made their contribution. Thus Denmark, with its diminutive community, produced in the past generation Georg Brandes, Professor of Aesthetics at the University of Copenhagen, and one of the outstanding literary critics of his age, who did more perhaps than any other man to enhance the reputation of Danish intellectual life abroad. Of his brothers, Eduard Brandes was one of the most successful Danish playwrights of the last decades of the nineteenth century, while Ernst was a prominent economist. Slightly before their day was Meir Aaron Goldschmidt, who, prevented from qualifying as a physician owing to the prevailing anti-Jewish prejudice, became a stormy petrel in journalism and a successful novelist. To him and Georg Brandes is due the opening of Danish intellectual life to modern ideas. Both retained their interest in Judaism—the latter to a marked extent. Henrik Hertz, on the other hand, one of the most prolific and widely translated Danish poets of the nineteenth century (no less than ten German versions of his *King René's Daughter* exist) was baptised in middle life. Henri Nathansen is another modern Danish-Jewish playwright of international reputation.

Sweden provides us with the names of Ludwig Oscar Josephson, dramatist, critic and theatrical producer, pioneer of the New Drama and one of the staunchest supporters of Ibsen and Strindberg; of Sophie Elkan, well-known as an historical novelist; and of the poet and critic Oskar Ivar Levertin, the foremost of the Swedish romanticists. Holland contributes Herman Heijermans, one of the outstanding modern Dutch novelists and dramatists and leader of the naturalistic school: Isaak Costa, a famous poet: Israel Querido, who demonstrated his origin by turning to the Bible for inspiration: and many others. Hungary's great names include Franz Molnar, Ludwig Biro, Ludwig Hatvány, Melchior Lengyel: in Czechoslovakia there are Ottokar Fischer and Frantisek Langer: in Poland, Julian Tuwim and Antoni Slonimski: in Russia, Isaac Babel the novelist and Boris Pasternak the lyricist. The greatest poet that anti-Semitic Roumania has as yet produced is the Jew Ronetti Roman, whose play, *New Lamps for Old*, is one of the very few specimens of Roumanian literature known abroad.

Italy in particular, with its handful of some 40,000 Jews, certainly provides a disproportionate number of names—from poets of a century and a half ago, such as Salamone Fiorentino, to classical prose-writers like Giuseppe Revere; from popular romancers like Guido da Verona to more profound imaginative novelists like Italo Svevo; from playwrights like Sabbatino Lopez to critics like Eugenio Camerini; from Alessandro d' Ancona, the literary historian, who introduced the historic method into Italy, to Graziadio Isaia Ascoli, the foremost Italian philologist of all time, both leaders of that group of thinkers to whom the renewal of Italian culture in the nineteenth century was due. The Jewish interest in the last-named branch of study has been particularly marked in every land. It owes its origin indeed to the Jewish savants of the Middle Ages who, through the intimate relations of Hebrew and Arabic, made their grammatical studies the beginning of comparative philology; and great scholars such as Sanders in Germany, or the brothers Darmesteter in France, demonstrate the universality of interest in the subject in our own day. Nor should one forget that remarkable genius, Lazar Geiger, whose bust stood until recently in the entrance-hall of the Frankfort Public Library. His researches on the origin of language were of sensational importance and led him to the same conclusions as Darwin, that evolution reigns in all nature. It is said indeed that he died from grief (he was only thirty-one) when it became clear that the English scientist had anticipated him.

Nothing indicates more clearly than these names, and the innumerable others which could be mentioned, the complete fusion of the Jewish element in the intellectual life-blood of Europe. The antecedents of these writers may have helped in some cases to widen their horizons, but did nothing to narrow their sympathies or to qualify the fidelity with which they mirrored the tone, the atmosphere and the fashions of their environment.

Appendix to Chapter V

JOURNALISM AND THE JEW

THE dictum, "Let me write a people's ballads: I care not who makes their laws", needs revision in the light of conditions of the present-day, when the written word and the power of the Press have attained an influence unknown in any former age. (The implications of this should not of course be exaggerated: for recent experience in England and America has shewn that on great public issues the popular suffrage has sometimes gone in a diametrically opposite direction to the general consensus and advice of the popular newspapers.) In this connexion, the same picture presents itself as in so many other branches of activity, intellectual and economic. In the first impetus of their emancipation the Jews flocked to journalism and played a considerable part in that profession. But there was never any distinctively Jewish quality in their contribution (it is difficult, indeed, to see how there could be): and the new conceptions and ideas which they introduced became common property before long.

The rapidity with which the Jews grasped the potentialities of the new instrument may be realised from the fact that in the seventeenth century two Jewish newspapers were established in Amsterdam—one in Spanish and one in Yiddish. The former, at least, was probably intended to cater for a wider circle. Yet for Jews to engage in general journalism was as yet impossible. It is true that Oliver Goldsmith writes of a Jewish journalist in 1771, in his *Haunch of Venison*. But this instance, if not jocular, was isolated: and from certain points of view the earliest English journalist in the modern sense was Lewis Goldsmith, a violent pamphleteer of the Napoleonic era, whose daughter married the great Lord Chancellor Lyndhurst and founded a famous salon.

It was in German journalism that the influence of Jews in the early nineteenth century was most pronounced, and they made a permanent mark. In particular, the contributions of Marx to the *Rheinische Zeitung*, and the brilliant feuilletons contributed from Paris by Heine and Börne (in particular to the *Augsburger Zeitung*) aroused the German periodical press from its traditional pompous lethargy, and set a fresh example for European (above all Central European) journalism as a whole. In Austria, L. A. Frankl and particularly Ignaz Kuranda, in his audacious *Grenzboten*, performed a somewhat similar function, though with more explosive objects. It is significant that, once this semi-subterranean periodical had achieved its end and a constitution had been granted, Kuranda founded the *Ostdeutsche Post*, which was of conservative tendencies and even over-emphasised the Pan-German standpoint. This in turn disappeared ultimately before the once-famous *Neue Freie Presse*, in its day one of the most important journals in the world, which was founded and managed by a group of Jews. (It was due to his brilliant feuilletons in the columns of this periodical that the founder of political Zionism, Theodor Herzl, owed his original reputation.) The same period saw the establishment, in 1872, by Rudolf Mosse and Georg Davidsohn (its first editor) of the *Berliner Tageblatt*, which speedily became known as one of the world's great newspapers. But the leading German journal was (and still is) the *Frankfurter Zeitung*, which was begun by Leopold Sonnemann. Other great figures in pre-war journalism in Germany included men like Maximilian Harden, the greatest opponent of William II's megalomaniac absolutism, and, a little later, Theodor Wolff, editor during a long and critical period of the *Berliner Tageblatt*. A rôle of real importance was played, too, by men like David Kalisch, who founded in 1848 the famous German humorous weekly, *Kladderadatsch*, or Moritz Gottlieb Saphir, the best-known humorist in Continental Europe, who laughed Metternich out of the Dual Empire. Kalisch's principal collaborator was Rudolf Loewenstein, the famous poet, whose verses were to be found prior to 1933 in every First Reading Book used in German schools.

In England, the most notable Jewish figure in the newspaper world in the nineteenth century was J. M. Levy, who created, not merely the *Daily Telegraph*, but thereby, popular journalism as a whole in England. (It was left to another agency to confuse popularisation with vulgarisation.) Contemporaneously, there were a few outstanding figures such as Blowitz, the great Foreign Correspondent of *The Times*. The latter's attitude was one of the many indications that Jewish sympathies have on the whole been markedly absent in the more prominent Jewish journalists; for he was so "objective" as to maintain a somewhat shameful detachment even during the progress of the Dreyfus Case. In this, however, he was outdone by Arthur Meyer, editor of *Le Gaulois*, which became under his direction the mouth-piece of the Clerical, Monarchist and anti-Semitic parties in France: so much for "Jewish solidarity."

The nineteenth century witnessed in addition the emergence of various Jewish newspaper administrators of genius—men like Adolph Ochs, who made the *New York Times* one of the most powerful stabilizing forces in American public life, and Leopold Ullstein, founder of what was in its day the most important German publishing-house. One of the rare common features about these enterprises was that in so few cases has the control continued in the same family down to to-day. Thus, no member of the Levy (Lawson) family is now associated with the *Daily Telegraph :* while the Ullstein Press was "co-ordinated" by the Nazi government. In fact, Jewish influence in contemporary journalism has not been particularly great. In Germany, before the Nazi Revolution, it was fashionable to describe all papers of the Left (i.e. Democratic and Socialist) as "Jewish". Really, no more than ten out of the eighty-five more prominent German papers had a Jewish editor-in-chief; while there were fewer than twenty Jews on the editorial staffs of the entire German Socialist Press, out of some 400. In England, the influence is even less. To-day, not a single important English daily paper is controlled by a Jew: only one has a Jew as Chairman of its board of directors: and not one has a Jewish editor-in-chief.

In the development of the news service, which is all-important for modern journalism, Jewish pioneers took a vital share. Two, and possibly three, of the pioneers in the establishment of European news-agencies were Jews—Reuter, Wolff and Havas[1]. The greatest of these three was indubitably the first. Havas operated at the outset chiefly in France, and Wolff in Germany. But Reuter boldly made London his base, transferring

[1] Havas' Jewish origin is often stated, but I have no means of verifying it.

himself from Germany to England and assuming British nationality : and the pre-eminence which was established by his enterprise has never been challenged. It is characteristic of what has happened in so many other branches of endeavour that the Jewish element in all three of these organisations has now entirely disappeared. The Wolff agency (which played so important a rôle in Germany during the war of 1914–18) retained some sort of Jewish direction longest : but it has now come under Government control, its former "non-Aryan" directors having been extruded from it.

In the realm of publishing, Jewish participation has been more important than extensive. It is sufficient to mention that greatest of German publishing houses, the firm of Fischer, whose intellectual guidance was largely responsible for the revitalisation of German literature at the close of the last century. Bernard Shaw is one only of the foreign authors whose introduction to the German public was entirely due to them. To suggest any 'racial' bias in such activities becomes all the more preposterous when one recalls the strange irony that even Nietzsche, the major prophet of National Socialism, was discovered and supported by Jews.

CHAPTER VI

ART, MUSIC, STAGE

§1

IT was long believed that the Jewish share in the visual arts was negligible, until modern times, owing to the excessively rigorous interpretation of the third commandment. One of the most sensational of recent archaeological discoveries has made it necessary to revise this view. At Dura Europos, formerly a frontier city on the borders of the Roman and Persian Empires, there have been discovered the remains of a third-century synagogue, in a remarkable state of preservation. The walls still stand to a height in some places of nearly twenty feet. They are adorned with frescoes of amazing vitality, representing Biblical scenes, the visions of the Prophets, the Temple at Jerusalem, and so on. Contrary to all preconceived ideas, no qualms whatsoever are entertained at representing the human figure, notwithstanding the religious nature of the building. The overthrow of the Egyptians in the Dead Sea, or the Dedication of Aaron, leaves nothing to fantasy: while a portrait of a Priest (probably intended to represent the Prophet Jeremiah) closely resembles the early representations of Jesus of Nazareth. These frescoes, in fact, display remarkable affinities with those discovered in the Christian catacombs and the mosaics in the earliest Roman churches.

In view of these discoveries, some scholars go so far as to suggest that the ideas previously held with regard to the origins of Christian Art must be radically revised. It was formerly considered that it had its roots in pagan Egypt; now, it appears highly probable that (as in so much else) the Church simply carried on the tradition which already obtained in the Synagogue. But the whole of European painting depends, in the last instance, on ecclesiastical and early Christian origins ; hence, if this new theory is correct, the tradition of Giotto and of Cimabue goes back ultimately to a Jewish prototype.[1]

Whether or no this is the case, the Jewish inspiration of much of European art cannot be denied. Three-quarters at least of European paintings before 1500, and a very high proportion after that date, deal with Biblical—i.e. Hebrew—characters and scenes. It is difficult to conceive Italian art of the Renaissance without such familiar episodes as the Creation, the lives of the patriarchs, the triumph of Judith and so on : while (though the fact was not realised or conveyed in pictorial art until the last century) the central subject of all—Jesus and the Madonna—was essentially Hebraic.

It was Dutch painting which first made a definite breach in the ecclesiastical tradition in art. Yet this by no means signified a revolt against the Hebraic subject-matter. Rembrandt, for example, turned again and again to the Bible for inspiration, though he was more attracted by its dramatic than its spiritual values. Moreover, his realistic sense led him to the Jewish quarter of Amsterdam in order to obtain local colour : with the result that his purview extended from the Hebrews of old to the Jews of his own day, depicted with a characteristic intermingling of realism and romanticism. For many years of his life, Rembrandt lived among Jews, painted Jews, and worked frequently

[1] It may be added, in connexion with this, that a professional Jewish animal-painter named Eudoxios lived at Rome in the Imperial period.

THE PROPHET JEREMIAH
From a third-century synagogue fresco at Dura Europos
(*From Reifenberg, Denkmäler der jüdischen Antike, by courtesy of Schocken Verlag, Berlin*)

under Jewish auspices. (It is interesting to recall in this connexion that he illustrated a book for Menasseh ben Israel, the founder of the modern Jewish settlement in England.) In view of all this, it has often been suggested, though without any documentary evidence, that he was himself of Jewish blood.[1]

For the paradoxical reason that art was so specifically Hebraic in character, the Jews could participate in it to only a very limited degree in the great age of European painting. It occupied itself largely with New Testament scenes : it was destined to a large extent for ecclesiastical decoration—or, rather, veneration. Hence a very large proportion of the training, the activity and the livelihood of the artist were cut off from the Jew. He compensated himself by interpreting with increasing rigour the Biblical prohibition to forbear from making graven images or any likeness, this fortifying still further the prevalent tendency. Finally, social prejudice prevented him from entering the profession which, of all handicrafts, postulated the most intimate and friendly association between patron and worker.

§II

Hence, from the close of the classical age down to the period of the disintegration of the Ghetto, Jewish artists working for the Gentile world, though not absolutely unknown (a few instances have been given above,

[1] Other Dutch and Flemish artists who have been suspected to be of Jewish extraction include the fifteenth century master-engraver, Lucas Jacobsz (known as Van Leyden) son of the painter S. H. Jacobszoon: the family of engravers and artists of the seventeenth century, the De Jodes: and the Ruisdaels—Izaak Jacob, Jacob Salomons and Salomons. Evidence based on names is however a little tenuous, particularly in the seventeenth century, when the Puritan tradition became so strong. It is believed on the other hand that the great Spanish painter Bartolomé Bermejo, of Cordova, was of Marrano (or crypto-Jewish) extraction.

pp. 53–4), were few and far between. However, immediately art lost its ecclesiastical bias, and social prejudices decreased, they began to play a more active rôle. They began with a branch of art in which social connexions and religious allegiance were unimportant. In particular, as a natural outcome of their commercial interest in precious stones, they mastered the art of gem- and seal-cutting, which developed into engraving and medal-making. In Germany, in the seventeenth and eighteenth centuries, these professions were very commonly followed by Jews. Many of the petty courts had a Jewish seal-engraver in their employment: and some of the best medallists of the period were Jews. It is enough for our purpose to mention that Jacob Abraham who held an official appointment in the Court of Prussia in the second half of the eighteenth century, and his son, Abraham Abrahamson, both prolific workers.

From gems and seals, there was an easy transition to miniature-painting, exemplified in the eighteenth century by Raphael Bachi in Paris, the Pinhas and Treu families in Germany, and, at the beginning of the nineteenth century, by David Alexander Fiorino, one of the best miniaturists of his day, in Dresden.

Thus, by gradual degrees, the Jew began to acclimatise himself in the artistic world. By the close of the eighteenth century, a couple of figures of first importance were of Jewish origin. Anton Rafael Mengs (Court Painter at Madrid, a much-read writer on the theory of art and the first person to recognise the genius of Goya), was the son of a converted Danish-Jewish enamel-worker named Ishmael Mengs. The younger Mengs' reputation in his day was enormous—probably exceeding his merits. He had, moreover, a lasting influence in the history of painting as the founder of the neo-classical school, which received its greatest development in that superb painter David.

The latter's name has made it suspected that he, too, was of Jewish extraction. So, according to the latest researches, was John Zoffany, one of the original members of the Royal Academy in London and a master of the conversation-piece; he was, it appears, born at Frankfort of Bohemian Jewish parentage, and certainly lodged in the house of a Jew when he first came to London.

This brings us to England, which exemplifies most strikingly the rôle of the Jew in painting—always in essence a child of his environment and of his age. It is worth while, for that reason, to deal with this country in a little greater detail.

The English miniaturists of the Stuart period, Samuel and Abraham Cooper, are said to have been Jews, though on questionable evidence. It is significant nevertheless that in England, where social emancipation started so soon, Jews began to play a definite part in artistic life earlier than in any other modern state. The features which characterised (it would not perhaps be fair to say distinguished) English painting were on the whole faithfully imitated, the English Jew showing himself as conservative as his Gentile neighbours. Casanova tells us how on one occasion, desiring a portrait of one of his mistresses, he requested a friend to send him the best miniaturist in London: "and he sent me a Jew." Solomon Polack (whose son married Queen Pomare of Tahiti) was a constant exhibitor at the Royal Academy between 1790 and 1831: and Frederick Benjamin Barlin —son of the Minister of the Chatham Synagogue—in 1802 and 1807. Abraham Ezekiel, of Exeter, miniature-painter and engraver, was sufficiently distinguished to merit a place in the *Dictionary of National Biography*. If Solomon Alexander Hart, Professor and Librarian of the Royal Academy, was a noteworthy exponent of what may be termed the pontifical school in British

K

painting, that wayward genius, Simeon Solomon, was not the least remarkable member of the pre-Raphaelite group. His brother, Abraham Solomon, was a painter whose merits are once more gaining recognition; while his sister, Rebecca Solomon, also deserves mention. Another distinguished exponent of the classical tradition in England, both as portraitist and as painter of figure compositions, was Solomon Joseph Solomon, President of the Royal Society of British Artists. During the War of 1914–18 he was sufficiently versatile to turn his talent to the perfection of the military system of camouflage, which was placed on a scientific basis for the first time under his direction. In view of the early Jewish association with the art of miniature-painting, it is interesting to note that it is a Jew, Alfred Praga (for many years President of the Society of Miniaturists), who was responsible for the revival of the art in England. To-day, Sir William Rothenstein and Philip Laszló (both of Jewish birth) represent the conservative tradition, in contrast to those younger artists—Mark Gertler, David Bomberg, Bernard Meninsky, Jacob Kramer, and so on— who have shared with their non-Jewish comrades in the exciting struggles of the modern movement.[1]

[1] A few additional names of Anglo-Jewish artists deserve mention. In the Victorian period, there were Felix Moscheles, H. Lemon (the famous steel engraver), E. B. S. Montefiore (the animal painter) and his brother, E. F. Montefiore (etcher): while E. P. Fox was one of the earliest Australian painters. More recently there has been a remarkable group of Anglo-Jewish women artists including Clara Klinghoffer, Clara and Hilda Montalba, Constance Halford, Mary Davis, A. Elias, Dorothea Landau, Ethel Henriques, Flora Lion and Mary Raphael. Other contemporaries include J. H. Amshewitz, whose panels may be seen in South Africa House and the Royal Exchange; Isaac Cohen, the eminent portrait painter: Benno Schotz, Edward Wolfe, Edmund Kapp, P. Naviasky, A. J. Lyons, I. Snowman, A. Wolmark, J. Oppenheimer and Meyer Klang, to name only a few out of many. Etchers include Lionel Phillips, T. Friedenson, F. L. Emanuel, S. van Abbe, A. Gross, S. E. Pecher, and Herbert Cutner. Pilichowski and Lucien Pissaro may be reckoned English through long residence: while Ospovat enjoys international reputation as

§III

It was characteristic that, while in England Jewish artists were typical members of the placid British school, on the Continent they were caught up in the feverish new tide which had its origin in France. During the course of the nineteenth century, Paris became the artistic centre for the whole world : and under the inspiration of Manet and Monet, Millet and Renoir, a new tradition in art began. It is not generally realised that one of the founders of the New School was a Jew, Camille Pissarro, who had a profound influence on the earlier development of Cézanne. The peculiar atmosphere of the streets and boulevards of Paris have had no more faithful chronicler than in his "luminous vibration", though he brought to his work as well something of the atmosphere of his West Indian birthplace ; and his landscapes are among the most solidly constructed achievements of the Impressionist movement. But more important was his warm humanity. It is to this common factor that one seems forced back in considering the Jewish contribution in whatever sphere.[1]

With the twentieth century, the stream of Jews who went to study and work in Paris grew greater and greater, producing painters of the calibre of Chagall, Pascin, Soutine and Kisling, and above all, Modigliani, the

---

caricaturist and book-illustrator. Isaac Rosenberg, that fine poet killed at the Front in 1918, was also an artist of considerable interest. In America modernism in art owes its introduction to Max Weber and Abraham Walkowitz, and the part played to-day by men like Louis Lozowick is of the utmost significance.

[1] Before this period, France produced at least one outstanding Jewish artist—Rosa Bonheur, the famous animal painter (whose father, Raymond Bonheur, had also enjoyed a high reputation.) Her work was remarkable for the firm handling of the subject, coupled with extraordinary accuracy. She was the first woman to receive the Grand Cross of the Legion of Honour (1894).

Botticelli of the twentieth century, who before his untimely death had become one of the really great figures in contemporary art.

It was in the generation following on Manet, that the characteristic Jewish function of acting as intellectual intermediary began to make itself felt: for it was to a large extent by Jews that the spirit of the Impressionists was carried beyond France, to initiate a new tradition in painting throughout Europe. Thus, Serafino de Tivoli, who had studied in Paris, brought the new conceptions back to Italy, where he founded what was irreverently called the school of the "macchiaiuoli". Josef Israels took it to Holland, becoming the most significant figure in Dutch art since the seventeenth century, and certainly the nearest in spirit to Rembrandt van Rijn. It was typical that this Jew was the first person of his age to enter into the spirit of the people, and to go to the fisherman, the peasant, and the artisan for inspiration, unmingled with any sense of patronage, amusement, or charity. A similar democratisation was achieved in Russia by Isaac Levitan, of whom the anti-Semitic *Novoye Vremya* wrote: "This full-blooded Jew knew, as no other man, how to make us realise and love our plain and homely country scenes."

In this, Israels and Levitan were at one in spirit with their great contemporary, Max Liebermann, who, on the authority of the *Encyclopaedia Britannica*, is one of the two first-rate figures in German painting. There had been eminent German-Jewish painters of the conventional school in the generation which had preceded him—Veit and Oppenheim and Possart and the Bendemanns, father and son. It was Liebermann, however, who, by bringing the Impressionist school to the knowledge of his country, disturbed the complacent traditionalism (shared by these Jewish painters) which had previously prevailed. Germany was for a long while reluctant to recognise him: it was only when his fame had re-echoed back from abroad that his supremacy was at last realised. Following the example of Israels and their common master, Millet, he devoted himself to depicting the life of the poor, finding his best subjects in orphanages, asylums, peasants, and villages (a characteristic reaction from the former cult of the Battle Piece). He democratised, as it were, the subject-matter of German painting. "His pictures hold the fragrance of the soil and the breezes of the heavens," states the *Britannica*. But his influence was not exercised only through his painting. It was he who in 1900 organised the first Berlin Sezession, a landmark in the history of German art. In 1919, he was elected President of the Berlin Academy of Fine Arts, maintaining that position until the Nazi Revolution, and distinguishing himself by a receptiveness of new ideas and appreciation for new currents most unusual for one in such a position.

Liebermann was almost unique among academicians in his realisation of the fact that, in art, the revolutionary of yesterday is the conservative of to-day. The absence of any stylistic coherence among Jewish artists may be realised from the fact that Jews were so prominent among the German Expressionists and their successors, whose rise in the first decades of the twentieth century marked the decline of his influence. Among the leaders of this movement was Max Pechstein: the Sturm group which began to supplant it was formed by the Jewish critic, Herrwarth Walden; but this in turn had to yield before a new reaction, a leading member of which was the modernist animal-painter, Franz Marc, killed at the Front. The most distinguished Jewish artist of the pre-war period, after Liebermann, was probably Lesser Ury, a genius in colour: while Yankel Adler subsequently made his name known among the radicals. But there was nothing in the artistic temperament of the Jew which inclined him to revolutionary idealism : and, when the *Neue Sachlichkeit* sounded the call for the movement back to nature, one of its leaders was Josef Bato.

Sculpture was, for centuries, the most ecclesiastical branch of art, and this is perhaps the reason for the comparative lateness of the Jew's entrance into it. In the romantic period, Mark Matveyevitch Antokolski was easily the most eminent Russian sculptor, gaining the first prize in the international competition of 1878. As the Russian art-critic, Stassov, wrote : "He is the greatest sculptor of our age. He represents in his personality something altogether different from what all the rest of our sculptors stand for—both ancient and modern." Important, too, at this time, though far inferior to Antokolski in ability, was Moses Jacob Ezekiel, perhaps the most distinguished American-born sculptor of his age. The next generation produced Henryk Glicenstein, N. Aronson, Arrigo Minerbi, and some others of equal reputation. To-day, the magnificent virility of men like Jacques Lipchitz, Osip Zadkin, and Jacob Epstein is leavened by the classical purity of Arnold Zadikow : while Benno Elkan leads a return to the Renaissance ideal in wedding a sculptor's imagination to sober utilitarianism.

§IV

In architecture, the Jew had little opportunity to demonstrate his talent until comparatively recent years. The Temple in Jerusalem was reckoned almost among the wonders of the ancient world : but there was no possibility of emulating this achievement on however much reduced a scale in the Diaspora. The mediaeval synagogue was, of necessity, modest and unpretentious to a degree. It

is remarkable how faithfully this reflected the fashions
of the environment. The earliest German synagogues
are perfect specimens of the romanesque style (as in the
case of that of Worms, constructed in the eleventh
century) or of the Gothic (as is to be found in the Alt-Neu
Schul of Prague): those of Spain (e.g. at Toledo, Segovia
or Cordova) reproduce the flowing Arabesques of the
neighbouring mosques: Italy, at Venice or Padua or
Ferrara, brings in the baroque influence: while the
wooden synagogues of Russia and Poland are thought
to reproduce the style and fashions of the ancient Pagan
temples, of which no other trace survives.

In only one respect does it seem that the mediaeval
Jew was responsible for an important architectural
innovation. The precariousness of his existence made it
desirable for his dwelling-place to be as strong as possible,
and his wide-spread connexions indicated the means.
Accordingly, it appears that he was the pioneer of domestic
architecture in stone in Northern Europe. It seems more
than a coincidence that all over England ancient dwelling-
houses of especial solidity are even now associated with the
names of the Jewish owners of seven centuries ago. In what
was formerly the Lincoln Jewry, above all, some admirable
specimens survive—said to be the oldest dwelling-houses
in Europe (outside Spain) which are still inhabited.

The nineteenth century at last opened the doors of
architecture to the Jews: and they were not slow to
take advantage of the fact. English Jewry provided at
least one important figure—George Basevi, whose works
include that perfect specimen of the neo-classical style,
the Fitzwilliam Museum at Cambridge. In Germany, in
the middle of the century, the most prominent name in
this sphere is that of Georg Hitzig, President of the
Academy of Art, who designed the Bourse (1859-64) and
the Reichsbank (1869-77). Many of the local branches

of this institution, in the full fortress-like floridity of the close of the last century, were erected by E. Jacobsthal; while in Austria, a new tradition in theatrical architecture was started by Oscar Strnad. Hyper-patriotic admirers of the neo-Gothic style of architecture in Germany date the revival from 1905, when Alfred Messel completed the Wertheim Building in Berlin, and (according to the reactionary *Freiheitskampf*) "a new epoch opened for German architecture". To-day, there is one Jewish figure of European significance in architecture—Erich Mendelssohn, who, ruthlessly sweeping away traditional forms, summoned the sun and air to collaborate with bricks and mortar. His style symbolises, and has assisted, the modern insistence upon the sun as a therapeutic agency; while his interplay of horizontal and vertical lines has aided the American sky-scraper in its evolution from a utilitarian curiosity to an unprecedented architectural form of rare beauty[1].

In artistic criticism and history, in every branch, the part played by Jews has been of the utmost importance. Thus, one of the greatest living authorities on Italian art of the Renaissance is Bernhard Berenson, an American critic of Lithuanian birth; while there was no greater authority on mediaeval Italian sculpture than Senator I. B. Supino. Germany has provided a greater number of workers in this field—Marc Rosenberg, the outstanding expert on goldsmith's work; Adolph Goldschmidt, authority on mediaeval sculpture and manuscript illumination; and Max J. Friedländer, author of a monumental work on Dutch painting. Some of England's

---

[1] Another name associated with the development of the sky-scraper is that of L. J. Horowitz, head of the company which erected the Woolworth Building. In the previous generation, Dankmar Adler (who designed the Chicago Stock Exchange) was a notable figure in American architecture; while among contemporaries who deserve mention is the Swiss Julius Flegenheimer, architect of the Palace of the League of Nations at Geneva.

most eminent art-critics and historians, too, have been Jews. The name of Sir Isidore Spielmann, for over forty years a leader of the world of art in this country, was outstanding in the last generation. His brother, Marion H. Spielmann, was editor of the *Magazine of Art* and the recognised authority on Millais and Ruskin, as well as on the portraiture of Shakespeare and Chaucer and on the history of "Punch". Sir Charles Walston, Slade Professor at Cambridge, wrote extensively on the aesthetics of art, besides being a great archaeologist. Malcolm Charles Salaman is a distinguished critic, and the greatest English authority on coloured prints and woodcuts; while in the field of etching a standard work is Frank Emanuel's *Etching and Etchers*. The name of Salamon Reinach is famous, not only in France, as author of what is perhaps still the best introduction to the history of Art—*Apollo*.

§v

Music, like painting, is a particularly faithful index of assimilation: and Jewish religious and folk-music have on the whole reflected with the utmost fidelity the atmosphere of their environment. Northern Jewry generally imitates, in home and synagogue, the German musical tradition of the Middle Ages; Southern, that of Spain; and the melodies common to both elements, which might therefore be presumed to be of ancient Palestinian origin, are conspicuous by their rarity. Indeed, there is a higher probability that the tradition of Temple cantillation may to-day be traced in the oldest music of the Catholic Church than in that of the Synagogue. On the other hand, in a later age, synagogue music has occasionally been drawn upon by Gentile composers. Thus Benedetto Marcello found the settings for many psalms in the Ghetto at Venice, while the historic tune to the English hymn, "The God of Abraham praise", was carried away from the Great Synagogue in London one Friday evening in 1772 by the Wesleyan minister, Thomas Oliver, after hearing Leoni chant the doxology, *Yigdal*. But the tide has generally flowed in the other direction. Students of mediaeval Spanish music, for example, are now beginning to devote increasing attention to the folk-music of the Jews in the Levant, who still possess a vast store of uncontaminated folk-songs and ballads of the age of Columbus.

Jewish musicians, whose performances were eagerly listened to by non-Jewish audiences, were indeed to be encountered throughout the Middle Ages. As with their neighbours, it was only with the Renaissance that individual composers began to emerge. The first known to us by name was one Joseph ("Giuseppe Ebreo"), who flourished at the court of Lorenzo de' Medici, where he collaborated with the Jewish writer on the art of dancing, Guglielmo da Pesaro. At the court of Mantua, there were also a number of singers and instrumentalists and composers, some of whose work—mainly of secular interest—was published. Among these may be mentioned David Civita, whose *Premitie Armoniche* appeared at Venice in 1616; Allegro Porto, who dedicated three volumes of compositions to the Emperor Ferdinand; and Salamone de' Rossi, who divided his attention impartially between compositions intended for synagogal and profane use. In Venice, the Jews had in the Ghetto their own Musical Academy, which exchanged courtesies and compositions with other similar bodies in the city.

The development of the Catholic Reaction destroyed this promising beginning. With the Jews cooped up in their Ghettoes and forbidden ordinary intercourse with their fellow-citizens, and with Church compositions the easiest (if not the only) avenue to recognition, the tradition languished. Hence it was only in lands of greater freedom that the Jewish musical ability found its outlet.

The pioneers were the instrumentalists. Thus, in the first half of the eighteenth century there emigrated from Verona to England a certain Jacob Basevi Cervetto, a superb performer on the violoncello—almost unknown in the country before his day. For some forty-five years he was one of the best-known players in London : it is said that the Gallery cry, "Go it, Nosey", was originally used in reference to his physiognomy. In addition, he composed a fair amount of music. His son, James, was the heir to much of his ability as well as to his considerable fortune.

Jewish singers, too, began to come into their own in England at the same period. The best known was John Braham, by far the most celebrated vocalist of his day, whose voice is said to have had a range and beauty equalled by no other recorded English singer. Starting life as a choirboy at the Great Synagogue, he ultimately became estranged from his co-religionists : and his daughter married the Earl of Waldegrave, her *salon* subsequently becoming a great force in London life. Braham's original work is not of any particular merit : but he is noteworthy as the composer of what was long one of the most popular English songs, "The Death of Nelson." (See above, p. 108)

Isaac Nathan is best remembered to-day for having instigated his friend Byron's "Hebrew Melodies", which he set to music. He was at the time a considerable figure in the musical world, being historian of music to George IV, and instructor to the latter's daughter, the Princess Charlotte. Later, he emigrated to Australia, where he rendered great service in developing musical talent and improving Church music and choral societies. His *Don*

John of Austria has an importance of its own, as the first Australian opera. Among his numerous other works was a life of the great operatic singer, Madame Malibran de Beriot, also a Jewess. Another well-known figure in English musical life of the Regency period was Michael Bolaffi, Musical Director to the Duke of Cambridge, who published a 'sonnet' in the style of the period in memory of Haydn. There is nothing very sensational, indeed, in all this: it is typical (as it should be) of the placid, harmonious, somewhat amateurish course of musical activity of that period in England as a whole.

It was Germany which led Europe in music, and it was natural that German Jews shewed a greater prominence in this than their co-religionists across the Rhine or the North Sea. Here Felix Mendelssohn-Bartholdy, the baptised grandson of the great Jewish philosopher, exercised an influence so potent that it can hardly be credited that he died before attaining his fortieth year. England knows him as a composer, almost the last real genius of the melody which was once music. His *Midsummer Night's Dream* all but enhanced the charm of Shakespeare; more than normal obtuseness was necessary to have this masterpiece of harmony banned in Nazi Germany, on the ground that its composer was "Non-Aryan". His sacred oratorios—a branch of music to which he gave a new lease of life—meant more in England than they did in his own country: and his *Elijah*, first performed in Birmingham in 1846, has not only preserved its classic popularity but had almost too potent an influence on composers of English Church Music[1].

In the words of Sir Hubert Parry, one of England's greatest musical scholars, "he was one of the few composers to whom, in his best moments, all the resources of art

---

[1] It may be recalled that the most popular of modern Christmas carols, *Venite Adoremus*, is also Mendelssohn's work.

were equally available. His choral writing was, on the
whole, the most practical and the most fluent that has
been seen since Handel and Bach, and for mastery of
choral effect he had no real superior in his time. His
harmony is full of variety and sufficiently forcible, and
his facility in melody quite unlimited".

But, even had he not composed a note, Mendelssohn
would still be an important figure in musical history.
In 1827-8, in the face of considerable opposition, he
began propaganda on behalf of the music of Bach,
which finally resulted in the formation of a Bach Society
and the publication of his Masses and Cantatas; it was
to this that the renaissance of Bach, long forgotten among
his countrymen, is to be traced. Mendelssohn's transference to Leipzig in 1835, as conductor of the Gewandhaus
Orchestra, made Leipzig the musical centre of Germany,
as Germany was of Europe. He founded, too, the Leipzig
Conservatoire, upon the staff of which were a number of
eminent Jewish instrumentalists, many of whom were
at the same time composers of note. They included
Ignaz Moscheles, founder of a new school of pianoforte-
playing, whose long life enabled him to link the pianistic
tradition of an earlier day with modern times: Joseph
Joachim, "one of the loftiest names in the history of
the violin" and the interpreter *par excellence* of the
classical tradition, whose "Hungarian Concerto" and
"Hebrew Melodies", for viola and piano, testify to the
range and catholicity of his musical sympathies: and
Ferdinand David, who combined the qualities of the
classics with the technical skill and brilliance of the
moderns, and to whom it was due that Leipzig long
remained the centre of violin-playing in Europe. "Leipzig is a Jewish metropolis," grumbled Wagner in 1869.

Contemporary with Mendelssohn was a group of other
Jewish composers, almost on the same plane. The

"Cyclopaean" Giacomo Meyerbeer, son of a Berlin banker, became famous in the one sphere all but untouched by his great contemporary—namely, Opera. He anticipated, or instructed, Wagner in his genius for matching the pageantry of scene with that of tone: and a more immediate influence is sometimes discernible. His works still hold the stage, on the Continent especially: while his influence in style, setting and orchestration have had a subtle effect on many subsequent composers. The travelling fellowships which Meyerbeer established by his will were then something novel in musical annals, and have not been without their permanent influence. His work shews considerable analogies to that of Jacques François Fromenthal Elie Halévy who may be reckoned one of the great figures in French music, by the side of Thomas, Gounod, Bizet or Saint-Saëns, and barely second to them. In Paris at least (where a street is named after him) his works are still regularly played and enthusiastically received. Alone of the more eminent Jewish composers of the nineteenth century, his name is associated with a work on a Jewish theme, though indeed shewing no Jewish influence in its music—his masterpiece, *La Juive*, still a favourite.

Jacques Offenbach linked Germany with France, being the son of a synagogue cantor at Cologne, but passing his most active years in Paris, where during the Second Empire he was one of the outstanding figures in the musical world. He was the father of the Opéra Comique. The artistry of his hundred or more compositions makes them of living interest to the present day: and among them there is one at least which is assured of immortality—*The Tales of Hoffman*. More solid was the operatic work of Karl Goldmark, especially remarkable for the rich splendour of the orchestration. Gustav Mahler was a composer in the grand manner, whose works evoked enormous devotion and are marked by a spiritual power of moving impressiveness. In England, though no names of equal calibre have as yet emerged, Sir Frederic Cowen, conductor as well as composer, had a prolific output of songs, instrumental music and choral work of abiding value.

The nineteenth century produced a number of other Jewish composers, perhaps less universally known than those mentioned above, but of considerable reputation nevertheless—Salomon Jadassohn, Ignaz Brüll, and Moritz Moszkowski in Germany and Austria; John Barnett, Julius Benedict and Isidore de Lara in England, as well as Charles Kensington Salaman, who founded the Musical Association in 1876 and instituted the Concerti da Camera in 1835; Camille Erlanger and Paul Dukas in France; Federigo Consolo and Alberto Franchetti in Italy.[1]

In the modern school of music, Jews—at last afforded ampler opportunities—are among the leaders. It is enough to mention Arnold Schönberg, "the first musician since Debussy to have carried forward the form of Opera" whose innovations have profoundly affected a large body of disciples but who now is an exile from his native Germany; Darius Milhaud, the outstanding member of the modern French school, with the distinction that his revolutionary music often expresses religious emotion; Mario Castelnuovo-Tedesco, one of the most gifted of the younger Italian composers of our time; and Ernest Bloch, Swiss by birth, widely considered to be one of the outstanding composers of the day, who, as Director of the San Francisco school of music, had a great influence on the younger American composers. He is one of the few modern Jewish musicians who has devoted

[1]According to some authorities the names of Sullivan, Leoncavallo, Costa and even Beethoven should be added to this list, as having been of Jewish extraction.

his talent to Jewish themes. Far, however, from diluting the pure source of European music with an extraneous element, he has endeavoured (though not all agree, with success) to put a Jewish content into modern European musical forms, as for instance in his recent titanic experiments in Synagogal composition.[1]

§VI

In music, unlike any other branch of art, interpretation is all-important : and, since the first half of the nineteenth century, Jews have figured in utterly disproportionate numbers among the instrumentalists in every land. Indeed, the concert hall of to-day would be inconceivable without the Jewish *virtuosi* who constitute no mean proportion of its major attractions. The violin has had a particular attraction for the Jews (particularly, by some freak of environment, for those of Russian birth): witness the names of Joachim, David, Elman, Heifetz, Kreisler, Zimbalist, Achron, Auer, Seidel, Menuhin, Szigeti, Hubermann, Pollitzer (Elgar's master), and so on. Pianists include Anton Rubenstein (one of the greatest the world has ever known, and at the same time a composer of merit) and his brother Nicholas, founder of the Russian Musical Society : and, nearer our own day, Myra Hess, Ossip Gabrilowitch, Moritz Moszkowski, Moriz Rosenthal, Harold Samuel, Moiseiwitsch, Consolo, Horowitz, Solomon, Hambourg, Schnabel, Arthur Rubinstein, and so on. Among 'Cellists, the names of Feuermann, Piatigorsky, and Bernhard Cossman are preeminent. Mention should be made also of Eli Parish-Alvars, of Teignmouth, "the Paganini of the Harp",

[1] In order to avoid any controversial claims, mention has not been made here of Maurice Ravel, who, though bearing a distinctively French-Jewish name and attracted by Jewish themes, is stated authoritatively not to be a Jew.

one of the most distinguished harpists of any period and almost the earliest English instrumentalist to achieve a great reputation abroad.

Great singers have not been quite so common, yet they include Giuditta Pasta (for whom Bellini wrote "La Norma"), Pauline Lucca, the first "Africana", and Lilli Lehmanns (a half-Jewess), as well as Julius Lieban, Joseph Schwarz, Alexander Kipnis, Hermann Jadlowker and Richard Tauber.

Among the great Jewish conductors may be mentioned Walter Damrosch and his family, whose services for the upbuilding of the great musical tradition of the United States have been so conspicuous: and Hermann Levi, one of the most notable Wagnerian conductors and producers. Nearer to our own day and equally famous are Bruno Walter, Otto Klemperer, Ossip Gabrilowitch, Ferdinand Hiller, Léo Blech, and the Frenchman, Pierre Monteux, who (it is said) was engaged to replace Bruno Walter at a concert in 1933, under the impression that he was "Aryan".[1] In England, Sir Julius Benedict was for a long time a leading figure in the musical world. Sir Landon Ronald is pre-eminent not only in the sphere of conducting, but also as head of one of the leading British Conservatoires of Music.

Critics and theoreticians include Heinrich Porges, Wagner's greatest champion, and Eduard Hanslick, his greatest opponent; Guido Adler, leader of the "Vienna School"; Max Friedländer, the great authority on German folk-music; Oscar Bie, historian of the dance and the opera; and Egon Wellesz, one of Schönberg's foremost followers in Austria and the great authority on the music of the Orient. In England Alfred Kalisch, in his day, was particularly highly-esteemed as a critic.

[1] Arturo Toscanini, it may be added, married a Jewess, and thus falls in Germany under the operation of the "Aryan" Laws.

L

As patrons of music, moreover, the role of Jews has been all-important. They have been among the most sedulous frequenters of concerts, the most discerning appreciators of talent, the most receptive students of new ideas, currents and methods. "How can I be anti-Semitic when I know that without our Jewish friends all our opera-houses and concert-halls would be more than half empty?" asked Richard Strauss. This would have been true, and is still, not only of Central Europe, but also of London, Paris, and New York. Nor is the phenomenon a new one. In eighteenth-century England, when Handel was sedulously neglected by the nobility and aristocracy (if only because of the patronage he received from the Sovereign), he found encouragement and support from the London Jews, who thus had their part in identifying with this country what has been among the most potent influences on English music. Rossini's life was rendered possible through the friendship and unflagging support of James de Rothschild in Paris. (Perhaps it is for this reason that his works are at present banned in Germany, for he had no traceable Jewish blood.)

Even Richard Wagner, notwithstanding the anti-Semitic extravagances which he expressed in his *Judaism in Music*, found that the Jews were not only among his finest interpreters, but also his most practical supporters. Jewish subscriptions poured in for the foundation of the Bayreuth Theatre, while it was the Jewish pianist, Karl Taussig, who devised the plan to raise 300,000 thalers for the actual construction. Attempts have been made to trace Semitic influences in the glitter and elaboration of Wagner's music. Rather is it to be found in the essentially Teutonic themes which he developed for his story; for the action both of *Tannhäuser* and *The Flying Dutchman*, which he himself ascribed later to some unspecified, and untraceable, collection of legends, were dependent upon the genius of Heinrich Heine. "In Heine's truly dramatic treatment of the redemption of this Ahasuerus of the Sea," Wagner had written with reference to the latter, in his *Autobiographical Sketch* of 1843, before his anti-Jewish prejudice had developed, "I found all I wanted to make of the Saga an opera subject. *I came to an understanding in the matter with Heine himself.*"[1]

That there is anything Semitic in the compositions of Mozart has never been suggested: though it is a fact that the handful of Jews of London were among the first persons to shew him encouragement, during his visit to England as an infant prodigy in 1764. However, no small part of the enjoyment of the myriads who listen to his operas—particularly *Don Juan* and *The Marriage of Figaro*—comes from the extraordinary ability of his librettist. This was Emanuel Conegliano, of Ceneda in Italy, better known under his baptized name of Lorenzo da Ponte. He rivalled Casanova in his amorous adventures and autobiographical audacity, contributed considerably to the success of the most famous of Mozart's operas, brought the first Italian opera company to America, and closed an eventful life at New York, at a venerable old age, in 1838. Similarly, the libretto of Richard Strauss' *Rosenkavalier* was written by that stylistic genius and Liberal reformer, the half-Jew Hugo von Hoffmansthal.

§VII

One of the most important strands in the complex history of the Theatre is, of course, Biblical. The mediaeval Miracle Play, presenting to the people in dramatised form the familiar episodes of Scriptural

---

[1] It may be added that there is strong ground for suspecting that Wagner himself, for all his anti-Semitism, was half-Jewish by blood, his real father being named Geyer.

history, was generally based upon the Old Testament or Apocrypha when it was not upon the Passion or the Nativity of Jesus. The stories of Joseph and his Brethren, of Susannah, of the Deluge, of the Sacrifice of Isaac, were especially favoured: and it was from these simple representations that the modern stage emerged.[1]

This universal European practice was paralleled (to say "copied" would be to anticipate the answer to a question which has not yet been adequately examined) by the Jews in their Ghettoes. It was perhaps symbolic that, while among their neighbours these dramatic representations were associated especially with the seasons of greatest solemnity, among the Jews they took place above all at carnival-tide, at the feast of *Purim*. In these circumstances, it was inevitable that the story of Esther and Mordecai, commemorated at that season, was a specially favoured subject. However, there were others—the Sale of Joseph, David and Goliath, and so on. Precisely when this tradition started is uncertain.[2] Traces of it may be discerned in the Dark Ages, in the East; in the late Middle Ages, it took on a more elaborate development: and at the period of the Renaissance, the performances made by the Jews were famous, and attracted numerous Gentile spectators. Thus we are

---

[1] Hebraic echoes are to be discerned even in some of the Morality Plays. Thus the famous *Everyman* has its analogue in a familiar passage in the collection of Rabbinic apophthegms known as *The Ethics of the Fathers* : "When a man departs from this world, there accompany him neither silver nor gold nor precious stones nor pearls, but only learning and good works". The thought is natural enough: but it is significant that in the English version (in which, incidentally, God is referred to as *Adonai*) "knowledge", corresponding to *Torah*, accompanies "good deeds"—a typically Hebraic conception, as it would seem. The more elaborate version of this contained in the *Chapters of Rabbi Eleazar* is even closer in spirit to the Morality Play, introducing the dramatic form.

[2] Jewish actors had of course been known even in classical times: Josephus mentions one, Alityros, who was a favourite with the Emperor Nero.

informed by the industrious Marino Sanuto how, at Venice in 1531 "there was performed by the Jews in their Ghetto a very fine Comedy: but no Christian was permitted to be present, by order of the Council of Ten". Ultimately, it seems that a permanent theatre was instituted in the Venetian Ghetto, where there were presented plays composed by writers not unknown to the outside world.

This practice certainly had some influence on the Italian theatre and indirectly on that of modern Europe generally. Jewish interest in the drama appears to have been particularly strong at Mantua, where the actors of the Ghetto were famous for their histrionic ability. Accordingly, during the sixteenth century, whenever it was desired to give a dramatic performance at the Court of the Gonzagas, in honour of some visiting Prince or Grandee, the obligation (and, incidentally, the expense) generally devolved upon the Jews. We are informed that on Friday the performances had to commence betimes, so that they would end before the Sabbath: while on Jewish feast-days they either had to be postponed, or else shorn of their most attractive features. Thus, at the formative period of European drama, when the influence of Italy was felt throughout Europe and Italy looked with interest to Mantua, the Jewish community of that city was closely associated with, if not responsible for, the dramatic performances at that Court.

The Jews of Mantua did not provide the actors only. Leone de' Sommi Portaleone (by profession a scribe, by predilection a Hebrew Poet, and founder of a synagogue in his native city which existed for many generations) was a prolific writer of Italian prose and verse, and composed in addition several plays of the somewhat insipid pastoral character then fashionable—of course of a specifically non-Jewish nature. He was impresario and producer at the Ducal Court; and the poet Manfredi entrusted him with the production of at least one of his plays. But above all he is remembered as author of a volume, *Dialogues on the Dramatic Art*, composed in 1556 —the first work of that nature ever written in a European tongue. It is a body of sane theory and pioneer understanding of stage practice, in some respects in advance of its age. The work was not published in full until recent years. Nevertheless, the author had many opportunities of putting his theories in practice, and some at least thus became commonplaces of the Italian, and ultimately the European, theatre.[1]

Considering this long tradition of Jewish association with the Theatre, it is not surprising that Jewish writers of to-day have furnished so high a proportion of dramatists. Jews have written for the stage in England ever since the days of Moses Mendes (*supra*, p. 101), whose *Double Disappointment* was produced at Drury Lane in 1746. More recently, in the English-speaking countries, we have had (*supra*, pp. 103–104) Pinero Sutro, Zangwill, Merrick, Benn Levy, Belasco, and among the disturbing figures of the younger generation in America, Elmer Rice, George Kaufman, and Lilian Hellman; in France, Bernstein, d'Ennery, Porto-Riche, and the two Bernards, father and son; in Denmark, Henrik Hertz; in Sweden, Josephson; in Holland, Heijermans; in Italy, Sabbatino Lopez; in Hungary, Franz Molnar, Melchior Lengyel; in Germany, Schnitzler, Fulda, Rilke, Hoffmansthal, Wedekind; in Russia, Semjon Juschkewitch and Ossip Dymow . . . their name is legion. In our own day, the Palestine Arts Theatre, *Habimah*, has elevated the drama into a spiritual experience. And it is

---

[1] It is noteworthy that the greatest authority on the history of the mediaeval stage, Gustave Cohen, of Paris, is a Jew, as was also Alessandro d'Ancona, the great historian of the Italian theatre.

remarkable that the one Nobel artist-prizeman is a
Jew—Leo Bakst, the scenic artist whose presentation of
Scheherazade in 1910 brought him international fame,
and whose designs for Russian ballet had so profound
an influence on the modern stage even in England. But
neither the eye of prejudice nor of enthusiasm can
possibly find any common factor in all these strangely
diverse types, at one only in fidelity to their age and
environment.

§VIII

Jewish actors of genius, to whom Europe and America
have owed no small part of their dramatic enjoyment
in the course of the past century and more, are too
numerous to specify, and include some of the greatest
names of all. If Rachel, the Queen of Tragedy—a Jewess
—had an equal, it was the half-Jewess, Sarah Bernhardt.
Necessarily less widely known than either of these, but
hardly less talented, was Esther de Boer, for half a
century Queen of the Dutch stage. Their spiritual heiress
to-day is Elizabeth Bergner, an exile from Germany
owing to her Jewish stock. Nazimova, too, is a Jewess.
And in the eighteenth century, the fortunes of the newly-
opened Covent Garden Theatre in London were decided
by the astonishing performance of Hannah Norsa as
Polly Peachum in *The Beggar's Opera*.[1] Ada Isaacs
Menken is hardly to be mentioned in the same breath
as these, yet Swinburne could write of her: "Lo! this is
she that was the world's delight."

If Jewish actors have not quite attained the overwhelming place of the Jewish actresses who have been
mentioned, they have nevertheless provided some of the

[1] Hannah Norsa's niece, Maria (daughter of Maria Norsa and
Sir Edward Walpole) married, first, the second Earl of Waldegrave,
and, secondly, the Duke of Gloucester, brother of George III. This
match was immediately responsible for the Royal Marriage Act of
1772.

great names in the history of the theatre. When Sheridan's *Duenna* was produced at Covent Garden in 1775, the part of Isaac was taken by "Mr. Leoni" (Myer Lyon) on whose account performances were suspended on Friday nights. A century ago, London flocked to see and to hear actors like Isaac Isaacs, whose daughter, Rebecca, enjoyed an equal reputation,[1] or the Solomon family—Charles (Sloman), Henry and Edward (father of Claire Romaine). In the Edwardian era, the English stage was almost dominated by Sir Beerbohm Tree (Sir George Alexander was also said, though apparently without justification, to be of Jewish birth). Holland has never had an actor to equal Louis Bouwmeester, one of the most remarkable figures of the European theatre of his day. Two Hungarian Jews, Ludwig Barnay and von Sonnenthal, played a leading role in the theatrical history of Germany and Austria respectively. On the German and Austrian stages Jews have been prominent for upwards of a century: and in the last generation especially they included some of the foremost actors in their number: it is sufficient to mention Emanuel Reicher, Rudolf Schildkraut, Fritz Kortner, and Max Pallenberg.

As theatrical entrepreneurs, too, Jews have been prominent: though they shewed a tendency, which to some professionals may have seemed distressing, to proceed from the parallel (and normally non-convergent) functions of management to more intimate participation. In London, the St. James's Theatre was built by that phenomenal tenor of the Hanoverian era, John Braham; while Benjamin Lumley (author, astonishingly enough, of a standard Parliamentary handbook on Private Bills) revolutionised Grand Opera in England while managing His Majesty's Theatre in the 1830's. In New York,

[1] The report that Edmund Kean was a Jew has no foundation in fact; the same applies to the American Edwin Booth.

similarly, Italian Opera was first introduced by Lorenzo da Ponte, Mozart's Jewish librettist. It was Oscar Hammerstein who attempted (though without success) to popularise Grand Opera in London at the new Opera House which he erected in the Kingsway; and, if the experiment ended in failure, the fault lay with the public, not with the courageous pioneer. In America, his work was more spectacular: and, besides managing many theatres, he introduced a galaxy of new stars to the operatic world at the Manhattan Opera House, which he built. David Belasco dominated the American theatre for many years, as producer as well as actor, and sometimes playwright.

In Germany, Otto Brahm, founder of the Freie Bühne (whose thirty years' activity at the Deutsches Theater left an indelible mark on German stage history), and Leopold Jessner, formerly Director of the Berlin Staats Theater, who introduced expressionism to the stage, are among the foremost figures. They would be even better known were it not for the activity of Max Reinhardt, whose rationalistic productions have completely revolutionised the art of the theatre in our day and who, with Brahm, was responsible for the intimate atmosphere which led to the evolution of the fashionable "little theatres". In fact, the modern German theatre, which came to mean so much in European cultural life in the post-war period, is all but a Jewish creation. To quote a recent work, "the Jew has been foremost in raising the activity of the stage-director from a perfunctory job to an art characterised by imagination, style, and creative approach".[1]

In the new art of the Cinema, where there were no established traditions or prejudices to hamper their

[1] Myerson and Goldberg's *The German Jew, his Share in Modern Culture*—an admirable work to which I owe more in the compilation of certain portions of this book than I can adequately acknowledge.

progress, the Jews entered whole-heartedly. They found it a starveling newcomer, relegated to back-streets and uncomfortable halls, and occupying itself in cheap extravagances. It was largely under Jewish auspices that it developed from this to a great industry, not challenging but supplementing the theatre; the centre of a new art which brought a new standard of comfort as well as of achievement to the reach of the poorest pocket. There was a period when the subject-matter (reflecting post-war moral standards) tended to be sordid and sex-centred. If the Jews were associated with this, they were associated no less with the subsequent regeneration, which in recent years has made such remarkable progress. No man, for instance, did more to enhance the dignity of the cinema industry than Irving Thalberg, whose death in 1936 was mourned by critics all over the world as a major disaster.[1]

§IX

Much has been said, from the days of Wagner onwards, of the contamination of the pure source of European inspiration by the "alien" element introduced by the Jew. An examination of the facts assembled above shews that this suggestion is in complete variance from the truth. In music, in art, in literature (as, indeed, in science and in medicine) the Jew has brought to bear a keen critical faculty, highly developed through centuries of intensive culture and an innate respect for intellect and intellectual achievement. This is coupled with great receptivity, a reluctance to accept tradition *per se*, and perhaps a critical aloofness, natural in those whose identity has for centuries been maintained as that of a small minority in a hostile world. Thus there is inherent

[1] The screen has proved a stimulating, if dangerous, rival to the stage. But it was disastrous to the old-type Music Hall, with which Jews were hardly less intimately associated than they are now with the Cinema (See also below, pp. 253-4).

perhaps in the Jew a mental attitude which qualifies him peculiarly to collaborate in brushing away the cobwebs of the dead conventions, though rendering him no less receptive of prevailing tendencies.

The Jew, hence, is very often found in the vanguard of a new movement. But, on the other hand, he is less frequently responsible for the first revolutionary step. He generally works through the medium most favoured at the time; with the romantics he is romantic, with the impressionists impressionistic, and with the moderns ultra-modern. There may conceivably be something Jewish in the essence—a feeling that spirit is more important than form, or some other mystical abstraction which defies analysis. In certain instances, there is a tendency to seek relief from everyday drabness in a riot of colour. There is generally (as indicated elsewhere) a warm feeling of humanity. This, however, is all that can be conceded. The style is that of the moment; the subject is the environment, or what is demanded by convention. Thus Israels, Auerbach, Levitan, were the interpreters in paint or in prose of the Dutch, German, Russian countryside: only, coming out as they did from the obscurity of the Ghetto, they were perhaps able to see in it more than those whose fathers had been familiar with its tints and folds and figures for centuries past.

If there is any other common factor about the Jews' contributions to art, music and letters, it is due to the simple fact that, forming as they do a single sociological group and being brought up in a similar environment, they tend to reflect something of that group's outlook. There are signs that a new art, in the wider sense, may perhaps develop in Palestine. But it is an art rooted in the European milieu and using a European technique. If anything specifically Jewish may evolve, it is still to make itself known.

CHAPTER VII

THE JEW IN EUROPEAN THOUGHT

§1

It is commonly assumed, perhaps too hastily, that the Hebrews of the Biblical period were uninterested in philosophy. A courageous attempt has recently been made to correct the impression. The Old Testament, it is now suggested, shows trace of a native Hebrew philosophy, Platonic in type but not in origin, which is especially noticeable in the Book of Ecclesiastes. In particular, the well-known "wisdom" passages of the 4th and 8th chapters of Proverbs are held to be the "remains of generations, and indeed centuries, of keen and devoted thinking on the problems raised by the phenomena of life".[1]

That this is in the main true is clear. The Old Testament is obviously the product of profound and exhaustive meditation on divine purpose and human destiny. But a distinction should be drawn between philosophy as a technical discipline and thought in the wider sense which includes feeling. The Book of Job gives classical expression to the rebellion of the human heart against the apparent tyranny of the ways of the universe; but its protest is not made in the technical forms of the syllogism, and its ending is as illogical as it is magnificent. In the same way the Hebrew Bible as a whole offers a view of life which is both consistent and rational, but it

[1] Macdonald, *The Hebrew Philosophical Genius* (Princeton, 1936), p. 49.

would not seem to have been "thought out" in terms of logical analysis and is not therefore in the strict sense of the term philosophy.

Yet men live by feeling and not by logical analysis, and the influence of the Hebrew Bible on European philosophy is greater than that of any philosopher or philosophical system. The reason is simple. The Hebrew Bible laid down for the European peoples, largely though not solely through the channel of Christianity, certain leading principles concerning the ultimate origin and nature of the world, and these principles thus became the data of philosophical speculation, setting its problem even if not being accepted as that problem's solution. Hebraic theism gave Europe its vision of supreme reality and is thus at the base of the European intellectual outlook. We may rebel against it, but our very negations affirm it. It is there, inescapable, an integral part of our minds.

It may be thought that with the Old Testament the Jews' work was finished, to be gathered up and merged into the New Testament and Christianity. Yet it is an interesting and typical fact that the theology of Christian theism itself was built up, after the completion of both Old and New Testaments, with help derived from Jewish thinkers. The work of the Jew Philo, the first who offered a synthesis between "revealed" and "philosophical" religion, passed into the structure of Patristic Christianity, while in the great age of the Schoolmen, when Christianity boldly undertook to embrace the whole intellectual world, the way that was followed was that traced out by the Jew Maimonides.

The last-named is so important as to merit more than passing mention, but before we turn to him it should be asked what were the elements in the old Hebraic

outlook which offered something fresh to the world. The
answer is an old one, although none the less true for
that. Hebraism has always meant what it means to-day
and will mean to-morrow : monotheism and its attendant
ideas. That well-known passage of Longinus which has been
referred to above (pp. 86–7) quotes the verse of Genesis :
"God said let there be light, and there was light." This
verse is typical of the Old Testament—of Genesis, of
Isaiah, of Job. It expresses the idea that behind the
manifoldness and the discord and the contradictions of
the world in which we live there is one supreme source
to which the whole owes its being. And this source is
active, creative. "God said : let there be light, and
there was light"; by his "word" the "heavens were
made".

The God of the Old Testament is thus not a mere
hypothesis to account for the wheels of the world going
round. But neither is he a mere cosmological force.
Among the "work of his hands" are human beings, and
he is interested in them *because* they are the work of his
hands. The creator is the father, not in the physical
sense of the old Greek mythologies, but in the moral
sense that he *cares :* that he approves and disapproves,
that he punishes and forgives, loving those who live as
he would wish, hating those who live as he would not
wish. We have all heard of the dark side of this picture,
especially in these easy-going days when the word
"puritan" has become a term of reproach. Yet Cromwell's Ironsides were men of whom any people might be
proud, and men who recognised by the Biblical names
they gave themselves what spirit it was that made them
what they were. The Hebrew genius is ethical, and it
is its ethical quality which has affected men's lives both
in the daily grind and in those outbursts of enthusiastic
return to religious faith heralded by Luther, Milton,

Wesley and, in our day, Karl Barth. What has mattered in history is not so much the Jewish revelation of the unity of God as the Jewish intuition of that God's moral nature.

But men's lives rest not only on what the great Hebraic Christian moral teacher and philosopher Immanuel Kant called the "categorical imperative", the austere command "Thou shalt" or "Thou shalt not" by which we do the right because we must. Men need a vision which gives meaning to moral striving. This can take the form of one of two ideals in which present inequalities are re-dressed, the one that of a perfected social order, the other that of a perfected individual life-cycle. Both these ideals took shape in the Hebraic tradition, the former receiving more stress in Judaism, the latter in Christianity. Although obviously compatible with one another they have appealed separately to different persons and different ages, and both have stimulated reflection, the one on the practical problem of social justice, the other on the religious problem of immortality. If one adds the institution of the Sabbath, which is nothing other than the voluntary limitation of the hours of labour which raises man above the beasts and asserts man's moral dignity as a human being, we have a trio of Hebraic ideals directly derived from the Old Testament which yet have a role to play in our civilisation.

§II

Mention was made of two Jewish philosophers, Philo and Maimonides, whose work is woven into the texture of Christian theology. But the world-outlook of the mediaeval schoolmen was not merely theological in the narrow sense and they took, as we saw, all knowledge to be their province. This mediaeval world of knowledge is, almost as if by deliberate intention, an object lesson in the inextricability of the heterogeneous strands which go to make up any culture worthy of the name. The ultimate base of Scholasticism religiously is Hebraic. But philosophically and scientifically it is Greek, and the Greek came through Syriac and Arabic (and often Hebrew) before it assumed its Latin dress. The fathers of the Church were content to draw on them all without discrimination; and Greek, Arab and Jew jostle one another on their pages in complete promiscuity.

In the fashioning of this syncretistic and surprisingly unified world of knowledge the Jews played a large and important part, in the field of philosophy as well as in those of medicine, mathematics and astronomy (see pp. 170 f., 193 ff.). Among the best-known was the physician Isaac Israeli ("Isaac Judaeus") of Kairouan, whose surviving works include a logical treatise *On Definitions* and an exposition of Aristotelian physics called *On the Elements*. The former in particular comprises a treatment of various philosophical terms, derived ultimately from Aristotle, which were taken over subsequently by the Schoolmen and became the basis of mediaeval Christian philosophical terminology. More important as an original thinker (as it seems, at least, for much of Israeli's work has perished) was Avicebron (Ibn Gabirol), the synagogal poet living under Moslem rule in Spain in the eleventh century, whose *Fons Vitae* (the first philosophical treatise compiled in that country) was accepted for centuries as the production of a Christian thinker and approved—or disapproved—as one of the typical expressions of Neo-Platonic metaphysics (see pp. 50, 90.). The anti-Semitic William of Auvergne, not suspecting his real identity, termed him "unique, and most notable of all philosophers". It was this remarkable treatise which introduced Neo-Platonic thought among the Arabic-speaking thinkers of the Iberian peninsula, and popularised it ultimately among the Christian schoolmen. Thus when the reaction against Aristotelianism and its exponents began, thinkers like Duns Scotus (following in this the great Franciscan, Alexander of Hales) leant heavily upon Gabirol, though it is doubtful whether they would have done so had his Judaism been known. One of the principal points of difference between the two schools was that the latter adopted the Spanish thinker's theory of the existence of a material substratum to spiritual beings, and declared the essence of the Divine nature to be in will rather than in intellect. The special ferment of thirteenth-century scholasticism may hence be traced in large measure to the impingement of Gabirol's thought.

Greatest of all was Moses Maimonides ("Rabbi Moysis" as he was known to generations of schoolmen) whose epoch-making work, the *Guide for the Perplexed* (completed in 1190), was translated into Latin shortly after its composition and was followed by Thomas Aquinas on almost all the great issues common to Judaism and Christianity. The later history of this remarkable book is illuminating. The early Latin version was re-issued in the sixteenth century (Paris, 1520) and superseded by the new one of the Christian Hebraist Buxtorf in the seventeenth (Basel, 1629), this in turn to give way to the French version of Munk (Paris, 1856–66). In the interim it had inspired Spinoza (not necessarily always to agreement); stimulated the social and political enquiries of men like Bodin, Selden, and Grotius; presided over the birth of modern anthropology in Spencer's *Laws of the Hebrews* (1685), and been made the subject of a series of penetrating comments and summaries by Leibniz. It is now a standard repository for students

M

of the conceptions forming that common mediaeval world-view which in many respects still provides some of the permanent elements in European civilisation.

§III

At the time when these philosophers, translators and scientists were helping to erect the structure of mediaeval rationalism, a mystical revolution was preparing itself which became of hardly less significance, although doubt may be felt as to its real value. Gathering up elements the origins of which are lost in the remotest antiquity, the Zohar, the book of "Splendour", flashed on the Jewish world in the beginning of the fourteenth century, and Christian Hebraists soon discovered that this "secret doctrine" of the Hebrews contained hints of the mysteries of Christianity. It is difficult to exaggerate the influence exerted by these writings (the Zohar and its kindred literature), the obscurity of which is only equalled by the insight of their occasional inspiration. They shew remarkable affinities with the lucubrations of Raimon Lull and other contemporary Spanish mystics, whose influence reverberated through Europe. They entered deep, through men like Reuchlin and Pico della Mirandola, into the harmonising temperament of the Renaissance. A by-product is said to be a metaphysical theory of space which commended itself to various philosophers, from the Italian Patrizzi to the Englishman John Locke, to the latter as the result of a conversation with no less a person than Isaac Newton. Since the conception would seem to have reached Newton through the Cambridge Neo-Platonist Henry More, we have here another suggestion of the tangled origin of modern ideas. But be that as it may, it is important to note that no account of the Renaissance would be complete without an enquiry into the so-called "Cabbala" of the Jews, and there is little doubt that its traces are to be found within such broad boundaries as the humanist martyr Giordano Bruno in Italy and the creator of the Biblical epic, John Milton, in England.

Not that the stream of mysticism ever was, or ever is, unmixed. Both in its sources and its later history the Cabbala was always infected with some philosophical elements, and an interesting instance of the resultant is offered by one of the now forgotten but once famous books of the sixteenth century, the *Dialoghi di Amore* of Judah Abrabanel ("Leone Ebreo"), son of the last Jewish scholar-statesman of Spain, Don Isaac Abrabanel. Composed originally, in all probability, in Hebrew, and published originally in Italian, this work ran through edition after edition in half the languages of Europe. It exerted a great influence on Castiglione's *Il Cortegiano*, which provided the seventeenth and eighteenth centuries with its new ideal of aristocracy in which the old knight merged into the modern gentleman; and this book, translated into English, was one of the most widely read books in Shakespeare's England. The conception of "Platonic love" is one of the heritages of the *Dialoghi di Amore* to the modern world.

§IV

It is with the seventeenth century that the greatest of Jewish philosophers, one of the outstanding names in modern thought, emerged. Though the Synagogue of Amsterdam cast him out, nervous lest his impiety should endanger its newly-won religious liberty, Spinoza was Jewish in feeling, in background and largely in equipment.

Volumes have been written about the Jewishness of
Spinoza, and it has been denied as vigorously as it has
been affirmed. But all would agree that his peculiar
flavour owes at least something to his origin. By "origin"
is not meant some mysterious and indefinable, but no
less actual, quality of the blood which made Spinoza,
from his very first embryo stage, what is called a monist;
but only that the cultural tradition from which Spinoza
sprang and in which he spent his early and impressionable
years, a tradition rooted as it was in an austere monotheism, was such as to suggest a monistic key to the riddles
of existence. Monism is, of course, not monotheism, and
the religion of the Synagogue which Spinoza left is not
the five books of the *Ethics* which Spinoza bequeathed
as a new Pentateuch to mankind. But if the Synagogue
taught anything it was the unity of God, and Spinoza's
philosophy is a hymn to the unity of God's work or
nature. The characteristic dogmas of Judaism and
Spinozism are thus closely akin. Whatever Spinoza
derived from other sources is subordinated to this ultimate vision, and the unitary character of the resulting
system, crushing in its simplicity, is only another sign
of its primary inspiration.

The extent and profundity of Spinoza's influence on
modern thought is a matter on which two opinions
cannot be held. He is one of the great thinkers of the
world. It is common to mention him with Plato, and
like Plato he has survived even his admirers. Indeed,
he is most like Plato in that he is a fruitful source of
ideas even for those who profess themselves his opponents.
Personal intercourse with Leibniz at the very close of his
life gave the determining influence to the latter's thought,
which was destined to dominate the eighteenth century.
No book on Spinoza fails to tell of his position in the
history of the formation of the German mind in its days

Benedictus Spinosa.

BENEDICT SPINOZA

of true greatness, the days of Lessing and Herder and Goethe. And no student of Hegel can avoid seeing the debt owed to Spinoza by that dominating and seminal personality. But it is absurd to lengthen the string of names. Spinoza is Spinoza, and there is nothing to it but that.

§v

As one looks at the present-day scene, one may observe an outpouring of talent among Jews which is clearly phenomenal: and this is as true in philosophy as in any other sphere of human activity. It is not so much the power to see new things: it is also—what is of even greater importance—the power to see old things in a new way. We may remark this gift in some—it is pointless to catalogue all—recent Jewish thinkers who have displayed it most obviously.

Bergson, it has been said, has re-discovered time, and it is as the re-discoverer of time that he will probably be remembered. And so Einstein, among his many other fruitful ideas, re-discovered space and Freud re-discovered dreams. Each of these men started as it were anew. They looked on old problems with new eyes. They brought to the tired discussions of centuries the freshness of approach of a child. And their results, too, are elementary, elementary in the profound sense that they reach deep, offering a foundation for a whole world-view. These Jews, and innumerable lesser ones with them, are among the master-builders of the modern intellectual world, and it is not for us to "claim" or "reject" them as "Jewish" or "un-Jewish"; they are men. If the fruitful doctrines of Creative Evolution and Dialectical Materialism are due to Jews; if the Jew, Hermann Cohen, founded a new and fruitful school of Kantian criticism, or the Jew, Meyerson, indicated new paths in the interpretation of science, or the Jew, Durkheim, stimulated new ideas in the study of human society, or the Jew, Worms, established the International Sociological Institute, or the Jew, Husserl, initiated a new movement in logic and metaphysics—these are contributions freely given to civilisation as a whole and, in civilised times, as freely received. Who cares, and who should care, when considering Lévy-Bruhl's work on the mind of the primitive or Léon's life of Fichte or Cassirer's history of the theory of knowledge or Brunschvicg's edition of Pascal or Samuel Alexander's massive defence of the realistic attitude in metaphysics which begins with space-time and ends in Deity—who cares and who should care that these men are Jews, and as such have given of their best to the world? And the list could be extended ten-fold. It is not only that the Jew is in every movement, old and new. It is that he is there as an integral part of the movement, a powerful leader, a faithful comrade, a courageous follower.

As an instance of the part taken by Jews in the humbler, but possibly in the last analysis more important, work of secondary interpretation rather than primary discovery, one may note the part taken in France by the centres of publication and discussion put to the service of the community by Jewish savants. In France the traditions of Renaissance humanism survive undisturbed, and the study of philosophy has always been a part of the official system of national education. But it would be difficult to overestimate the assistance given to the maintenance of philosophical thinking by such reviews as the *Revue philosophique* directed now for many years by Lévy-Bruhl, or the *Revue de Métaphysique et de Morale* founded and edited until his recent death by Xavier Léon; and to the latter is due too the "Société française de Philosophie" (with its Bulletin now in its thirty-fifth year) and the initiation of the series of international Congresses of Philosophy. With the fate of the *Kant-Studien* and its exiled editor before one's eyes, it is good to end on this note of modest and prolonged public service.

CHAPTER VIII

SCIENTIFIC PROGRESS

§1

THE question is often asked, why the Romans, with their high powers of organisation and their remarkable technical ability (as shewn in their buildings, their baths, and especially their roads), never made any greater progress than they did in engineering science. One answer out of the many is particularly cogent. The reason lay above all in their cumbrous and elementary system of numbering. If a simple figure, such as 478, has to be represented by a long and complicated row of letters, cccclxxviii, it is obvious that arithmetical calculations are difficult, the study of higher mathematics closed, and many scientific and engineering developments which are dependent upon mathematical calculations enormously hampered. It was only when the western world was introduced to the more convenient, so called "Arabic" system of numbers, and with it to higher mathematics, that the path to the material civilisation of to-day was opened. One may affirm then that the introduction of the Arabic numerals to Europe, with the use of the zero and decimal system, was one of the landmarks in the history of Western civilisation. It is hardly too much to say that our mathematical system is the key to the material pre-eminence achieved by European culture in the past four centuries.

The so-called Arabic numerals are not however, in fact, Arabic. They originated in India, where they were familiar twenty centuries ago: thence they were carried westward by the Arabs, from whom in turn they were taken over by mediaeval Europe. Recent enquirers have suggested that the introduction was due in the first instance to the "Radanite" Jewish traders of the Dark Ages, who penetrated as far as India and must necessarily have spread abroad a knowledge of the number systems used in recording prices or market computation.[1] There is extant, however, a more circumstantial account, preserved in the writings of the mediaeval Jewish philosopher and exegete, Abraham ibn Ezra (who visited London in 1158 and whose character inspired Robert Browning's famous poem). He writes:

"In olden times there was neither science nor religion among the sons of Ishmael . . . till the great king, by name Es-Saffah (750-5) arose, who heard that there were many sciences to be found in India. . . . And there came men saying that there was in India a very mighty book on the secrets of government, in the form of a fable . . . and the name of the book was *Kalilah and Dimnah*.[2] . . . Thereupon he sent for a Jew who knew both languages, and ordered him to translate this book. . . . And when he [i.e the King] saw that the contents of the book were extraordinary—as indeed they are—he desired to know the science of the Indians, and he sent accordingly the Jew to Arin, whence he brought back one who knew the Indian numerals, besides many other astronomical writings."

A Jew was thus responsible (if this account is to be believed) for the transmission of the Hindu numerals from India to the Arabic-speaking world. How did they make the next, and more vital, transition—from the Islamic world to the Christian?

In this process, too, Jewish agency is to be traced. One of the most active of the band of translators of

[1] Smith and Karpinski, *Hindu Arabic Numerals*, p. 101 and below, pp. 217-9.
[2] For this famous work, see above, p. 46.

Jewish birth who worked at Toledo in the period after the capture of that city by the Christians was, as we have seen, Johannes Hispalensis, or John of Seville, whose Arabic name, Ibn Daud, was corrupted by the schoolmen into Avendeath. The most important of the compositions which were introduced to the Christian world by his means was a work of the Persian, Muhammad al-Kwarizmi[1] (fl. c. 830) on practical Indian arithmetic. In this, the so-called Arabic numerical notation is used for the first time in Latin literature—a milestone in the history of western culture. So fundamental was al-Kwarizmi's work that, for centuries, what we now call mathematics was known after him as "Algorism". Though it was not till the sixteenth century that the new method was completely acclimatised in Europe, it may be said that the whole of modern mathematics (and with it, a great part of modern science and philosophy), dates back to this translation from the Arabic, by a Jewish scholar, of a system first introduced to the Arabic world by a Jew.

Even before this period, mathematics had come under the influence of a very ancient Hebrew composition, *The Treatise of Measures*, ascribed to Rabbi Nehemiah and probably composed about A.D. 150. This remarkable work has many an original approach to mathematical problems, and exercised considerable influence on Arabic—and hence, mediaeval—science generally.

At approximately the same time as Indian mathematics, or a little later, Indian geometry also was introduced to the Latin world. The medium was in this case a work by a famous and devoted Jewish scholar and religious philosopher, Abraham bar Hiyya of Barcelona, or Savasorda (d. 1136), whose *Treatise on Geometry* was

---

[1] The town of Kwarizm is the modern Khiva.

translated from the Hebrew into Latin during his lifetime by Plato of Tivoli, under the title *Liber Embadorum*. This work, together with that of which we have been speaking above, was used by Leonardo da Pisa as the foundation for his text-books on Indian arithmetic, geometry and trigonometry, on which the whole of mediaeval mathematical studies were based. It is upon them, ultimately, that the technical progress and the material civilisation of the present day depend.

§II

In the blundering progress of scientific and technical achievement in the Middle Ages, the Jews of Europe did not fail to play their part. Throughout the period one finds mention of them—now translating a fundamental scientific work, now introducing a new process from one country to another, now referred to as authorities, now making their original contributions.

An impressive list of Jewish inventors and scientists of the Middle Ages could be compiled. Many of them have been mentioned above, in connexion with the evolution of various nautical instruments and tables. But their interests were not by any means confined to this. The fourteenth-century philosopher Levi ben Gershom, inventor of the so-called "Jacob's Staff" (*supra*, p. 66), is distinguished in the history of science also as discoverer of the *Camera Obscura*, of which he gave a detailed description, many generations before Alberti and Della Porta, in a mathematical work soon translated into Latin. (His interest was of course dependent on the fact that the device could be used for astronomical observation.) The importance of this become apparent when it is realised that on this simple idea depends the whole of photography and cinematography as we know them to-day.[1] Levi ben Abraham, a little-known Provençal scholar of the thirteenth century, whose mathematical writings are just beginning to receive the attention which they deserve, is memorable for having recognised heat as a form of motion, centuries before the days of Robert Boyle.

Here and there, throughout the course of the Middle Ages and the Renaissance, other Jewish inventors and scientists make their appearance. According to some authorities, Typsiles, who re-invented gunpowder in Augsburg in 1353, was not a Byzantine but a Jew. In anti-Semitic Venice of the fifteenth century, a certain Jew named Solomon enjoyed a high reputation as a hydraulic engineer, and was granted special privileges on that account. At the Court of Ferrara, Abraham Colorni distinguished himself as a military engineer, and devised a primitive quick-firing gun, as well as a taximeter and an instrument for measuring distances by means of reflectors. A Jewish engineer was employed to build a bridge in Brazil in 1640. Jewish mining engineers are found in Germany, Italy, even England—where, in the reign of Elizabeth, a certain Joachim Gauns, of Prague, directed smelting-works both in Cumberland and in the West Country.

Many other instances may be adduced, serving to indicate that, in the gradual, anonymous, development of technical progress before the nineteenth century, Jews collaborated with other sections of the European population. It is not perhaps without its significance that one of the earliest chemical utensils, the *Bain Marie*, or "water-bath" of our modern chemical laboratories, is legendarily associated with the name of its hypothetical discoverer, a Jewess named Maria.

[1] It may be added at this point that in a later age the use of sensitised paper for photography was the invention of the younger Herschel.

This same intellectual alertness was given a fresh outlet after the breakdown of the Ghetto. In the course of the nineteenth century, the energy and inventiveness which had previously been almost confined to Talmudical studies (with their philosophical and mathematical corollaries), or to the difficult task of earning a living through menial occupations, began to be turned to science in its wider sense. Jews now not only earned distinction but produced a few scholars who are the unchallenged leaders in their particular branches of research. The institution of the Nobel Prizes, as has been indicated above, provides some sort of index. Jews who were given that coveted award down to 1934 numbered at least seventeen (in addition to whom there were at least four half-Jews). Of the seven American prize-winners, two were Jews; and while the Jews do not exceed 1 per cent of the general population of the western world, they contributed 9 per cent (or, with the half-Jews, 12 per cent) of the Nobel Prize-winners. Numerically, they exceeded all but the French and Germans—several of whom, *per contra*, were Jews. (In fact, of the thirty-eight Germans who have been awarded Nobel prizes nine were Jews and one partly Jewish: while the case of two more is doubtful.) Proportionately, Jews were exceeded only by Scandinavians—but it must be recalled that the Nobel Prizes are a Scandinavian foundation. As will be shown elsewhere, a majority of the Jewish Nobel Prizemen received the award (characteristically, it may perhaps be added) for services to medicine. Proportionately, the next highest number were rewarded for their services to the cause of Peace. There has been one reward for scenic art, and one for literature. The remainder were singled out for their services to one branch or the other of scientific enquiry in the more restricted sense.

§III

The characteristic feature of our modern civilisation is a technical progress, which has had a widespread influence upon the amenities of life in all countries and in every class of the community. This, in the last resort, is dependent to a very large extent upon physical and mathematical advances: with the result that those who have led in these spheres may be reckoned among the benefactors of the modern world. It is perhaps in instinctive appreciation of this fact that Albert Einstein, the full implications of whose Theory of Relativity can be appreciated only by very few, has received in our day an unexampled degree of public recognition. But, among the workers in the same field whose names are indubitably in the first rank, are several more of Jewish birth or descent; the great physicist, Niels Bohr, Danish on his father's side and Jewish on his mother's: James Franck, youngest of all Nobel Prizemen, who received the award in 1926 for his experimental confirmation of the Quantum Theory, and his associate, Gustav Hertz, given the prize in Physics for research in the theories of atoms: Albert Abraham Michelson, the American whose experiments broke down the theory of a stationary ether which had previously prevailed, through which all motion took place and the transmission of light and electricity was conditioned: and the great mathematical physicist, Max Born, formerly editor of the *Physikalischen Zeitschrift*.

The mathematical propensity of the Jews—traceable perhaps to the rigidly logical character of their training— continued the notable mediaeval tradition to which allusion has been made. Ozanam, the greatest French mathematician of the seventeenth century, is generally reported to have been of Jewish extraction: and the nineteenth century produced a remarkable galaxy in this field. It is believed that even Lobatschewski, one of the discoverers of absolute geometry, was the son of Jewish parents who had been converted to the Greek Catholic faith. The great pioneers of the last century include, too, K. G. J. Jacobi, of dynamical as well as pure mathematical fame: George Cantor, "The Classic of Mathematicians", and his namesake Moritz Cantor, the historian of Mathematics: Immanuel Lazarus Fuchs, Leopold Kronecker, Vito Volterra, Leon Königsberg and many others of equal note. In the younger generation there were Edmund Landau and Helloch Berliner in Germany; J. Hadamard and G. H. Halphen in France. Pre-eminent, too, was Hermann Minkowski, who gave a great impetus to the mathematical basis of relativity, following upon the conception of a four-dimensional time continuum: while Tullio Levi-Civita—one of the most distinguished figures in Italian academic life to-day —developed the absolute calculus, which was the mathematical instrument necessary for the fashioning of Einstein's ideas.

It was on the basis of the work of Michelson, Minkowski and Levi-Civita that Einstein developed his remarkable thesis. If it is possible to say that there is something Jewish in the tenacity which can persist in a long sequence of thankless research, in the flash of genius which can evolve a new explanation of the data so laboriously collected, and in the courage which can maintain an unpopular theory in the teeth of opposition and contempt, then the Theory of Relativity is (as the adverse critics of its author maintain) essentially Jewish. But scientific research knows nothing of racial and religious distinctions, and in point of fact this, like every other conquest of knowledge, is a human achievement, built up on human experiments and human theories, in which a Jewish strand can no more be set apart than any other.

England, for some reason, has not produced the same long sequence of distinguished Jewish students in this field as Germany. There are, however, a handful of the highest eminence. Thus the greatest English pure mathematician of the nineteenth century (with the possible exception only of his collaborator, Cayley) was James Joseph Sylvester, Savilian Professor of Geometry in the University of Oxford, and the first professing Jew to enter the University of Cambridge. He was placed as second wrangler in 1837: but, owing to the religious intolerance which still prevailed, it was only in 1872 that he was able to take his degree! With Cayley, he shared the work of founding the doctrine of invariants in algebra, and he enriched the science of number with a body of doctrine on partitions. In addition (a surprising diversion for a mathematician) he was the author of a considerable body of verse of high quality, as well as translations from foreign languages and a theory of versification. The Sylvester Medal established by the Royal Society commemorates his outstanding services to learning. It was an English Jew, too, Benjamin Gompertz, who laid down the principles as to the decline of resistance to death which are the foundation of all actuarial tables in use. "Had the principle [i.e. Gompertz' Law] been propounded in the days of Newton," affirmed the late Professor de Morgan, "Vitality would have been made a thing of, like attraction." [1]

[1] Obituary notice in *The Athenæum*, July 22nd, 1865 [The meaning is clear, though the phrasing is awkward].

§IV

Chemistry, similarly, furnishes a few names of first importance, the results of whose investigations are felt in every branch of our daily life. It was in 1859 that Adolf Frank began to study systematically the plant-consumption of potash, which had been noticed by the great chemist Liebig. In 1861, as the results of his researches, he set up his first factory, thus founding the great (and until recent years, exclusively German) potash industry. In addition, he developed all the commercial by-products—bromide, ammonia, and the various chlorides —which themselves became the nuclei of great industries. Frank's collaborator, Nicodem Caro, one of the most prolific workers in German chemistry, joined with him in perfecting a method for obtaining nitrogen from the air—a discovery of great practical significance. Fritz Haber carried these discoveries a step further, when he devised his method for producing ammonia from the nitrogen in the air and hydrogen, thereby rendering unlimited supplies of natural fertiliser available for the soil. (For this discovery, he was given the Nobel Prize in 1919.) It was his discoveries which enabled Germany to withstand a world in arms, between 1914 and 1918. Nevertheless, he died in voluntary exile: and it was in England that his services to science were formally commemorated. Another great German Jewish chemist whose work links up with that of this group was Victor Meyer, a brilliant worker in Stereo-chemistry, whose apparatus for the determination of vapour-densities is the most widely used, and who did much brilliant work in elucidating the constitution of molecules. In 1882 he discovered in impure benzine the sulphur-containing compound thiophene, and thereby did a

N

good deal to further the production of cheap industrial chemicals, now so necessary.

The dyeing industry is a typical demonstration of the interaction of science and industry. Not only does it give employment to tens of thousand of hands, but in addition its modern development has had a marked effect upon the life and the aesthetic outlook of the ordinary man and woman. In the Middle Ages, as will be demonstrated, Jews were prominent in this calling, until the Italian cities secured the monopoly. Later, in the nineteenth century, with the evolution of aniline dyes, Germany took the lead. Two of the most important names which must be mentioned in this connexion are those of Jews. Heinrich Caro, director of a great industrial concern in Baden, discovered aniline red, induline, eosine, Manchester brown and Victoria blue, and was the co-discoverer of phosgene dye-stuffs. His work revolutionised the dyeing industry, and even facilitated important technical advances in the field of medicine by rendering possible the colouring of various tissues. Later on, the researches of Richard Willstäter, one of the greatest living chemists, were in large measure responsible for the superior position of the German dye industry in our own day. In the field of biochemistry, too, his work has been of paramount importance, in determining the chemical structure of the colours of flowers and of the haematin of the blood: yet he was forced to vacate his chair at Munich through the post-war anti-Semitic agitation—a fate shared by many other contemporary German scholars, who have been spoken of in these pages.[1]

[1] The only name to be mentioned by the side of these two is that of the Nobel Prize-winner and founder of the great Baeyer A.-G., Adolf von Baeyer, who discovered eosin (much used in medicine), artificial indigo, and many other aniline dyes; he was a half-Jew, his mother belonging to the Hitzig family.

In England, work on similar lines was done by the eminent naturalist and chemist, Raphael Meldola, who discovered many important compounds and coal-tar dyes, some of which proved to be of great commercial importance. He was, in addition, one of the greatest recognised authorities on photo-chemistry, a biologist of considerable distinction, and a valued friend of Charles Darwin (his intellectual interests may perhaps be ascribed to the fact that he was descended from a long line of Rabbis). Ludwig Mond, a German, who settled in England in 1862, revolutionised the chemical industry of the country by his process for the recovery of sulphur from alkali waste. Subsequently, he perfected the Solvay process for the recovery of ammonia soda, and by his discovery of nickel carbonyl devised a process for the extraction of nickel from its ores. The British chemical industry, now of such vital importance both industrially and from the point of view of national defence, owes more to him than perhaps to any other one person. Later, during the war of 1914–18, his sons took a foremost share in acclimatising the new German dyeing and metallurgical methods in Great Britain.

In the new branches of science, such as colloid chemistry, Jewish investigators have played a noteworthy part. Jacques Loeb left Germany at the close of the last century for the United States, where he was a pioneer worker on colloid science as well as (below, p. 209) a leader in physiological research. More recently, Herbert Freundlich, perhaps the foremost authority on colloids to-day, was forced by reason of his partly Jewish origin to leave Germany for the benefit of the University of London. In the same sphere, one must mention Jerome Alexander in America, Emil Hatschek in England, I. Traube, P. Rona, and a host of younger workers. And, among contemporaries, two more names cannot be

neglected: Kasimir Farjans, formerly director of the
Physical Chemical Institute at Munich and one of the
best-known physical chemists of our day: and Friedrich Adolph Paneth, formerly of the University of Berlin,
famous for his fruitful work on radio activity.

§v

The most dramatic technical triumph of modern
times is the astonishing improvement in communications.
Until the close of the Napoleonic era, these had hardly
overtaken the standard which the Romans attained
eighteen centuries before. Since that date, distances
have been annihilated by successive inventions. The
reactions on economic organisation, on social life, on
intellectual outlook, have been immeasurable.

The first stage, the Steam Age, was in the main the
result of the activity of English and American inventors.
Jews did not play a part of any importance,[1] except that
some of the wealthier among them, quick to realise the
implications of the new inventions, took an active share
in making possible their practical application—the
Rothschilds in Austria, the Péreires in France, the
Josephs in Canada, de Hirsch in Turkey, and so on. The
Railway Age was, however, challenged by two new
inventions. At the close of the nineteenth century, the
automobile made its appearance; and, at the beginning
of the twentieth, air communications began to develop.
By this time, the Jews had emerged from the Ghettoes,
to which they had hitherto been compulsorily confined.

---

[1] This is not to be interpreted too rigidly. Joseph Simon, of Lancaster, Pennsylvania, was closely associated with the genesis of the
steam-boat; it was in their joint workshop that his partner, William
Henry, made his first unfortunate experiment in 1763, and under their
tutelage that Robert Fulton, who constructed the first effective steam-
boat in 1807, developed his abilities.

Their collaboration was therefore possible; and it was considerable.

It is said that the earliest electrically-driven automobile was made and driven in the streets of Darmstadt, in Germany, in 1854, by a Jew named M. Davidsohn. For the moment, however, this means of traction was premature; and the subsequent development was based upon an oil-driven engine. A short while before petroleum was first refined and utilised in America, in 1854, the discovery was anticipated by a Galician Jew, Abraham Schreiner, who thus paved the way for the modern system of transportation. His amateurish efforts robbed his discovery of real significance and he died in penury. The direction was maintained by another Jew, Siegfried Marcus, inventor of the automobile. It was in 1864 that he built his first horseless carriage, and in 1875 the second, which was the first benzine-driven vehicle to function (this earliest motor-car is now in the possession of the Vienna Automobile Club). This he drove about the streets of Vienna, amid general astonishment. His automobile patents were registered in Germany in 1882 (it was not until four years later, in 1886, that the first Daimler motor-car was built). A tablet was affixed by the Town Council of Mecklenburg outside the house in which he was born, in honour of his invention: no doubt it has been removed in the course of the past few years, when men's ancestry has come to attract more attention than their achievements.

Aviation, too, owes a distinct debt to Jews. One of its pioneers was a certain German Jew named David Schwarz—so far forgotten even by his co-religionists that he does not figure in the columns of most Jewish works of reference. It was in 1890 that he first devised a rigid airship, with a gas-container made of metal. He presented his scheme to the Austrian War

Ministry, which rejected it on financial grounds. Not discouraged, in 1892 he went to Russia, where the first rigid airship was constructed under his direction at St. Petersburg. Unfortunately, the container was made of inferior metal, and the experiment was only a qualified success. However, the German government became interested, and invited him to Germany to make a trial flight. The excitement was too much for him, and when he was handed the official telegram he collapsed and died in the street. His widow, however, carried on the work, and a new airship was constructed under her supervision. At the trial, a certain Count Zeppelin was present, and was so impressed that he purchased the patents from Frau Schwarz: so that the successful dirigible which finally resulted bears (not improperly) his name alone. But Jewish collaboration did not end: for Karl Arnstein was chief construction engineer in the Zeppelin works, and in 1924 piloted the first Zeppelin across the Atlantic to America[1].

§VI

Let us now consider another aspect, with which modern technical progress is intimately bound up: the advance in the harnessing and utilisation of electricity, with its many varied outlets—power, lighting, communications, telegraph, the radio, and so on. Joseph Popper (Lynkaeus) —a pioneer also in the theory of flight—is said to have been

[1] Other important inventions in connexion with flying which are due to Jews are those of Emile Berliner (for whom see the following pages) who devoted his later years to devices for stabilising aeroplanes: and of Theodor von Karman, who occupies a premier position among mathematicians in aviation. Mention should be made also of the services rendered to aviation by Henri Deutsch de la Meurthe by his writings (especially *Le pétrole et ses applications*), the prizes which he instituted, and his foundation of the Aerotechnical Institute of St. Cyr.

There is nothing but the name to support the belief that Otto Lilienthal, who first put forward seriously the idea of a heavier-than-air flying machine, was a Jew.

the first person to suggest the possibilities of transmitting electrical power, in a paper submitted to the Imperial Academy of Sciences at Vienna in 1862. Other names in this field, however, enjoy a less vulnerable distinction.

Foremost among the physicists of the nineteenth century was Heinrich Hertz—a half Jew—who, bringing optics and electro-dynamics under one doctrinal discipline, made an important advance towards the unification of modern physics. His *Principles of Mechanics* is still considered, after many years, the fundamental work in this branch of study. The great discovery with which his name is associated is the possibility of the transmission of electro-magnetic waves through space—the basis of the wireless system suggested first by Clerk Maxwell and subsequently applied to commercial purposes by Marconi, and of the radio system which has assumed such importance in every household during the past two decades. He died, not yet forty years of age, in 1894, when he is believed to have been on the point of anticipating Röntgen in the invention of the X-ray[1]. In this connexion, mention may be made of Leo Graetz, son of the famous historian of the Jews, the first person to investigate the dispersal of electrical waves, whose name is thus intimately associated with the whole range of modern science.

So far for the theoretical side. On the mechanical, there is fully as much to be said. It was a Jew of German birth, Philip Reiss, who was responsible for the genesis of that every-day necessity of modern life, the telephone. The son of very poor parents, and almost self-educated, he began to be interested in the possibilities of controlling

[1] It is a little absurd to try to evaluate the paternal and maternal contribution to genius. But it is not without its significance that Hertz's cousin on the side of his Jewish father was the Nobel Prizeman, Gustav Hertz; this seems to indicate that, in this instance, the Hebraic factor was decisive.

sound-devices before he was twenty years of age. At first he copied the structure of the ear, making an electrified ear-drum, which was improved upon until it could be shewn at a meeting of the Frankfort Physical Society, and again in 1864 before a conference of physicists in Giessen. But (alas for the theory of unlimited command of money by Jews for all purposes!) he had neither the means nor the health to develop his invention, his "telephone", commercially : and it was left to Graham Bell to elaborate the device, in conjunction with Edison, and to place it on the market. Nevertheless, the standard works of reference record Reiss's name as the first inventor of the telephone, and a monument to his memory was erected by physicists in 1878.

The microphone, on the other hand, was the invention of Emile Berliner, a German Jewish scientist who lived in America, whose work is hence associated with the telephonic and gramophonic devices now in general use. Indeed, the claim has been made with a considerable degree of justification that he was the true inventor of the gramophone, though the commercial triumph of Edison has obscured his claim to recognition. What has been said above does not of course belittle in the slightest degree the discoveries of the latter, the greatest inventor, perhaps, of all time. But it is worthy of note that the two devices with which his name is particularly associated owed a great deal to Jews, but for whom their perfection would certainly have been retarded, and might have been impossible. Similarly, Lord Kelvin's system for multiple telegraphy, elaborated in 1858, was based upon a discovery of that astonishingly versatile Russian-Jewish genius, Hayim Selig Slonimski, who two years previous had produced an electro-chemical device for sending four telegrams simultaneously. Another name which deserves mention in this connexion is that of John Lewis Ricardo, nephew of the great political economist, who established the first Electric Telegraph for national purposes. Later on, the copper alloys which made possible long-distance telephoning were first used in Europe by Lazare Jean Weiller. And it was Robert von Lieben who invented the radio amplifier which made possible the development of modern radio, as well as of the sound film—an achievement which earned for him (until they discovered his Jewish origin) the enthusiastic plaudits of the anti-Semitic Press in Germany.

§vii

Minor mechanical devices and processes of Jewish origin which are in daily use are numerous. The sewing-machine, which made possible the immense reduction in the price of clothing, was developed to a high pitch of efficiency by Isaac Singer. Nahum Salamon, a London Jew, established the first bicycle factory in Coventry: and it was his invention of the spider-wheel which made the modern safety-bicycle possible. The Luxemburger, Gabriel Lippmann, was discoverer of the capillary thermometer and of colour photography (gaining the Nobel Prize for the latter): the Italian, Samson Valobra, invented the safety-match: Abraham Stern made the first calculating machine: L. B. Phillips (an able etcher of the last generation) invented the keyless watch, which is now almost universally used: Aaron Hirsch introduced various improved metallurgical processes: Moritz Hermann Jacobi, a prominent German architect of his day, was the inventor of galvanoplasty, with all its manifold subsidiaries (including electrotyping): Joseph d'Aguilar Samuda, the most eminent nautical engineer of early Victorian times, was the pioneer in the use of iron for the construction of steamships.

In our own day, Mrs. Ayrton (Hertha Marks) made her scientific reputation with her researches into the electrical arc, going on from this to elucidate various problems connected with the search-light. (During the war of 1914–18, she invented an anti-gas fan which was used to some effect.) The great humanitarian, Lewis Gompertz, devised the expanding chuck, still widely used in industry, from which a more practically-minded person might have made a fortune. This was one only of his thirty-eight inventions—mostly designed, it may be added, for the purpose of rendering the lives of dumb animals more bearable.

§VIII

Jewish interest in natural history and allied branches of science goes back to a remote period. When in the tenth century a copy of Dioscorides' work on Botany reached Cordova, it was the Jewish physician, Hasdai ibn Shaprut, who turned it into Arabic, with the aid of a Byzantine monk. It was thus that the work of the great Greek scientist became available to the Spanish schools, and ultimately to mediaeval Europe as a whole. This was typical of the share of the Jews in spreading mediaeval science.

Mention is made elsewhere (pp. 200-1), in connexion with his vastly important medical work, of the Marrano physician, Garcia d'Orta, founder of tropical medicine. But his famous *Colloquies* (first published at Goa in 1563) marked an epoch, too, in the history of botany; for it has the earliest scientific description of a large number of plants, and is the first work that treats a flora different from that of the classical writers—Dioscorides, Theophrastus, and so on. D'Orta's botanical work was further developed by another Marrano scholar and traveller, Christoval Acosta, whose *Treatise on the Drugs and Medicines of India*

(Burgos, 1578), is still much more than a bibliographical curiosity (see below, p. 201).

One of the earliest Jewish natural scientists who attained a European reputation in modern times, was Marcus Eliezer Bloch (1723–1799) who, unable to read German until he was nineteen years of age, nevertheless had such a passion for learning that within eight years he was able to take his medical degree at the university of Frankfort-on-Oder. His passion, however, was the study of fishes. (His collection of specimens, acquired by the Prussian government, was until recently to be seen in the Zoological Museum in Berlin.) In 1781, he began to publish his superbly illustrated *Allgemeine Natur-geschichte der Fische*, which was completed in fifteen years, in twelve volumes. This work, considered to have laid the foundations of the science of ichthyology, for many years remained the standard work on the subject and even to-day may be consulted with profit.

While Bloch was at work in Germany, the wayward Emanuel Mendes da Costa was active in England, where he was considered the greatest living authority on fossils and conchology. The twelve volumes of his correspond-ence with contemporary savants, English and foreign, preserved in the British Museum, is a remarkable monument of eighteenth-century encyclopaedic scholar-ship. The name of Moses Harris, the great English entomologist of the same period, would similarly seem to indicate a Jewish origin. There is no doubt as to Nathaniel Wallich, the eminent Anglo-Indian botanist, whose best work was accomplished in the first half of the following century and who was father of the marine biologist, George Charles Wallich, one of the founders of deep-sea exploration.

This tradition was carried on by such eminent German botanists as Ferdinand Cohn (whose researches led to

his epoch-making discoveries in the field of bacteriology),
Julius von Sachs (especially associated with the development of plant physiology and micro-chemical processes),
Nathaniel Pringsheim and Eduard Strassburger—all
figures of the utmost importance in the history of the
study of organic life. In England, the second Lord
Rothschild ranked among the foremost natural historians
of our day, his writings and his collections enjoying
a world-wide reputation.

§IX

In the study of the stars, in modern Europe, the Jews
were indubitably among the pioneers. The beginnings
do not redound altogether perhaps to their credit, according to modern standards. In the Middle Ages, they
believed for the most part, in common with their neighbours, that the actions of man were influenced by the
planets and could be predicted by their study. This
fact marks a regrettable recession from the earlier
standard, when (as Josephus and Tacitus agree) the
Jews were distinguished by their refusal to pay attention
to celestial indications. There were, of course, exceptions:
and no more authoritative voice was raised during the
whole course of the Middle Ages against the pseudo-
science than that of Maimonides, in an astonishingly
rationalistic communication sent to the Rabbis of Marseilles. But even his views did not command universal
acceptance: and, both before his day and after, Jews
were regarded as pre-eminent in this field. This was the
case especially in Spain, where both Moslem and Christian
courts frequently had a Jewish astrologer in their employment.

Yet astrology, however far-fetched its conclusions, was
dependent upon a careful and accurate observation of

scripta. Deinde iterū itra añū c⁹ reuolutioē q̄ris i mēse ppoito z ac⸱
cipe dies z horas z m̄ibi scripta z tūc miōre numez subtrahe amaio⸱
ri z illud q̄ remanetē dria āni radicis z añi reuolutiōis q̄ drīa sezua
z si numer⁹ radicis maioz fuerit āni reuolubilis tūc illam drīa minue
atēpore natiuitatis l rey reuolubilis p⁹ ƀuato z remanebit tibi tenp⁹
reuolu. Et si numer⁹ p⁹ accept⁹ fuerit minor secūdarie accepto tūc
pzeƀuatā diferētiā adde tēpori natiuitatis l rei reuolubilis z māebit
tibi tp⁹ reuolutionis. z hoc totū iteligif numerādo ānos amaztio.

Canō q̄rt⁹ de loco z̾o lune habēdo.

Debes pmo scire q̄ reuolutio lune ꝓplef i 31 ānis ideo ponūtuz 3r
table defʉiētes 31 añis. i quoz capite piotur numer⁹ añoz q̄b⁹ df⸱
uit talis tabla. radix z̾o haz tablaz añ⁹ 1473 Etiaz nota q̄ sup q̄ li
bz tablā i pte siniſtra ponūtur due litere q̄z pma sepē .b. q̄ denotat
añū bisextū z secūda denotat reuolutiones. z ꝓ clariori doctrina po⸱
nā ordinē iſtaz tablaz vt facili⁹ ea q̄ dico iteligāt. ponūtur q̄dē i ca⸱
pitib⁹ iſtaz tablaz mēses icipiētes a maztio secūdū ordinē mēsiū z
subt⁹ quolibz mēse dies hebdomade separatiz. Deide subt⁹ p totā
colunā s̄.ḡ.m̄.i q̄b⁹ ē luna i quolibz die talis mēsis. in pte z̾o siniſtra
tabule secūdū lōgitudiē ponunf dies mēsiuz coēs ꝓ oib⁹ in illa tabla
positis ponūtur etiā iter mēsez z mēsez eq̄tiones q̄ sūt note p titulum
positū i capitib⁹ tablaz. cū ergo uolueris scire i q̄ feria icipit q̄libet
mēsis q̄re tablā añi ꝓpositi z sub nominib⁹ mēsiū repies. df.heb. cuz
q̄tuor literis. pma litera denotat feriā i q̄ icipit ille mēsis i pma reuo⸱
lutiōe. ƀa z̾o litera de notat feriā i q̄ icipiet i secūda reuolutiōe. z
sic de allijs duab⁹ literis seq̄ntib⁹. trāsaetis z̾o hiis q̄tuor reuolutio
nib⁹ redde ad pncipiuz eodē ordie. Atamē debes addere ꝓ q̄b⁹ lib⁵
q̄tuoz reuolutiōib⁹ diē vnū. Si tamē uolueris scire pncipiū mēsium
añ radice .q̄re tablā cui⁹ titul⁹ ē. tabla ad sciēdū literā dōinicalē z pn
cipiū cui⁹ lbz mēscs. subtrahēdo ab añis tuis 1472 z cū residuis in⸱
tza tablā cū añis p lat⁹ z cū mēse i capite. z directoi uenies pzincipiū
mēsis. z hoc i reuolutiōib⁹ futuris. i pzeteritis z̾o vide quot añi sūt
āte radice aq̄b⁹ subtrahe 28 quotiēs potueris z cū residuo igzedere

PAGE FROM THE ALMANAC OF RABBI ABRAHAM ZACUTO
Printed at Leiria by Abraham d'Orta, 1496. This compilation accompanied
Columbus on his later voyages

the motion of the heavenly bodies. Hence, just as Alchemy and the search for the Philosopher's Stone did a good deal to advance Chemistry, so (but to an even greater degree) Astrology was the basis of the modern science of Astronomy. Above all, the instruments upon which astronomical study is based are a heritage from the mediaeval observers. The Alfonsine Tables drawn up by two Toledo Jewish savants (*supra*, pp. 67–8) form the basic document of all scientific astronomy. Mention has been made above of the improved astronomical instruments which are due to Levi ben Gershom of Bagnols, and of the Tables drawn up by Abraham Zacuto of Salamanca, which were of incalculable importance for the maritime discoveries at the close of the Middle Ages. These instances may be multiplied.[1] The names of no less than 252 Jewish astronomers who flourished, mainly in Europe, before the year 1500 have been enumerated—a remarkable figure, rivalled by very few European peoples during that period.[2]

This interest did not end with the Middle Ages. It is known that Galileo was on friendly terms with the Marrano poet, Immanuel Boccaro Frances, and that Tycho Brahe knew the Hebrew chronicler, David Ganz of Prague. It is probable, too, that Sir William Herschel, the greatest of astronomers, was of Jewish birth; for the name is typically Jewish, and he came over to England from Germany as a musician in a Hanoverian band. Benjamin Gompertz, who has been mentioned above, began the construction of tables for the mean places of fixed stars, but was anticipated by Bessel.

---

[1] It may be added that the earliest literary reference to a sun-clock occurs in II Kings xx. 9–11, in connexion with the illness of King Hezekiah of Judah.

[2] One interesting figure was the convert Pierre de Notre-Dame, physician to King René of Anjou, and grandfather of the famous Nostradamus.

Moderns include Hermann Goldschmidt, who, between 1852 and 1861 discovered fourteen hitherto unknown asteroids between Mars and Jupiter; Wilhelm Beer, brother of the composer Meyerbeer; Maurice Loewy, one of the greatest observational astronomers of the nineteenth century, who devised the two-part telescope now in common use; Sir Arthur Schuster, the famous physicist who headed the Eclipse Expedition to Siam in 1875; Max Wolf, of Heidelberg, who introduced the method of photography into astronomy; Rudolf Wolf, the great historian of the science; and, in our own day, Frank Schlesinger, an authority on stellar distances, with Erwin Freundlich and very many others.   In Astronomy, moreover, more almost than in other branches of study, the work of the cloistered observer, known to only a limited circle of enquirers, is essential to any advance of knowledge.   It is by these modest workers as well as by the giants that the cultural contribution must be judged[1].

[1] Arnold Zweig, in his *Insulted and Exiled* (published while this work was going through the Press) calls attention to one remarkable dynasty of German-Jewish scientists and scholars, that of Pringsheim. The founder achieved fame as a railway pioneer in the middle of the last century. One son was Nathaniel (already mentioned above, p. 188), an originator of the modern science of vegetable physiology (it was he who first discovered sexuality among the lowest forms of plant-life) and founder of the German Botanical Society. One of his brothers, Alfred, was Professor of Mathematics at Munich. In the next generation come Ernest Pringsheim the eminent physicist, Klaus Pringsheim the musician (now in Tokio) and a daughter who married Thomas Mann and bore children who have already achieved a reputation in the literary and artistic world.

CHAPTER IX

MEDICINE

§1

THE earliest, and what is perhaps still the noblest panegyric of the healing art appears in the Apocryphal Book of Ecclesiasticus, compiled by a Jerusalem notable, Joshua ben Sirach, in the second century B.C.: "Honour a physician with the honour due unto him, for the uses which ye may have of him: for the Lord hath created him. For of the Most High cometh healing, and he shall receive honour of the King. The skill of the physician shall lift up his head, in the sight of great men he shall be in admiration. . . . Then give place to the physician, for the Lord hath created him; let him not go from thee, for thou hast need of him. There is a time when in their hands is good success."

These glowing words make it probable, that even at this stage a flourishing school of medicine was to be found among the Jews. There is no trace of this in the Bible; but that work contains some remarkable illustrations of medical intuition. In the words of the great medical historian, Karl Sudhoff: "Two of the greatest hygienic thoughts of mankind owe their origin to 'Semitism' . . . the weekly day of rest and the direct prophylaxis of disease. The first will be immediately evident to all, even though it has not yet been clearly recognised and proclaimed as a hygienic manifestation of prime importance. . . . Had Judaism given nothing more to mankind than the establishment of a weekly day of rest, we should

still be forced to proclaim her one of the greatest benefactors of humanity. . . . It is a most interesting fact
that, despite its theory of natural causation, Greek
medicine was blind to the fact of contagion, or direct
transmission of disease. But in the Old Testament we
have a methodic inspection of a leper by the priest who,
according to the diagnosis, isolated the patient temporarily
or permanently, and admitted him again to free intercourse only after indubitable convalescence or cure. . . ." [1]

It is not remarkable, in the circumstances, that
throughout the ages the Jew has shewn a remarkable
predilection for the healing art, and that in all epochs
his skill has been recognised. In the Middle Ages, half
of the best-known Jewish scholars, philosophers, and
litterateurs—men like Moses Maimonides, Jehuda haLevi,
Immanuel of Rome, and so on—were physicians by
profession; a striking illustration of the respect in which
that calling was generally held. The great bibliographer,
Moritz Steinschneider, who devoted much of his life to a
study of the Jewish contributions to mediaeval science,
was able to enumerate no less than 2168 Jewish physicians,
who were of sufficient eminence to be recorded and
who flourished between the Dark Ages and the eighteenth
century: yet his list is manifestly incomplete, and for
some periods could easily be doubled. The record, deeply
impressive for the Middle Ages, becomes in modern
times of almost overwhelming importance.

The Talmud preserves some scattered notions of
ancient Jewish therapeutics. The earliest extant specifically medical document of Jewish authorship is, however,
the well-known compilation of "Asaf Judaeus" who
(according to the most recent researches) flourished in

[1] The idea of direct prophylaxis was first applied in Europe only
in the fifteenth century, when, subsequent to the ravages of the Black
Death, the public officials of Marseilles and Venice first organised a
system of sanitary control for incoming vessels.

Syria or Mesopotamia in or about the seventh century.
His famous medical treatise—the earliest experiment in
this genre of literature which has survived in Hebrew—
sums up the scientific outlook which prevailed at the
period. Nevertheless, in one important point he strikes out
for himself; for he is the first medical writer who seems
to have had any inkling of the hereditary character of
certain maladies.[1]

§II

After Asaf, the earliest of the great Jewish physicians
in the classical tradition was Isaac Israeli of Kairouan,
known to the European scholars as Isaac Judaeus. He
was described by a Muslim contemporary as a man of the
highest character who, though much occupied about
Court, was indifferent to wealth and personal advance-
ment. During the Middle Ages, he was one of the best-
known of his profession, and his views on fevers in
particular had the utmost influence. Like many another
Jewish physician, he was also a philosopher, and as
such, too, exercised great influence (already treated of
in another connexion in this work). To Israeli belongs
the credit of having introduced scientific medicine into
Northern Africa; and his writings later exercised no
small influence on mediaeval western medicine. His great
composition translated into Latin by Constantine the
African under the title *De Gradibus Simplicium* was
one of the few early standard works on pharmacology,
a main source and basis of most of the subsequent
mediaeval treatises on the same subject, and therefore
of singular importance for the history of medicine.

---

[1] Noteworthy, too, is Asaf's treatise on the medicine of the poor,
comprising remedies which required no outlay: for "he made his
pupils take an oath that they would accept no fee for this work, but
would attend the poor and needy free of charge, for the sake of charity."

o

One of the great thinkers who came under Israeli's influence was Avicenna, "the Aristotle of the East" who possessed powers of codification hardly surpassed even by his Greek prototype. His writings impressed mediaeval thought in every department: but his *Canon* especially was the most widely read of all medical compositions of the Middle Ages, continuing to be used as a text-book in the European universities until the middle of the seventeenth century. Avicenna is said to have been of Jewish origin.[1] There is, indeed, nothing improbable in this; for near Bokhara, where he was born, the Jews had been settled from time immemorial. But, whether it is so or no, it is a fact that a large proportion of Avicenna's writings reached Europe through the medium of the Jewish scholars and translators who worked in Spain, Italy, and Provence, and whose activity (as has been indicated above) was so important an influence in the earlier stages of the Renaissance. The material on which they worked was partly Avicenna's own (thus his treatise *On the Soul* was translated by the Jew, John of Seville, in collaboration with the Archdeacon Dominicus Gundissalinus), partly that of the series of scholars who carried on and developed his tradition.

Foremost among these, and among the physicians of Moslem Spain, was Avenzoar (d. 1162), friend of the great Averroes. He, though a Moslem, was of Jewish descent, and may thus be included among the great Jewish physicians of history. His most important work was his *Taysir*, or Aid to Health, one of the most widely-read medical works of the entire epoch. At an early date, it was translated into Hebrew—the language of the author's forbears. From Hebrew it was turned into Latin in 1280 by a Paduan physician working in collaboration with a converted Jew, Jacob of Capua, thus reaching

[1] See A. Soubiran, *Avicenne, Prince des Medicins*, Paris, 1935.

the European world. It was at Padua, too, that the Jew Bonacosa translated into Latin the *Colliget* (or General Rules of Health) of Averroes, which was long used as a medical text-book and frequently published even after the invention of printing.

Similarly, the most popular of all mediaeval books of remedies, which goes by the name of *Mesue* (itself based in part on Jewish sources) was translated into Hebrew, and thence into Latin. This version was printed no less than thirty times between the invention of printing and 1581, and its influence is even now to be traced on the modern pharmacopoeia. So is that of the drug-list associated with the name of *Serapion Junior*, a joint production (based on Hebrew and Arabic sources) of the Christian Simon Cordo of Genoa, and the Jew Abraham ben Shemtob of Tortosa.

A foremost figure in this band of translator-scientists was the enigmatic character of the eleventh century known as Constantine the African (above, pp. 49, 193), who was the ultimate source of much European medicine. The works which he translated and thus introduced to Europe were largely of Jewish origin. His main sources, in fact, are the works of Isaac Israeli and the latter's pupil, also a Jew—Ahmed ibn al Djezzar. That he was materially assisted in his work by Jews is certain. Indeed, there is ground for believing that he was himself of Jewish birth.

The most important name of the Middle Ages in Jewish life was that of Moses Maimonides. His overwhelming importance as philosopher and codifier half-obscures the fact that he was by profession a physician, and that his achievements in the field of medicine were such as to have secured him in any case a high place in the annals of science. The volume of his written work in this field was considerable; much of it was translated into other languages, and continued to be published and re-published long after the invention of printing. Of his *Treatise on Poisons and Antidotes*—a work which was cited in the thirteenth and fourteenth centuries by writers like Henri de Mondeville and Gui de Chauliac—a modern authority states: "The book is written in so scientific and independent a spirit, with such practical advice, that one often feels in reading it that it is a modern work." [1] More popular still was Maimonides' *Aphorisms*, of the Latin translation of which no less than five editions appeared, for the use of European physicians, between 1489 and 1579, and which was praised by the great Mercurialis as being not inferior to the similar work of Hippocrates. As late as the close of the eighteenth century—six centuries, that is, after its original composition—it was still being quoted.

Maimonides' medical writings are in some respects astonishingly modern in tone. Modern writers stress his common sense, his rationalism, and his treatment of disease on scientific principles, rather than upon guesswork, mysticism and superstition. Even the exception which he makes to this rule shows him to have been far ahead of his time: he sanctioned faith-treatment in cases of dangerous illness on psychological grounds, *for the sake of the patient's peace of mind!* He believed in the strong curative power of nature herself, and the importance of proper diet. In an ultra-modern fashion, he stressed the superiority of prevention over cure, suggesting that the physician should be consulted regularly in order to keep the patient in good physical condition, instead of waiting till sickness supervened. He insists on the reciprocity between the mental and bodily state, emphasising the corollary that the physician should have regard for the former no less than for the latter.

[1] *Bulletin of the History of Medicine* (Johns Hopkins University, Baltimore), iii (1935) 571.

In other details, too, Maimonides is surprisingly up-to-date. He advocated something in the nature of eugenics, while insisting at the same time that, for the benefit of the offspring, there must be complete psychological harmony between husband and wife during sexual union. He commended exercise and sport, though only in moderation. He insisted on the importance of bodily cleanliness—baths, he said, should be taken weekly—as also on the beneficial effects of fresh air and sunshine. The house, he advised, should be properly ventilated, and plenty of natural light should be allowed to enter it, for "the sun is the best disinfectant".

In all this, as modern authorities agree, Maimonides shews himself surprisingly in advance of his age. In many respects, he was the most modern in spirit of all mediaeval physicians. The progress of medical science, between the thirteenth century and the seventeenth, owed much to his teaching; it would have been all to the good had his theories been drawn upon even more.

§III

Though the greatest names in mediaeval Jewish medicine are bound up with Spain and the Moslem world, it was by no means without its influence elsewhere. The foundation of the famous medical schools of Salerno and of Montpellier, by which the Arabic medicine was first acclimatised in Christendom, is traditionally associated with the work of Jews. The report is of such antiquity, and of such insistence, that it cannot be neglected entirely, notwithstanding the absence of documentary evidence. For the statement is in complete harmony with what we know of contemporary conditions. From the Dark Ages onwards, Jewish physicians had figured prominently all over Europe, in the service of

kings and princes. One of the earliest Italian physicians
whose record has survived was the Jew, Sabbetai Donnolo,
born at Oria in 913, whose extant works justify us in
considering him one of the most important figures in
the scientific life of Latin Europe in his age. (Incidentally,
he provides the earliest mediaeval description of a
magnifying- and burning-glass.)

Such was the reputation of the mediaeval Jewish
practitioners that, in the thirteenth century, the Count
of Flanders sent to England to summon the scholar and
physician, Master Elias of London, to cross the narrow
seas to attend upon him. Later on, after the Jews had
been expelled from England, Jewish physicians were
sometimes summoned from abroad when the occasion
demanded. Thus, in 1410, the ailing Henry IV sent to
Italy for a Jewish expert, to attend upon him in his
grave illness—Dr. Elias Sabot (i.e. ben Sabbetai) of
Bologna. In the previous year, Richard Whittington,
of nursery-tale fame, sent to France to fetch the Jew
Master Samson de Mirabeau, to come to England to the
sick-bed of his wife, the Lady Alice. In other parts of
Europe, similar conditions prevailed. It was seldom
that one or another of the Spanish courts did not have
a Jewish physician in its employment. The Kings of
France, no less than the Holy Roman Emperors and the
Doges of Venice, often consulted Jewish medical advisers
of the same stock; and at the curia of the Pope, in Rome,
there was a long succession of Jewish practitioners
considered in their day among the most eminent in
Europe. One of these, at the close of the fifteenth century,
conducted the first recorded experiment in the transfusion
of blood.

With the Counter Reformation, a determined effort
was made to drive the Jewish physicians out of practice.
The mediaeval regulations, which forbade them to

attend upon Christian patients (under the pretext that they might obtain too strong a hold over their minds) were renewed, and, for the first time, consistently put into effect. Henceforth, in Catholic Europe, it was only at times of emergency that the Jewish physician found his activity unhampered—as happened in 1630 during the plague of Venice, when Dr. Valensin extended his activities from the Ghetto itself to the neighbouring districts, which had been deserted by the Gentile practitioners : or during the War of Candia in the middle of the century, when Elkanah Circoletto attended the Venetian wounded in hospital without accepting any fee. Yet in the Catholic world as a whole, the old tradition of the Jewish physician, which had been the rule in the Middle Ages throughout Europe, was now at an end.

For some generations, accordingly, we must look for the manifestation of Jewish genius in this direction, not among professing Jews, but in the first instance among the Marranos or crypto-Jews of Spain and Portugal. The latter had been compelled to embrace Christianity at the time of the persecutions of the fourteenth and fifteenth centuries, culminating in the Edict of Expulsion from the larger country in 1492 and from the smaller in 1497. They still continued to cherish their ancestral faith in their hearts : and the enforced outward change of religion could obviously not affect their natural proclivities for the healing art. Accordingly, an overwhelmingly large proportion of the eminent Spanish and Portuguese practitioners, from the sixteenth century onwards, are known to have been of Jewish extraction, and in many cases gave formal expression to their religious allegiance, either by flight to a land of greater tolerance or at an auto-da-fè. It is obvious, however, that not all of them had the opportunity to manifest their Jewish sympathies in this manner, and that numbers remain unidentified. Were the list complete, it is doubtful whether many eminent Portuguese or Spanish physicians of the period would not be included.

The Pope of Rome and the Queen of England: the Doge of Venice and the Stadtholder of the Netherlands: the Kings of France, Spain, Portugal and Denmark: the Czar of Russia and the Sultan of Turkey: all had at one time or another Jewish medical attendants of Marrano birth, who had attained the very highest standing in their profession. It would take too long even to enumerate them all here: but space must be spared for the mention of a few who have left a lasting trace in the history of medicine.

"Among the Portuguese worthies who have established for their country a claim to permanent remembrance in connexion with the history of India and the Farther East, the name of Garcia d'Orta stands in first rank", wrote Sir Clements Markham. His services to medicine and to science were immense. D'Orta was in fact the most important figure in materia medica and pharmacognosy from Dioscorides, in the first century of the Christian era, to his own time. He was one of the first great philosophic naturalists, to be classed with such men as John Hunter and Alexander von Humboldt, who observed men in their relation to nature. His writings, particularly his *Colloqios dos simples e drogas medicinães* (1563)—the first scientific work published in Portuguese and the greatest scientific monument of the Portuguese Renaissance—give the earliest description by a European of tropical diseases; and the accounts which he furnishes of medicinal plants are still unsurpassed. Asiatic cholera was an undescribed, if not unknown, disease to European medicine before his time; the account given of it by him brought it to the attention of the western world, in so complete and circumstantial a form as to constitute a classic of clinical description.

Historians of medicine, both in Portugal and outside, had written rhapsodically about the medical importance of Garcia d'Orta, without having any idea as to his origin. A brilliant piece of research, by a Portuguese scholar, Augusto da Silva Carvalho, has, however, recently established the fact that this great figure in the history of medicine was a Jew in everything but name. His forbears had been victims of the Forced Conversion in Portugal in 1497: some of his closest relatives were persecuted by the Inquisition as secret Judaisers: one of his sisters was burned alive: and only his timely death saved the great physician himself from arrest and trial on the same charge (his bones were, in fact, dug up and burned). It is more than likely that other of the greatest Spanish and Portuguese intellectual luminaries of the period, of whose lives we are at present insufficiently informed, belonged to the same category.

D'Orta's work was further developed by Cristoval Acosta, known as "The African"—a distinguished Portuguese surgeon, physician, botanist and traveller, of Marrano extraction, who spent some years in India practising medicine and subsequently undertook many long journeys in tropical countries for the purpose of studying natural history. His famous *Tractado delos drogas*, first published at Burgos in 1578, and partly based on material supplied by his illustrious predecessor, is still regarded as an authoritative work on materia medica and drugs.

Amatus Lusitanus is another of the great names in European medicine of the sixteenth century. His books are referred to even to-day for the immense store of case-history that they contain. He was born at Castel-Branco in Portugal in 1511, as Juan Rodrigo (the name

Amatus, which he subsequently assumed, was a translation of Habib, the original Hebrew name of the family):
graduated at Salamanca: emigrated to Italy, where he was in attendance on the Pope and lectured at Ferrara:
and ultimately sought refuge from the rigours of the Inquisition in Salonica, where he died in 1568. Among his pupils was Giovanni Battista Canano, who during one of his lectures received the first impetus for his discovery of the importance of the valves in connexion with the circulation of the blood. His published works were numerous: but most important were the famous *Centuriae*, which, issued from 1551 onwards, had passed through a dozen editions, in five countries, by the beginning of the following century. Even to-day, the collection is regarded as a medical classic and one of the most valuable sources of medical practise of the sixteenth century.[1]

Rodrigo de Castro similarly, a native of Lisbon, sought religious freedom in northern Europe, settling ultimately in Hamburg. Here he distinguished himself by his self-sacrificing devotion in the plague of 1594, and for his outstanding services to the city in subsequent years. He did not lack contemporary recognition, being summoned to attend on the King of Denmark, the Archbishop of Bremen, the Count of Holstein, and other persons of eminence in the region. But he is best remembered for his *De universa mulierum morborum medicina* (1603), which is generally regarded as having laid the foundations of gynaecology as we know it to-day. Castro is also one of the fathers of medical jurisprudence and wrote one of the first books on the subject.

---

[1] Amatus Lusitanus was no connexion of Zacutus Lusitanus of Amsterdam, another important Jewish figure in medical history of the period, who was a descendant of the astronomer Abraham Zacuto; it has, however, been conjectured that he was related to Elijah Montalto, yet another very prolific Jewish medical writer, physician to Catherine de' Medici, Queen of France.

From England, the names of two Marrano physicians of special eminence, out of many, may be adduced. Jacob de Castro (1704–1789), was the first practitioner admitted into the corporation of Surgeons after their separation from the Barbers. He was one of the enlightened group who endeavoured to introduce vaccination against small-pox into England, advocating it in a succession of pamphlets, in English and Latin, from 1721 onwards—half a century, that is, before Jenner's activity commenced. He is frequently confused with his more ostentatious namesake, Jacob de Castro Sarmento (1691–1762), similarly author of a large number of medical works, who also practised in England and was a fellow of the Royal Society. The latter is memorable for having first popularised the use of quinine in Portugal, thus doing something to stem the ravages of malaria in that country. Curiously, his precursor in this was another Portuguese Marrano, Dr. Fernando Mendes, who had come over to England in the train of Queen Catherine of Braganza, the consort of Charles II, as her medical attendant. Ribeiro Sanchez, another Marrano physician, who lived for a while in England in the eighteenth century, introduced the Russian vapour-bath into Western Europe, but is more memorable as a pioneer of educational and prison reform. On the other hand, the Dutchman Hermanus Boerhaave, leader of the world of medicine in the eighteenth century, was so much under the influence of Spinoza that the latter, though no physician, has been spoken of as "father of Boerhaave's medicine".

§IV

With the eighteenth century, the regulations against the employment of Jewish physicians fell into fairly general desuetude. Jews were admitted to study at one or two of the Universities and medical Schools: and their natural ability reasserted itself.

Perhaps it is not altogether a coincidence that the rebirth of medical studies dates from this period; for it is no exaggeration to say that the world is indebted to Jewish workers for a very considerable proportion of modern medicine. It may be added that a remarkably large number of the eminent Jewish physicians of the nineteenth and twentieth centuries were Germans, just as a particularly large number of the eminent German physicians were Jews. German Jewry has, in fact, provided the world with a disproportionately large quota of its relief from suffering. To say that Jews dominated German medicine is an irrelevance. Jews took their share, and more, in the activities which were carried on in Germany, and assisted to bring them to their high level. To resent this participation, or to submit the proportions involved to microscopic examination, is absurd.

It is not intended to give here a detailed analysis of the Jewish contribution to modern medicine—indeed, it is impossible to disentangle the various strands in a complicated science—but simply to indicate some of the most remarkable contributions for which Jews have been immediately responsible.

Modern therapeutics are to a large extent dependent on the comparatively new science of bacteriology. In Classical times, and throughout the Middle Ages, the doctrine of spontaneous generation had obtained—that is, the idea that under certain circumstances living organisms and life could come into existence from inanimate nature, without any outside agency. This conception was destroyed by Ferdinand Cohn (*supra*, pp. 187–8)—a botanist, but one whose researches had far-reaching implications on medical science. His studies of the development of bacteria and investigations into their life history enabled him to dispose once for all of the theory which had previously prevailed. He is thus the father of bacteriology: and, without his preliminary investigations, the great discoveries of his pupil, Robert Koch (who found the organism of tuberculosis), and even those of Pasteur, would have been impossible. The last-named owed much also to Ignaz Semmelweis, who discovered the contagious nature of puerperal fever.

The great Frenchman's life work, too, was carried on by a Jew—a Russian, this time, Elie Metschnikoff, who was his real successor in France—a zoologist and embryologist of world reputation, a leader in the gallant campaign against infectious diseases and author of the theory of phagocytose. Of nearly equal importance was the deeply-religious Waldemar Haffkine, who, after working under Pasteur in Paris, discovered the method of inoculation against Cholera. In 1893, at the invitation of the Indian government, he went to India in order to conduct the campaign against the bubonic plague, then carrying off vast numbers. At the risk of his life, Haffkine continued his investigations and at last discovered a method of inoculation which reduced the mortality by over eighty per cent. In recognition of his work, the bacteriological laboratory at Bombay has been renamed the Haffkine Institute. When one realises the terrible ravages of the bubonic plague, not only in Asia but also in Europe, ever since the dawn of history (for it was the specific malady which led to the Great Plague of London in 1665), it will be realised how Haffkine's researches benefited the world. Later, the serum against typhus was invented at the Pasteur Institute by another Jew, Dr. Alex Besredka.

One of the best-known names in modern medicine is of course that of Paul Ehrlich, father of chemico-therapy and the greatest biochemical philosopher of all time. His most notable discoveries testify at the same time to the fact that his genius consisted in an infinite capacity for taking pains. With Karl Weigert, also a Jew, he introduced the idea that every cell and tissue of the human body had a specific chemical composition, which reacts differently to colouring matter and may hence be analysed by the use of dye-stuffs. This theory, worked out in painstaking detail, is the basis of the modern science of haematology, and is fundamental to modern therapeutics. Better known to the general world is Ehrlich's salvarsan, generally referred to as 606 because it was the 606th substance that he tried as a cure for syphilis. This preparation, which has saved the lives and careers not only of many men and women, but even of children yet unborn, won its author the Nobel Prize in 1908, and entitles him to be ranked among the great benefactors of mankind. "As a therapeutic achievement," declared Emil von Behring, "the production of salvarsan and neo-salvarsan has never been surpassed." In England alone, it is said, the lives of 5,000 babies are saved each year through Ehrlich's researches, and, through his discoveries, there is a reasonable hope that the disease will become extinct in this country.

It is remarkable that in this particular sphere, a majority perhaps of the other discoveries of foremost importance have been made by Jews. Ehrlich was himself greatly helped by Alfred Bertheim, who had previously worked on the arsenical preparation atoxyl. A further great name was that of August von Wasserman, who in 1906 discovered the famous Wasserman Test for syphilis, which ruled until it was superseded by a new method elaborated in 1927 by an American Jew, Reuben L. Kahn. (Kahn, too, was the first person to demonstrate the immunising powers of the skin.) Albert Neisser, an outstanding bacteriologist and clinician, discovered the organism of gonorrhoea. Indeed, the only name of first rank in the history of this branch of medical research which is not Jewish is that of Schaudinn, the Austrian who discovered the organism of syphilis.

Hardly less important than Ehrlich, though not so well-known to the outside world, was Jacob Henle— the greatest German microscopic anatomist of his day, and one of the greatest anatomists of all time. It was he who first accurately described the cellular structure of the skin and of the tissues lining the intestines and other parts of the body: he first investigated the minute anatomy of the kidney: and his researches on the ligaments, the muscles, the viscera and the vascular nervous system were without number and were of epoch-making importance.

The most eminent of the great Virchow's disciples, without a doubt, was Julius Cohnheim, professor of pathology at Kiel, who in the course of his short life (he was 45 years old only at the time of his death) did work of immeasurable importance in the field of pathology. In opposition to his master's views, he established the fact that the essential feature in inflammation of any part of the body is the passage of white blood-cells through the walls of the vessels, the migration of these corpuscles being the origin of pus. This discovery initiated a revolution in pathology. Cohnheim was moreover one of the founders of experimental pathology in the modern sense by his transmission of tuberculosis to the cornea of the eye. As a teacher, too, Cohnheim's position was of the utmost importance, among his pupils being Ehrlich, as well as the great American physicians, Welch and Councilman.

In the comparatively new science of endocrinology, or the study of the internal glands, one of the greatest names of all is that of Moritz Schiff, a German Jew who taught in Switzerland and in Italy. His investigations covered the whole field of the nervous system as well as of the glands, and he has been described as the "great anticipator" of many subsequent discoveries. Above all, he is famous for his researches into the function of the thyroid gland; and the gland treatment which has recently become so conspicuous is to be traced back to his researches. Similarly the brilliant if unconventional anatomist, Benedikt Stilling, was the first person in Germany and one of the first in the world to conduct operations on the ovary. More recently, superb work in the same field has been conducted by Bernard Zondek, one of a most able group of brothers, and co-discoverer of the remarkable Zondek-Ascheim test for pregnancy. Again, both the founders and most prominent workers in the field of otology—the study of the diseases of the ear—were the Austrian Jews, Politzer and Baranji, of whom the latter was awarded a Nobel Prize in 1914.

Some other names may be mentioned at random. Ehrlich's collaborator, Karl Weigert, was responsible for a famous explanation of inflammation as an over-eager attempt of nature to replace damaged tissue. This is the basis of all protein therapy, now so widely employed. Cellular formation in live tissues was discovered by Saloman Stricker, who introduced the use of wax and gum cells for microscopic work. (He was indeed so far ahead of his time as a physiologist that when, fifty years later, Krogh confirmed his theories as to the functions of the minute blood-vessels, it was sufficient to gain the Nobel award!) Gottlieb Glüge made special studies on the subject of inflammation and introduced the current treatment for rheumatic fever; he was the first person to examine diseased tissues microscopically, and conducted important investigations on influenza. The micrococci of pneumonia were discovered by the lung specialist, Albert Frankel. Jacques Loeb (head of the department of experimental biology in the Rockefeller Institute, New York), endeavouring to interpret physiology in terms of physics and chemistry, conducted experiments in artificial fertilisation, which seem likely to have far-reaching consequences on our understanding of the generation of life.

Dittel invented the operation for calculus : Hollander was the pioneer of modern scientific dentistry : Ferdinand Georges Vidal discovered the absolute diagnostic blood test for typhoid fever known by his name, which is now regarded as indispensable and is universally used. Theodor Rosenheim was the founder of oesophagoscopy. James Israel, a specialist in diseases of the kidney, was one of the greatest German physicians and surgeons of his day. Gustav Magnus, just a century ago, was responsible for the epoch-making discovery that all tissues "breathe," that is to say, they absorb oxygen and give out carbon dioxide. Ludwig Traube (to whom a monument was erected in the court of the Charité) conducted what was, in its day, one of the most celebrated clinics in Europe. He was the founder of Experimental Pathology in Germany, and his studies on digitalis, fever, and diseases of the lungs, heart, and kidneys brought him a great reputation.

Several Jews, in addition to those mentioned above, have received the Nobel Prize for their researches in medicine and allied sciences. One of the best known is Otto Warburg, who was given the award for his great work on the metabolism of cancer, which has afforded fresh hope for many sufferers. Another great worker in this field, director of the Institute for Cancer Research at Berlin, was George Klemperer. Yet another Jewish Nobel Prizeman is Otto Meyerhoff, who devoted his

P

life to the study of the dynamics of living phenomena and to the chemistry of the muscles.

Otto Loewi, who was awarded the prize in 1936, had attained international reputation through his researches on the chemical nature of the transmission of nervous currents and on the structure of the heart; his work is now regarded as fundamental, and is being actively developed in many countries. Otto Minkowski, the eminent endocrinologist, laid the foundation for the treatment of diabetes by his famous experiment of removing the pancreas and so producing the disease artificially. Simon Flexner (at present Director of the Rockefeller Institute for Medical Research) has discovered the germ of dysentery and developed a serum to cure meningitis. Karl Landsteiner's studies on the compatibility of types of blood have made scientific transfusion practicable.

Schenck was founder of modern medical embryology. Alexander Marmorek, the Zionist leader, opened a new epoch in the struggle against tuberculosis. Ludwig Gasper is father of criminal medicine—a notable advance in humanitarianism as well as therapeutics; Hugo Kronecker laid the foundations of the scientific study of the physiology of the heart; Sir Felix Semon, physician to Edward VII, was the most eminent throat-specialist of his day.

Modern medicine depends to a considerable extent on operative treatment; but this has become possible only through the vast improvement in the system of anaesthetics, which has robbed operations of much of their terror. In the development of this, too, Jews have taken a prominent share. The introduction of chloral and the scientific manufacture of hypnotic drugs —one of the most notable achievements of German medical chemistry—is due to Oscar Liebreich. Local anaesthetics were inaugurated by Carl Koller, of New York, an ophthalmic surgeon, who first made use of cocaine for this purpose. Similarly, the cold light apparatus for internal operations was invented by Isaac Michael. The list must here end, but it might well be continued to a wearisome length.

§v

The Jewish practitioner of the Middle Ages seems to have felt an especial interest in ophthalmology: a branch of medicine in which the writings of Isaac Judaeus once enjoyed a great reputation. The most renowned ophthalmologist of the period, in fact, was the Jew Benvenutus Grapheus, or Rapheus,[1] of Jerusalem, whose *Practica oculorum* was one of the most widely used medical works of the time; it was translated into Hebrew, Provençal, Old French and Middle English, and numerous Latin editions appeared. In the later Middle Ages, the Jewish oculist enjoyed great renown: one, for example, operated for cataract on King Juan of Aragon in 1468. In modern times, the interest has continued. One of the earliest writers on astigmatism was George Hartog Gerson, of Hamburg, who had served under Wellington in the Peninsula Campaign and superintended the Hôpital des Visitandines during the Battle of Waterloo. The first Atlas of Ophthalmology was published by Liebreich: Javal of Paris attained fame through his studies in physiological optics: Mauther of Vienna and Julius Hirschberg are recognised among the greatest authorities on the subject: the investigations of Herman Cohn, of Breslau (father of the more famous Emil Ludwig) laid the foundation of the school hygiene of the eyes, and Carl Koller, of New York (as we have seen)

[1] *Raphe* = Physician (Hebrew).

discovered the use of local anaesthesia for ophthalmic operations.

Other names in the history of ophthalmology are those of Joseph Aub, of Cincinnati, who first used the electric magnet for removing foreign bodies from the eye: Julius Jacobson, who improved the surgical treatment of cataracts and originated the operation for trachoma: and John Zachariah Laurence, perhaps the greatest English ophthalmologist of the first half of the last century, founder of what is now the Royal Eye Hospital. It is significant that the two greatest authorities on the history of the science were August Hirsch and Julius Hirschberg—both Jews.

The particularly deep Jewish love of children is perhaps responsible for the Jew's bent towards pediatry— the factual answer to the infamous Ritual Murder charge. This branch of medicine was, indeed, in large measure the creation of German Jews. One of the founders of the science was Eduard Henoch: Abraham Jacobi, a fiery German patriot who was forced to take refuge in exile after 1848, introduced the science into America, where he founded the first child clinic, and was at the time of his death one of the most honoured figures in American medicine. Until recently, the outstanding German pediatrist was Heinrich Finkelstein, who discovered new principles in infant feeding. Adolf Baginsky (co-founder, with Virchow, of one of the greatest Berlin hospitals, the Kaiser-und-Kaiserin Friedrich Krankenhaus) was one of the greatest pioneers in the clinical and scientific study of child life, and a voluminous writer on the subject. Alois Epstein, founder of the world-renowned Foundling Hospital at Prague, initiated various antiseptic measures in infant hygiene, by means of which the mortality in foundling asylums was reduced from 30% to 5% in the course of fourteen years.

The current medical insistence on vitamins is in itself homage to the genius of the Polish Jew, Casimir Funk, born at Warsaw in 1884, who, while working at the Lister Institute in London in 1912, named certain substances which he had succeeded in isolating 'vitamins,' because he thought that they belonged to a group of chemical substances which he called *animes* and which were *vital* for life. A good deal of modern medical treatment is based upon this discovery. Again, it was a German Jewish physician, Kurt Huldschinsky, who in 1919 first used artificial sunlight to cure rickets, then very prevalent in Berlin.

In neurology and allied branches of the medical profession, the part of Jews has also been particularly important. Moritz Heinrich Romberg is regarded as the founder of the science in the modern sense. Robert Remak (who discovered the cells which initiate the heart-beat, and thus has an important place in the history of embryology) described a type of nerve-fibre which has been named after him, and evolved the electrical treatment of nervous diseases. It was Moritz Schiff who first attributed cretinism or its converse to the activity or inaction of the thyroid gland. Cesare Lombroso, an Italian, described the nervous relationships of pellagra (a skin-affectation then widely prevalent in Italy which often ended in insanity). His discovery had no immediate result except that he was compelled to resign his chair, but it has since been universally accepted. In addition, he opened up fresh vistas by his theories on criminology. His ideas, by their positive approach, played a decisive role in the transformation of penology and criminal law.

But towering above all others is the commanding figure of Sigmund Freud, "The Columbus of the Subconscious World", founder of psycho-analysis. There have been excesses in the development of this science, due more to Freud's disciples than to himself. Yet there can be no question but that it has proved of inestimable value to countless sufferers—not only those from ostensibly nervous complaints. This, however, is only one aspect of its importance. No theory of modern times since that of Darwin has affected human thought so deeply; and every branch of intellectual life to-day—philosophy and literature, art and music, even daily speech—is profoundly influenced by the theories advanced by the Viennese Jewish psychiatrist.

To quote an English authority: "Sigmund Freud's name is as cardinal in the history of human thought as Charles Darwin's. Psycho-analysts, under his leadership, have created a new and dynamic psychology, one that thinks in terms of activities and strivings, of impulses and conflicts, in the place of a flat and lifeless picture of mental states."[1]

It must be added that very many of the outstanding exponents of Freudian psychology and psychiatry from the beginning have been Jews—Alfred Adler, Karl Abraham, Hans Sachs, Joseph Breuer, and so on. Antiquaries, on the other hand, trace the whole conception back to a remote Jewish pioneer—Hibatullah ibn Jami, physician to the great Saladin.

§VI

The essence and corollary of the foregoing pages has been summed up in an amusing statement drawn up recently by Dr. Lukatchewsky, a non-Jewish medical man, depicting the quandary of a conscientious anti-Semite who refuses to avail himself of any remedy invented by Jews:—

[1] Wells, Wells and Huxley, *Outline of Science.*

" A Nazi who has venereal disease must not allow himself to be cured by Salvarsan, because it is the discovery of the Jew Ehrlich. He must not even take steps to find out whether he has this ugly disease, because the Wasserman reaction which is used for the purpose is the discovery of a Jew. A Nazi who has heart disease must not use digitalin, the medical use of which was discovered by the Jew Ludwig Traube.[1] If he has tooth-ache he will not use cocaine, or he will be benefitting by the work of a Jew, Carl Koller. Typhoid must not be treated, or he will have to benefit by the discoveries of the Jews Vidal and Weil. If he has diabetes he must not use insulin, because its invention was made possible by the research work of the Jew Minkowsky. If he has a headache he must shun pyramidon and antipyrin (Spiro and Eilege). Anti-Semites who have convulsions must put up with them, for it was a Jew, Oscar Liebreich, who thought of chloral-hydrate. The same with psychic ailments: Freud is the father of psycho-analysis. Anti-Semitic doctors must jettison all discoveries and improvements by the Nobel Prizemen Politzer, Baranji, Otto Warburg; the dermatologists Jadassohn, Bruno Bloch, Unna; the neurologists Mendel, Oppenheim, Kronecker, Benedict; the lung specialist Fraenkel; the surgeon Israel; the anatomist Henle; and others."

It has been suggested in certain circles that the proportion of Jews engaged in the practice of medicine is too high. In 1895, it was reckoned in Italy that Jewish physicians of eminence amounted to 64 per 100,000 of the population, whereas non-Jews amounted to only 34. In Germany, in 1932, of a total of about 52,000 physicians, 8,000 were Jews (in Berlin, the proportion was higher). For some incomprehensible reason, this is regarded as a "problem". But every person is at liberty to choose his own physician, as he is to choose his own lawyer: and, if in these callings the number of Jews is particularly large, it can prove nothing other than their ability and devotion, and the manner in which these

[1] [This is not quite correct. Digitalis was introduced into medicine by the Englishman, William Withering, in the eighteenth century.]

qualities are recognised by their clients. The foregoing pages have demonstrated that the Jew has shewn a devotion to the art of healing which has known no interruption for the past thousand years or more, and that some of the most notable contributions to medical science have been due to him. If skill and understanding can be enhanced by generations of devotion, study, and practice, the Jew of to-day must be better qualified than most men to engage in the practice of medicine. To exclude or discourage him on the grounds of a numerical calculation is certainly a crime against the individual: it may be one against humanity.

CHAPTER X

§I

ABOUT the year 847, the Postmaster of the Caliphate of
Bagdad, ibn Khordadhbeh, compiled a way-book for the
guidance of travellers and couriers. A section of this is
devoted to "the routes of the Jewish Merchants called
Radanites".[1] Well-known though it is, it deserves to be
quoted here once again; for no source conveys more
strikingly the part which was played by Jews in commerce
at that period, when other international intercourse was
barely known:—

"These merchants speak Arabic, Persian, Roman
[i.e. Greek], the language of the Franks, Andalusians and
Slavs. They journey from west to east, from east to
west, partly on land, partly by sea. They transport from
the west eunuchs, female and male slaves, silk, castor,
marten and other furs, and swords. They take ship in
the land of the Franks, on the Western Sea, and steer
for Farama (Pelusium). There they load their goods on
the backs of camels and go by land to Kolzum (Suez)
in five days' journey, over a distance of twenty-five
parasangs. They embark in the East Sea (Red Sea),
and sail from Kolzum to el-Jar (port of Medina) and
Jeddah (port of Mecca); then they go to Sind, India, and
China. On their return they carry back musk, aloes,

[1] It is conjectured that this term derives from Rhodanus (the
Rhone), the estuary of which river was the base of these merchants;
or else from the town of Rhaga in Persia.

camphor, cinnamon, and other products of the Eastern countries to Kolzum, and bring them to Farama, where they again embark on the Western Sea. Some make sail for Constantinople to sell their goods to the Romans; others go to the palace of the King of the Franks to place their goods.

"Sometimes these Jew merchants prefer to carry their goods from the land of the Franks in the Western Sea, making for Antioch (at the mouth of the Orontes); thence they go by land to al-Jabia, where they arrive after three days' march. There they embark on the Euphrates for Bagdad, and then sail down the Tigris to al-Obolla. From al-Obolla they sail for Oman, Sind, Hind, and China. All this is connected one with another.

"These different journeys can also be made by land. The merchants that start from Spain or France go to Sous al-Akza (Morocco), and then to Tangiers, whence they march to Kairouan and the capital of Egypt. Thence they go to al-Ramla, visit Damascus, al-Kufa, Bagdad, and Basrah, cross Ahwaz, Fars, Kirman, Sind, Hind, and arrive at China. Sometimes they likewise take the route behind Rome, and, passing through the country of the Slavs, arrive at Khamlif, the capital of the Khazars. They embark on the Jorjan Sea, arrive at Balkh, betake themselves from there across the Oxus, and continue their journey toward Yurt and Toghozghor, and from there to China."

This classical passage is one of many which indicate the importance of the Jews in the mercantile life of the Dark Ages. The Roman Empire and its magnificence had crumbled to pieces, so far as the West was concerned. The amenities of life which it had introduced were forgotten by the nordic and semi-nordic states which had sprung up on its ruins. On the other hand, a new civilisation—that of Islam—had come into existence in the

Middle East, opening a new gateway to the ideas and the commodities of China and India. The new inhabitants of western Europe had little knowledge of, or interest in, what lay beyond their own borders: and it was natural for the Jews to step into the breach, in the role of intermediaries. Thus they contributed largely to the process by which the harshness of the Dark Ages was modified, and various refinements of life—later to be considered necessities—were introduced to the countries of the bleak north. According to one authority[1]

"Europe owes to the Jewish Radanites the introduction of oranges and apricots, sugar and rice, Jargonelle pears, and Gueldre roses, senna and borax, bdellium and asafoetida, sandal-wood and aloes, cinnamon and galingale, mace and camphor, candy and julep, cubebs and tamarinds, slippers and tambours, mattresses, sofa, and calabash, musk and jujube, jasmine and lilac. There is also evidence that some of the more important items of foreign trade came in with the Radanites, as was perhaps natural. Thus the word 'douane', for custom house, 'tariff', 'bazaar', 'bale', 'fondac' or factory, and 'baggage', all occur early, as well as 'barge', 'barque', and 'sloop' (Lammens). There is also probability that the royal breed of horses in France known as limousin, introduced in the ninth century, was due to these Jewish merchants. . . ."

Yet more can be added to this list. The Jews are a people "endowed by divine grace with special aptitude for handicrafts," wrote Cosmas Indicopleustes in the sixth century; and, so long as Christian intolerance permitted, it was as artisans rather than capitalists that they were distinguished. Various branches of manufacture were associated with them almost exclusively. In the early centuries of the Christian era—and for long

[1] Jacobs, *op. cit.*, pp. 203–4.

after—the Jews were recognised as the most skilled workers in glass: indeed, in the Dark Ages, Greek artisans in France boasted that they had mastered the Jewish methods of work. Throughout the Middle Ages—particularly in South Italy and Greece—the Jewish communities had almost a monopoly of dyeing and silk-weaving; and it is probable that a good deal of the products of their industry was exported to Northern Europe. There was one yellow, indeed, of which they alone had the secret, and which was known by their name. A remarkable contrast, this, to the other shade of the same colour called Isabella, to commemorate (it is said) the dingy shift of that arch-persecutor of the Jews, who vowed never to change it until Granada had been captured from the infidel!

The tradition of silk manufacture, above all, had a continuous history among the Jews. When Benjamin of Tudela travelled in the Eastern Mediterranean at the close of the twelfth century, he found this to be the mainstay of the Jewish communities everywhere. In Sicily and Southern Italy, they enjoyed all but a monopoly, until Christian competitors from Genoa and Lucca secured their expulsion from the coastal towns. But the struggle was not yet over. In the sixteenth century, a Venetian Jew named Meir Magino wrote a book on his improved method of silk-manufacture, which he attempted to introduce into both Italy and Lorraine. It was about the same time that the silk industry was first established in the Low Countries by Antwerp Marranos. Later, they transferred it with them to Holland; but even in this generally tolerant milieu, once their trade secrets had been learned, they were officially excluded from it by the jealous burghers (the subsequent decline may not be altogether a coincidence). Precisely the same took place at Padua, where the Jews, after having introduced the industry and practised it undisturbed for generations, were driven out at the close of the eighteenth century. As though to compensate, the silk manufacture was first established in Berlin almost simultaneously by a Jew, David Hirsch.

In all these cases, the function of the Jews was not merely that of *entrepreneurs;* they were also the technicians and (so far as was permitted) the labourers. It has been worth while entering into this case in some detail as an illustration of the manner in which the broadening of the basis of Jewish economic work was consistently impeded.

The story may however be duplicated with regard to many other branches of industry—especially the textile industry, with which the Jews of Spain in particular were long associated. They possessed above all the secret of certain methods of embroidery, such as the famous *Point d'Éspagne*, which was much used for Christian ecclesiastical purposes : it has been pointed out that even the pomp and glitter of the autos-de-fé was in part the product of Jewish skill! As goldsmiths and silversmiths, too, Jews were famous, especially in the Mediterranean countries, throughout the Middle Ages and after. It is noteworthy that it is precisely with these callings that they have remained associated down to our own day; there is thus no question of a sudden, and competitive, incursion.

§II

At a later stage, there were four commodities, the introduction or popularisation of which in Europe had a considerable influence on social life, and indeed on economic organisation. They were sugar, tobacco, coffee, and tea. In the diffusion of all these (excepting, until recent times, the last) the Jews were deeply interested.

It has been conjectured that sugar was introduced to the European of the Dark Ages through the medium of the Radanite Jewish traders. The commodity continued to be a special object of interest on the part of Jews. Towards the close of the Middle Ages, it was exported by those of Crete as far distant as Austria, and treacle, the principal by-product of sugar, was (it appears) first made by them.

The industry entered upon a new phase after the maritime discoveries of the fifteenth century, when from a luxury of the wealthy it became one of the necessities of life. In this process, the part played by the Jews was considerable. In 1548, Portuguese Marranos transplanted the sugar-cane from the island of Madeira to South America, thus initiating what was for a long period one of the staple industries of the New World. In 1654, when the vast majority of them emigrated from Brazil rather than imperil the religious liberty laboriously achieved under Dutch rule, they transferred their activity to the West Indies, establishing the commercial prosperity of these islands on a new basis. It was Benjamin da Costa, one of the refugees, who set up the industry in Martinique, while others brought it to the Dutch (at that time English) colony of Surinam. They were very prominent in this branch of activity also in Barbados, Jamaica, and the other islands. It was a Marrano, too, who introduced the first sugar-cane mill into the West Indies. (Long after, in the nineteenth century, it was a certain Aaron de Pass who introduced the sugar-cane to Natal.) Upon this industry, to so great extent of purely Jewish origin, the prosperity of the West Indies long rested, and the livelihood of a large number of the inhabitants still depends.

With regard to coffee, the most interesting sources of information at our disposal relate to England. The first recorded use dates from the Commonwealth period, and the scene is Oxford. "This year", writes Anthony Wood, *sub anno* 1650, "Jacob, a Jew, opened a Coffee House in the Parish of St. Peter in the East, Oxon; and there it was by some, who delighted in noveltie, drank." This Jacob may or may not have been identical with another person mentioned by Wood, "Cirques Jobson, a Jew and Jacobite, born near Mount Libanus, who sold coffee in Oxon. in a house between Edmund Hall and Queen Co. corner." Subsequently, according to the same authority, Jacob left Oxford and transferred his business to London, "in old Southampton Buildings in Holborne". He was still alive in 1671. The whole question calls for further investigation; what however seems to be quite clear is that coffee was first introduced to England by Levantine Jews, who already had a considerable interest in the commodity in their own country. In Egypt, indeed, coffee was already so much associated with the Jews that it was generally termed "Jews' Drink".

More important was the case of tobacco. When not long after the first landing, the ship's doctor on Columbus' first expedition, Mestre Bernal (who was of Jewish birth, and had indeed figured as a Judaiser in an auto-de-fé) returned to the Admiral's vessel, his companions were surprised to see him breathing smoke out of his mouth —a procedure which apparently had something to do with an imperceptibly-fuming tube which he held in his hand. This was the first recorded use by any European, or by any man whose name has been preserved to history, of tobacco. From that time onwards, the association of Jews with the tobacco industry was always intimate: and they contributed thereby incidentally, to a considerable degree, in laying the foundation of American economic prosperity.

The Rabbis, though they questioned the permissibility of smoking on Sabbaths and Holydays, never took up the same attitude as the Christian clergy, who considered it "offering incense to the devil", or James I of England, who devoted a special treatise to combatting its use. They considered it, rather, an aid to sobriety. It was a Jew, Daniel David da Pisa, who had the first tobacco-monopoly in Venice. The same was the case on the neighbouring *terra firma*: and in Spain, in the seventeenth century, persons engaged in the tobacco trade figure with significant frequency among the Marranos punished by the Inquisition. In Holland, tobacco was unknown until 1611. In that very year, a Jew named David Abendana sold a barrel of it to a merchant in Hoorn: and from that date, tobacco-importing and tobacco-working played a very important part in the economic structure of the Amsterdam community. In the seventeenth century, a good part of the tobacco consumed in Germany was imported through the Spanish and Portuguese community of Hamburg.

The Jewish interest in the tobacco industry, therefore, is not by any means a recent development: they have been interested in it from the first. It may be added that in our own days the cigarette-making industry, which now employs many thousands of hands, was established in England by Jews. It was first introduced by one working at the Player factory at Nottingham; while the beneficiaries of Bernhard Baron's munificent charities (to cite only one example) have good reason to remember with gratitude its subsequent development at their hands.

Besides tobacco and sugar, other American products owe their introduction in the first instance to Marrano agencies. Thus the first grant to export grain and horses to America was made by Ferdinand and Isabella to Columbus' "New Christian" patron, Luis de Santangel, to whom is hence due the genesis of two of the greatest American industries of to-day.

Vanilla, too, is said to have owed its introduction into general use to Jews: this report finds confirmation in the fact that when in 1684 a certain Salamon de la Roche died in the Dutch colony of Essequibo, the secret of preparing the vanilla-bean for the market died with him. Indigo was also a staple article of Jewish international commerce, and the cultivation was introduced by this agency into North America. This links up with the participation in the dyeing industry in the Mediterranean world in the Middle Ages in the one direction, and with the establishment of aniline dyeing in northern Europe, in modern times, in the other. As early as the thirteenth century, under the Emperor Frederick II, African Jews were given Crown lands to develop indigo plantations in Sicily. Five hundred years later, a certain Dr. Nuñes first introduced the growth to Georgia, while Moses Lindo, coming from London in 1756, invested a fortune in fostering it in South Carolina. It is a striking exemplification of the continuity of Jewish interest in certain types of industry, in all its branches, for very many generations.

It was perhaps fitting that Europe owed to the Jews some of its cleanliness as well as godliness. A great centre for the manufacture of Castile Soap in the Middle Ages was Marseilles: here, it was introduced in 1371 (it is said) by the Jew Crescas Davin, known as *sabonarius*. But the story does not end here. Four centuries later, in 1761, the same process took place in America, when the General Assembly of Rhode Island empowered James Lucena of Newport to set up a manufactory of Castile Soap according to the process which he had learned in Spain. At the same period, Jacob Rodrigues Rivera introduced to the Colony the Spermaceti industry, with its off-shoot of candle-making; and it was because of this that Newport became the great whaling

Q

centre which it was in the middle of the eighteenth century, when its importance almost exceeded that of New York.

The diamond industry was another in which the Jews played a not inconsiderable role throughout the ages. Here, the reason is plain. In the Middle Ages, dealing in precious stones was one of the few callings, other than money-lending, in which they were allowed to engage; and they found an added attraction in it by reason of their general insecurity, which made them desirous of having their property in an easily transferable form. Their international connexions, and their pawn-broking business, gave an additional impulse. From dealing in precious stones, they naturally became interested in working them. In the seventeenth century, they were regarded as the best gem-polishers in Venice, though the protectionist policy of the *Serenissima* subsequently excluded them (to the great loss of the city, as was subsequently realised). Possibly, it was by the refugees from Venice that the craft was established in Holland, where its introduction is associated with the Portuguese Jews. The latter were engaged in it in Amsterdam as early as 1612. From that date onwards, this has been one of the mainstays of the Jewish community of that city, still the greatest centre of business, where the proportion of Jewish workers employed has never been less than 70 per cent. When in 1748 their Gentile competitors petitioned for legislation to exclude the Jews from the industry, the Government refused to take action, on the grounds that "the Jews have established the diamond trade in this city".

A natural outcome of this interest was that Jews, proficient in gem-cutting, became expert seal-engravers. In the seventeenth and eighteenth centuries, they worked in this capacity in many Central European courts, some of them attaining a high degree of skill and reputation. Similarly, we find them active under more humble conditions in various English provincial centres. This was their introduction, in many cases, to engraving and to art in general (see above, p. 128).

Meanwhile, their interest in gem-purveying had continued. Just as in the Middle Ages (as early at least as the time of Charlemagne), Jewish jewellers made perilous voyages over land and sea to the East to bring back gems for the courts of Europe, so at a later date they went to India with the same object, this being the earliest settlement there of European Jews. Similarly, when the Brazilian diamonds came on the market in the seventeenth century, they were brought to Europe largely by Marrano agencies. There was therefore nothing novel, or unnatural, when Jews took such a large part in the development of the diamond industry in South Africa at the close of the nineteenth century; indeed, it was a new experience when they were subsequently ousted from their previous almost dominant position by the immensely superior financial genius of Cecil Rhodes.

§III

It is with the field of finance that Jewish economic achievement is usually associated. This conception, already widely held, was popularised by Sombart in his ponderous and, in many ways, impressive volume, on the Jews and Modern Capitalism. In this he maintains with a wealth of learning that the Jews, by the circumstances of their history and of their intellectual bent, are particularly qualified to participate in modern capitalism, and are largely responsible for its evils. Indeed, according to him, all the predominant features which distinguish modern capitalism from mediaeval trade and industry are directly due to Jewish influence. "Thus, the economic form of the modern state was due to the activities of the Jews as purveyors and financiers, in providing the state with capital for war and development. They helped considerably in the foundation of modern colonies, which has determined the policy and controlled the development of modern states, and quickened international trade by the large scale of their trade, the variety of their wares, and the introduction of new commodities. As a consequence, we find the centres of trade changing from one country or centre to another, according as Jews were expelled or found shelter ; Sombart gives as examples the transference of trade from Spain to Holland, from Antwerp to Amsterdam, from Augsburg to Frankfort and Hamburg. Above all, Jews have transformed economic life in commercializing it by creating credit instruments and introducing the custom of buying and selling securities, which supplied mobile capital for industrial undertakings. They thereby introduced their capitalistic point of view into modern trade, with its competitive (against 'just') prices, its advertisements, adulterations, payment by instalments, utilization of waste products, and general efficiency."[1]

This is a remarkable catalogue of achievement ; and, whatever its original object, and whatever its present utilisation, it is not a record which necessarily calls for apology. Sombart's theories, however (as has been shewn by Jacobs, Hofman, Steckelmacher, Waetjen and others), are based upon an arbitrary selection of facts. Isolated data are taken as representative : strange names are assumed without justification to be Jewish : theories are built upon a basis of assumptions. A more careful enquiry results in a very different picture.

The Jew was driven by the unfortunate circumstances

[1] For this analysis I am indebted to Jacobs, *op. cit.*, pp. 247–8.

of his history to be predominantly a townsman. He had to seek an outlet, despairingly, in every branch of urban economy. Yet even here he found himself hampered at every turn by repressive legislation—whether in buying, selling, or manufacturing. Hence he may make an intermittent appearance in any branch of industry: but it invariably happened that before long he was ejected. It was much the same even in finance, which he was supposed to dominate. It was only for brief periods, perhaps once or twice in history (as will be seen), that his influence was really considerable. At other times, he filled only minor functions. However, his quasi-exclusive association with finance conveyed the general impression that he monopolised it; while the fact that in the Jewish quarter there were invariably one or two wealthy householders gave colour to the popular delusion which identified all Jews with wealth. (Actually, as is pointed out elsewhere, one-third of the Jews of the Ghetto Age were dependent on charity, and as many more lived on the verge of the minimum subsistence-level.)

One simple fact goes to shew how slight the Jewish influence in finance really was. For the consistent exercise of an important role in economic life, a certain stability of fortune—like that which carried the Fuggers or the Medici through, from generation to generation—is essential. But the Jew generally lacked this. There were, in the Middle Ages, some Jews of great wealth. But it seldom happened that this wealth passed from father to son. Generally, it was strictly personal: and the confiscatory measures which followed the death of a wealthy Jew (the whole of whose fortune legally passed to the Crown) prevented his son from enjoying it. Hence, though in the Middle Ages we know of several wealthy Jews, it is difficult to trace any wealthy dynasties, of the type which exist to-day: the children of Aaron of Lincoln or Benedict of York enjoyed at the best a modest competence. Wealth, moreover, bred jealousy; and time after time Jewish financial magnates—such as Samuel Abulafia of Toledo, minister to Pedro IV, who built what is now called the House of El Greco—were hounded to a shameful and penurious death. It is not until the growth of the more or less emancipated communities of enlightened Holland, in the seventeenth century, that the Jewish capitalist in the real sense, in untrammelled enjoyment of a considerable capital for investment, came into being. In the countries where the Ghetto still prevailed—Germany and Italy—Jewish wealth remained strictly personal until the close of the eighteenth century.

There were (as has been indicated) two periods only when the Jewish financier played a part of real importance. One was at the height of the Middle Ages: the other at the height of the Industrial Revolution. Both were periods of change: and each, moreover, called for special qualities which the Jews, as it happened, could at that time provide.

The first of these two periods was between the eleventh century and the thirteenth, when the Jews, ejected from commerce and industry through the jealousy of the Gilds, were seeking another outlet for their capital. At the same time the Papacy, with an impracticable idealism, was endeavouring to suppress the institution of interest among Christians (*supra*, pp. 23–26). Hence, for a short period, the Jews, without being by any means the wealthiest persons in Europe (those whose property was measured in terms of land were more wealthy by far) were in certain parts the sole capitalists. They possessed their capital, in short, in mobile form: and it is mobile capital which is all-important in economic development. The transition of Europe from a barter-economy to a money-economy, in the two and a half centuries which succeeded the First Crusade, was certainly facilitated by their presence. The ready money which they could provide made possible the development of the system of "scutage", whereby the baron acquitted himself of his obligations to the Crown by a monetary payment instead of personal service. Incidentally, the process meant that the hands of the central government were strengthened as against the centrifugal powers of the nobility. Thus the dissolution of the Feudal System was facilitated—itself no negligible factor in the development of civilisation.

Moreover, for the two characteristic occupations of the Middle Ages—fighting and building—Jewish aid was at this time indispensable. The Crusades, fatal as they were to the Jews, would not have been possible on the same vast scale but for the capital which they had to provide. Even ecclesiastical foundations had recourse to them when any important undertaking was contemplated: thus Aaron of Lincoln, the great Anglo-Jewish financier of the twelfth century, is thought to have assisted in the construction of no less than nine of the Cistercian monasteries of England, as well as of the great Abbey of St. Albans and even Lincoln Minster.

This period of prominence, however, did not last for long. The recurrent massacres which accompanied the Crusades and followed them; the competition of Christian usurers, operating under the highest patronage; and finally the great expulsions at the close of the Middle Ages; drove the Jews into the position of mere pawnbrokers. From the thirteenth century to the eighteenth, their importance in the world of finance was, generally speaking, negligible.

The second period when the Jews were of real significance in this sphere began, then, in the eighteenth century, and reached its climax in the nineteenth, after
the Napoleonic Wars. It was a period of growing indus-
trialisation, of rapidly increasing manufactures, of rising
exports. National economy gave place to a world
economy; and it became necessary to perfect a method
for the balance of payments without the laborious and
superfluous process of transporting bullion. It was this
need which gave origin to the great international banks,
which played so important a part in the economic life of
Europe in the first half of the nineteenth century.

It was not remarkable that the Jews, newly released
from the Ghetto and ebullient with a pent-up spirit of
enterprise, played a prominent role at this stage. The
circumstances of their recent history had driven them
to occupy themselves in finance—petty finance, it was
true, but not essentially different from the larger-scale
operations. Their adaptibility enabled them to devise
fresh methods to cope with fresh problems. Above all,
their mobility, and the international connexions which
resulted from this fact, provided them with potential
agents and agencies in every commercial centre. This
was the secret of the prominence of the Rothschilds, the
Worms, the Sterns, the Bischoffsheims, and the other
international banking houses which played so prominent a part in European finance a century ago. The
Jews of Frankfort were particularly to the fore; for
Frankfort was the traditional financial centre of the
Continent of Europe, and it was now for the first time
that its Jews were able to enjoy the advantages of their
position to the full. On the other hand, the treatment of
the Jews in Germany, even at this period, was not such
as to encourage them to stay, the constant emigration
which resulted emphasising the international connexions

and outlook of those who remained. But the fact must not be overlooked that the success of these firms was ultimately dependent on their reputation for probity. As long back as the seventeenth century, an Elector Palatine—grandson of James I of England—was advised to entrust his treasure to the keeping of a Frankfort Jew, as it would be safe in his hands as in those of the Almighty. The legendary account of the foundation of the fortunes of the House of Rothschild, as a result of a quixotic honesty in their dealings with the Elector of Hesse, has in it an element at least of truth. Nor should it be forgotten, in this connexion, that none of the Jewish financiers of the nineteenth century ever earned anything approaching the obloquy which attached (for example) to some great American capitalists of the period.

One is accustomed to hear these nineteenth-century captains of finance designated as "bankers". It is very important therefore to realise that in the strict sense of the term (that is, "maintaining an establishment for the custody of money, which is paid out on the customer's order"—Oxford English Dictionary) the part played by Jews has been very slight, and in England particularly almost negligible. In addition to the "Deposit Banks" just described, there grew up in England in the course of the nineteenth century a new type of Bank which was styled an Exchange Bank, and which dealt in the main with the colonies and dependencies. Of these, the officials were nearly always Scotsmen, and Jewish influence was, here too, insignificant. On the other hand, there was an old form of Financial House which used to be styled simply "merchants". As a distinction from other sorts of dealers, they later called themselves "Merchant Bankers". Their business was international, and their principal occupation was to finance trade and industry—

either on short terms, by bill-discounting, or on long terms, by means of loans. It was with this type of banking only, together with bullion-dealing and transactions in foreign exchange, that Jews were at one time (and in a modified degree still are) prominently associated.

It is not to be contested that these Jewish bankers, like their non-Jewish colleagues and competitors, operated for their own advantage.[1] Yet their services for the economic development of Europe and of the world were incontestable. It was not that they provided the capital. But they made it mobile. They perfected the delicate machinery by which it was brought together and rendered available for industry, and they transferred it from country to country as and when it was needed. If during the course of the nineteenth century communications improved to such an extent that what had previously been a week's journey could be accomplished in a few hours: if what had previously been the luxuries of the rich became familiar to every class: if the outposts of Europe overseas were developed to such an extent that they were able to absorb vast numbers out of Europe's teeming millions—the new financial machinery alone made it possible: and the Jewish financiers should share the credit, even as they are made almost to monopolise the blame.

Yet, contrary to what is popularly thought, this period of quasi-hegemony lasted only for a very short time. The Revolution of 1848 implied the waning of the House of Rothschild in France, where its influence had previously been greatest: and simultaneously the introduction of the principle of public subscription for State loans cut off what had formerly been a steady source of income.

[1] There are exceptions even to this elementary generalisation. The Beit Bridge-building bequest to South Africa, though it happens to have achieved an outstanding material success, was intended as a pure benefaction.

Above all, in the middle of the century, the great Joint-Stock banks began to flourish. This was largely due (as will be seen later) to the equalitarian initiative of the brothers Péreire in France, and to the support of men like Sir David Salomons in England. But their rise inevitably implied the decline of the private banks, a great part of whose business they henceforth absorbed. The Jewish private banks (which had in many cases meanwhile become less Jewish, both in personel and in sympathies), suffered especially, for precisely the same reasons which had previously brought about their rise.

The process of decline, which had already made enormous progress in the later Victorian era, received an additional impetus with the outbreak of the European War in 1914, which violently disrupted the traditional structure of international finance. To-day, there are only five Jewish banking-houses in the City of London of any importance—and most of these have non-Jewish partners. All the private banks combined, moreover, are of little importance as compared with any of the five great Joint Stock banks, amongst whose 150 directors are only three Jews. So, too, the foreign exchange business in England, which was built up by Jews and at the close of the nineteenth century was largely monopolised by them, is now almost entirely out of their hands. The Jews introduced the new methods; but the machinery they constructed and the technique they developed were before long absorbed into the common stock of the country—just as centuries before, the Flemish and French refugees introduced fresh industrial processes which, at first exclusive, subsequently became common property and an integral factor in England's commercial greatness.

On the Continent, the importance of the private bank —and hence the "Jewish" private bank—is of course greater : but nowhere does the influence of the Jew even approach a financial monopoly. In the United States, for example, after the recent legislation by which financial houses are compelled to choose between the retention of the issuing or the banking sides of their business, Kuhn Loeb & Co. chose the former : and it may now be said that Jewish banks and banking, in the accepted sense of the term, have practically ceased to exist in the country. In Germany, the influence of such well-known private firms as Bleichröder, Mendelssohn and Warburg, all of which could boast more than a hundred years of existence, was even before the Nazi Revolution very small in comparison with that of the big Joint Stock banks, where Jewish directors were by no means the rule.

With the Stock Exchange, contrary again to the general impression, matters were much the same. At Ghent, where so far as is known the "Bourse" first assumed prominence, and at Bruges, where the name originated, there was at no period a Jewish settlement of any significance. In Antwerp, where what was to prove the prototype of the European "Exchange" was constructed in 1531, there was resident at the time only a handful of surreptitious Marranos : and the same applied to London in 1566, at the period of Sir Thomas Gresham's epoch-making experiment. When the Royal Exchange here was reorganised in 1697, the number of "Jew Brokers" was restricted to twelve, or rather less than one-twelfth of the total—a figure barely commensurate with their importance in the City.

The establishment of the Dutch East India Company in 1602 marks what is generally regarded as the beginning of the modern joint-stock method of trading. It has been alleged that the part taken in this by the Jews was overwhelmingly important. Actually, their contribution

to the original capital was trivial—4,800 florins out of
a total of 6,500,000, or less than one-tenth per cent
—approximately proportionate, that is, to their actual
numbers in relation to the general population. Moreover, Jews were rigorously excluded from the administration of the Company until the Age of Emancipation had
begun to dawn. It was only long after the original
establishment, when the institution had passed its apogee
and the Amsterdam Jews had lost their pioneering spirit,
that they began to invest their funds in its stocks on a
large scale, for the sake of security: a procedure which
was to entail almost fatal consequences to the community as a whole at the time of the great slump in
the eighteenth century, when the shares fell to one-tenth
of their previous level, never to recover. Similarly, on
the establishment of the Dutch West India Company
in 1621–3, the original Jewish contribution to its capital
was no more than one-half per cent, to rise to four per
cent half a century later.

It is true that a Dutch Jew of Portuguese origin,
Joseph Penso de la Vega, wrote in 1688 the first handbook on the theory and practice of the bourse—characterised as being still, to the present day, the best
description, both in form and substance, of dealings in
stocks and shares. Similarly, Isaac de Pinto's remarkable
Traité de la circulation et du crédit, of 1771, has been described as standing at the beginning of the modern era,
in which joint-stock enterprises have become the centre
of economic activity. But from these isolated illustrations of theoretical comprehension it is absurd to draw
any far-reaching conclusions.

The Stock Exchange in London was organised only
at the close of the eighteenth century. There was a
time, in the heyday of nineteenth century expansion,
when Jews were perhaps prominent upon it out of

proportion to their numbers. This period, however, was short-lived. To-day, the Jews on the London Stock Exchange number only some 5 per cent, and include no house of the first importance; while of the thirty members of the Stock Exchange Committee, only one is a Jew. Similarly in New York the Jews, numbering some 25 per cent of the total population, contribute (surprisingly enough) only 15 per cent of the members to the Stock Exchange.

§IV

This is not to suggest that the Jewish share in modern capitalistic development was negligible. In view of the circumstances of their history, it was inevitable that they should have played a part of some importance in the evolution of the present financial system. From the simple money-lending, to which they were driven in the Middle Ages by religious prejudice and persecutory legislation, sprang commercial money-lending. This developed into anonymous lending—i.e. the purchase of bonds from States and issuing them to the general public. Hence grew up stock-dealing and, finally, stock-broking and bill-broking. And, in all these various stages of development, the part played by the Jews was of solid—though not decisive—importance.

It is generally stated, for example, that the Letter of Credit was a Jewish invention. Hardly a particle of evidence can be found to confirm this assumption. Yet the theory is not unlikely. Though the Jews may not have been familiar with the institution of "credit" in the technical financial sense, they knew it as a social reality. If a Talmudic scholar resident in London, at the end of a scholastic communication to a Rabbi of Marseilles, requested him to oblige a client on his way to Palestine with an advance, he could rest assured that the other would carry out his wishes, realising that the same service would be performed for him in London should the necessity arise. Similarly, in mediaeval England or Germany or France, a bond of indebtedness to a Jewish financier in one part of the country, duly endorsed, was equivalent to a draft or a letter of credit in the hands of the person who held it. The network of Jewish friends, relatives and correspondents, spread throughout Europe and the Mediterranean world, had therefore in it the germ of a highly developed financial system. It is even suggested, though on slender authority, that the Bill of Exchange owes its origin to the exigencies of the Jewish refugees expelled from Spain in 1492.

In view of all this, it was natural for Jews to take a solid share in the genesis and development of banking, the corner-stone of modern economic organisation. As early as the tenth century, their activity is associated with the beginnings of the banking system in the Islamic world at Baghdad. When the famous Venetian Bank, the Banco Giro, was founded in 1619, its organisation owed a great deal to the financial acumen of Abraham del Banco. In the same year, the Marrano community of Hamburg took a prominent part in the foundation of the Bank of Hamburg, forty of its members being included in the earliest roll of shareholders. Towards the close of the century, a Jew named Jacob Henriques (if the magniloquent petition subsequently presented by his son is to be believed) played some part in the establishment of the Bank of England.[1] It is remarkable, though, that while the Jews collaborated in the establishment of these institutions both with

[1] To these earlier instances may be added the participation of Bernhard Eskeles in the foundation of the Austrian National Bank in 1816, and the great work of Ludwig Bamberger for the establishment of the German Reichsbank in 1870.

advice and with capital, they played only the smallest share in their administration. The Banco Giro, in Catholic Venice, never of course admitted a Jew to any responsible post: while there was no Jewish Director of the Bank of England until the election of Alfred de Rothschild in 1868—the only Jew who has figured on the Board till our own day. (The old legend that Anthony da Costa and Sampson Gideon served in that same capacity in the eighteenth century cannot be substantiated from the records.)

The case was of course different (as has been indicated above) with the private banks, the heyday of which lay in the period which followed upon the conclusion of the Napoleonic Wars. Their influence, however, dwindled with the growth of the joint-stock banks in the middle of the century, which gave banking the form which the ordinary person knows and has experience of to-day. By a coincidence the great impetus in the establishment of these institutions, which undermined the position of the Jewish private banks, came from the brothers Péreire (grandsons of that Jacob Rodrigues Pereira who invented the system of teaching deaf-mutes). Among Saint-Simon's earliest and most devoted disciples, they felt that the instrument for the management of credit should be controlled by those for whose benefit credit was intended, and that in consequence the banking system should no longer be concentrated in private hands. In pursuance of this theory, they founded, first the Crédit Foncier, and then the Société Générale du Crédit Mobilier—the first joint-stock banks of the modern type. (The former was the prototype of the Agricultural Mortgage Banks which have continued to do good work for one hundred years, are still being imitated with beneficial results, and play an important part in the financial mechanism of modern states.) As bankers they were drawn insensibly into other interests, and a good deal of the railroad development of modern France was due to them. In this, their principal competitor was the House of Rothschild. This fact, combined with the disaster which the establishment of the joint-stock institutions brought upon many Jewish bankers, is yet another outstanding instance of the complete absence (contrary to the anti-Semitic allegation) of unity of aim among the Jewish capitalists. In England, the new methods owed a good deal to that doughty fighter for Jewish rights, Sir David Salomons, who was one of the founders of the Westminster Bank, and is described by the official historian of that institution as "one of the great architects of the whole joint-stock banking system".

Three names only are necessary to indicate how far Jews were associated with the process which made London the centre of the world's money-market. The Goldsmid family were the first to break down the old banking monopoly of loan-mongers, and to give the Government and the country the advantage of the best market-terms for money. It was the genius of Nathan Meyer Rothschild which made London the centre for financing the remarkable industrial expansion of the early Victorian era. Finally, the first Lord Swaythling (according to the impartial authority of the *Dictionary of National Biography*) helped to make London the clearing-house of the international money-market. It may thus be said that England is indebted to the Jew to a greater extent than to any other class of immigrant for the great edifice of her modern finance, which has stood up in recent years to a strain unexampled in modern history.

On more than one occasion, indeed, financiers who happened to be Jews (to speak of "Jewish Financiers" is to make an invidious and unjustifiable distinction) have done a great deal to restore public confidence at

R

times of strain, and sometimes to uphold public credit in a crisis. As long back as 1745, the Jewish merchants and magnates of the City took a particularly important part in maintaining confidence when the Young Pretender was advancing on London. They poured specie into the Bank of England; and they collaborated more than in proportion to their numbers in the association of merchants who bound themselves to accept bank notes at their face value, notwithstanding the general feeling of insecurity. Sampson Gideon it is said, parted with every guinea he possessed and pledged every stick of his property to support the public credit. Eighty years later, at the time of the 1825 panic, the Provincial Bank of Ireland passed a vote of thanks to one of its directors, Moses Montefiore, for his skilful management of its interests.

The work of the House of Rothschild in this connexion has been continuous. During this same crisis, the Duke of Wellington sent for Nathan Meyer Rothschild, the founder of the London house, to ask his advice. Two generations after, in 1886, the head of the Rothschild house was raised to the peerage in recognition of his courageous assistance to the Egyptian Exchequer at a critical moment, under circumstances which elicited cordial recognition in both Houses of Parliament. "Egypt was in imminent danger of bankruptcy," stated the Chancellor of the Exchequer. "In fact, it was saved only by monthly advances made by Messrs. Rothschild, upon no legal security, but simply on the security of a private note from the late Foreign Secretary." The firm enhanced its reputation by its conduct during the Baring crisis, in 1890, when the difficulties of that great house produced a Black Friday in the City, and every effort was needed to stave off a catastrophe. It was New Court which took the lead in the measures to save their rivals from disaster, and the actual scheme followed was that of another Jewish banker, Henry Raphael. And David Lloyd George, then Chancellor of the Exchequer, has paid a generous tribute to the manner in which his old political opponent, Lord Rothschild, received him and gave his collaboration on the outbreak of the War with Germany in 1914. So, too, in 1913, Paul M. Warburg successfully carried through the reorganisation of the American banking system (at which he had been working, together with Senator Aldrich, since 1911), thus thoroughly consolidating the currency and finances of the United States.

§v

It is too often overlooked that the vision and courage of the financial magnate—not necessarily altruistic in intention, but essential to the working of the economic system as we know it—is frequently responsible for achievements which may be of enormous benefit to the public. Failure does not win him sympathy: while success may win envy and obloquy. It is possible to cite here only a very few of many possible illustrations. Sir Isaac Lyon Goldsmid took a very prominent share in organising the London Docks, and thus making the modern port of London. Major Samuel Isaac carried through the Mersey Tunnel, after the project had long been in abeyance: while Sir Ernest Cassel financed one of the most gigantic, and most beneficial mechanical enterprises of modern times—the construction of the Assuan Dam. The latter, too, took a leading part in securing the construction of the first underground tube in the Metropolis, the Central London Railway, which he opened for traffic in 1900. Cecil Rhodes' earliest audacious enterprises in South Africa were rendered possible only through the support of the London Rothschilds, made available with a confidence which to some contemporaries seemed almost excessive.

We have seen above something of the share which Jews took in the great maritime discoveries. More than this, to be sure, was needed to open the ocean highways of the world to travellers and commerce—the enterprise of those who made international shipping the wonderfully-organised thing that it is to-day. In this, too, Jews played their part. The first ship which went to the Western hemisphere under the Venetian flag, at the close of the eighteenth century, and thus raised hopes that the glories of the Serenissima might be restored, was despatched by the firm of Treves de' Bonfili. Joseph Henry was the first person to build ships in Canada for the Transatlantic trade, thus founding the Canadian Mercantile Marine: while the earliest service between Montreal and Antwerp was established by Jesse Joseph. Emile Péreire, of Paris, took part in the organisation of the first French Transatlantic steamboat service. Joseph Samuda (as has been mentioned) was the pioneer in building iron vessels, before the days of steel, while Sir Alfred Yarrow, the great engineer and shipbuilder of the last generation, was semi-Jewish. The German Mercantile Marine was raised from nothing to the remarkable position which it enjoyed before 1914 by the genius of Albert Ballin, the only German in a prominent position who found the disgrace of his country's defeat too great to bear, and died at his own hand. Yet notwithstanding these services the Jewish influence in the world's shipping to-day is negligible: and even the Hamburg-Amerika Line, which owes its existence to Jewish genius, is now *Judenrein*.

Part of Sombart's thesis of the position of the Jew in modern Capitalism is that, while his part in the distributive trades has been disproportionately large, he has played an insignificant role in the so-called "heavy" industries. This is by no means justified by the facts. Many Eastern European Jews are coal-miners, like their neighbours; while the development of the mining industry in Germany (for example) owed a good deal to the Friedlaender-Fuld family. Similarly, Frankfort's pre-eminent position as a manufacturing city is largely due to the fact that it had an intelligent and industrious Jewish population. Nothing in its earlier history marked it out as a manufacturing (as distinct from financial) centre: but to-day the ring of factories that surrounds it owes its origin in a majority of cases to Jewish effort. (A secondary result of this was that for a long time Frankfort led Europe in Social Welfare work.) Another section of this work dealt with the participation of the Jews in establishing the chemical industry—Adolf Frank in Germany and the Mond family in England doing particularly important work in this connexion. The development of the electrical industry, with its far-reaching results on social as well as economic life, owed an enormous amount to Emil Rathenau, founder of the German Allgemeine Elektrizitäts Gesellschaft, who to-day may perhaps be said to have his counterpart in England in the person of Lord Hirst.

This type of activity may be paralleled all over the world, but a few illustrations only must suffice. One of the staple South African products to-day is mohair. This was originally exported only from Asia Minor, to which the breeding of the Angora goat was jealously confined by the Turks. Numerous experiments had been made to introduce the industry to South Africa, where climatic conditions were not dissimilar from those in Anatolia, but without success. At last, after the Crimean War, Adolph Mosenthal (a brother of the Austrian dramatist, Solomon von Mosenthal) managed to bring to the Colony, via England, a consignment of Angora goats, purchased with great difficulty in Turkey. The monetary loss on this original enterprise was considerable. Nevertheless, it was now demonstrated that the Angora goat could not only survive the long sea voyage, but could flourish in Cape Colony: and thus one of the great South African industries was established.

Participation in the South African mining industry was in the same tradition. When in 1885 rumours of new discoveries of gold arrived in Kimberley, they were not taken too seriously—they had been only too common before. However, Alfred Beit optimistically put £25,000 at the disposal of Joseph B. Robinson; and this was the beginning of the Rand mining industry and of Johannesburg. The work of the Jewish financiers in the subsequent development of the South African mining industry is well-known. Yet it is not so widely appreciated that they did much also to increase the amenities of the territory, and to make the city of Johannesburg what it is to-day. It was "Barney" Barnato who started the waterworks —an impossible and indeed chimerical venture, as it seemed then. Samuel Marks provided the means for damming the Vaal river, and planted orchards: while, with his brother-in-law, Isaac Lewis, he invested vast sums in collieries, breweries, glass, steel, brick and tile works, and in this manner founded the industry of the country. Johannesburg and the Rand are in a way a monument to Jewish enterprise.

Or let us take another of the "new" countries, which has provided refuge, livelihood and happiness to untold thousands of the surplus population of Europe. The part played by the Jews in the development of the American "Middle West" has never yet been properly investigated, but it was of incalculable importance. The stretches of territory involved were of vast extent. Hundreds of miles divided city from city. Communications were primitive, roads were at the beginning non-existent, travelling was dangerous. The pioneer from the Atlantic coast or the European immigrant who took up a holding in this area cut himself off from civilisation. It was the travelling pedlar who brought the amenities of life to him and made his life bearable. And, in most cases, these pedlars were Jews—to a large extent, Jewish refugees from the intolerant policies of Central Europe. When after some time conditions improved, these pedlars settled down in the rudimentary urban centre, where they opened the first primitive general stores. It is a significant fact, though its importance must not be exaggerated, that the first brick house in Chicago was built by a Jew. Sombart, indeed, avers that the Jewish traders constituted one in twenty of the pioneers who went out to conquer the American wilderness. This is a palpable exaggeration. But the fact remains that in the process which carried America forward from Atlantic to the Pacific, gave the Middle West its prosperity and established the great urban centres of the area, the work of the Jewish petty-trader was of supreme importance.

§VI

Much is said about the power of the financier (the Jewish financier, for some reason, above all) in deciding War. Less—incomprehensibly—is said about his power in deciding Peace. Yet his influence in the latter direction is the more usual: for the financier is more capable than most men of realising the terrible wastage of war, and the permanent impoverishment which almost invariably succeeds an international conflict.

This fact is brought out in a very marked fashion in the most authoritative *History of the House of*

Rothschild, by Count Corti, written by a non-Jew in a spirit which on the whole is far from friendly. There is no instance in this of the encouragement or even financing of a war on the part of this most famous of international Banking Houses, but there are several of the reverse. At the height of its power, in the early nineteenth century, it threw the whole of its weight, which was at the time very considerable, on the side of peace: and it seems that the intervention was sometimes decisive. This was so particularly during the crises of 1830 and 1840. In 1831, when the Austrian troops intervened in North Italy, James de Rothschild "did everything to allay the indignation which was flaring up in Paris, and to prevent any hasty action being taken." When in 1839 the Belgian Government applied to the House for an advance on the security of Treasury Bills, with a view to rearmament in preparation for hostilities with Holland, it encountered a point-blank refusal. "Our goodwill necessarily stops short of the point of providing the rod with which we are to be beaten, that is to say, providing the money wanted to make a war, which would destroy the credit that we are applying all our energies and resources to maintain", wrote the head of the Vienna branch. At the time of the Russian crisis in 1854, Von Hübner, the Austrian Ambassador, found James de Rothschild, of Paris, "positively demoralised" by fear of war. In 1866, the House did its best to avert the Austro-Prussian conflict, and three years later its heads were expressing "absolute panic" at the possibility of Franco-Prussian hostilities.

In the period before the war of 1914, the international influence of the House had dwindled, yet it continued to throw its influence on the side of peace. "If ever the archives of this period should be made available to the public, it will probably be possible to show, by documentary evidence too (what we can now deduce only from the consistency of the Rothschild policy during a century, as shown by various indications and the information derived from certain responsible persons) that immediately before the World War the Rothschilds . . . did everything possible to avert the catastrophe", writes Count Corti. A little is known of the part taken by Alfred de Rothschild at this time, to improve the prospects of world peace. It was he who succeeded in arranging the friendly encounter between Joseph Chamberlain and the German Ambassador, which took place under his roof, to discuss various points of friction between England and Germany without the encumbrance of diplomatic formality. His efforts were nobly seconded by two other Jews—Sir Ernest Cassel, who did everything possible to smooth the way for Haldane's despairing visit to Berlin in 1912, and, on the other side, Albert Ballin, head of the Hamburg-Amerika Line and founder of the German Mercantile Marine.

The classical example, constantly repeated, of the method in which hostilities can be exploited for the private benefit of the "financier" is the Waterloo Fable, which (notwithstanding the fact that it has been so ruthlessly exposed) continues to be repeated at intervals even to-day. The story goes that, in order to deceive the Stock Exchange, Nathan Meyer Rothschild followed Wellington to the field of Waterloo; that when he saw which way the battle was going he posted to London, depressed the market with hints of disaster and secretly bought the depressed stock; and that he thus contrived to clear several millions of pounds sterling when the official intelligence arrived. An alternative account tells how the news was received by pigeon post, of which the House was the first to make use.

In point of fact, Nathan Rothschild was nowhere near the field of battle, remaining in London throughout these critical days, and leaving for Belgium, *under instruction from the British Treasury*, only on June 20th—two days after Wellington's overwhelming victory. It was true that, owing to his admirable news-service, he had learned the result of the great encounter before anyone else in England. But, far from keeping it to himself or profiting by it, he hastened to communicate with the Prime Minister, Lord Liverpool, who refused to believe him. As for the allegation that he had depressed the market by hinting at a British disaster, the truth is that from the first (as the reports in the contemporary Press shew) he had bought openly and largely, in the face of an incredulous and falling market.

An episode of English history more glorious than the Battle of Waterloo was the abolition of slavery—"among the three or four perfectly virtuous pages in the history of nations", as Lecky called it. This culminated in the Bill of 1833 for the abolition of slavery in the British dominions—especially, of course, in the West Indies. A sum of £20,000,000 was necessary for payment as compensation to the slave-owners. It is significant that the finding of this amount was Nathan Meyer Rothschild's last great operation, before his death in 1836.[1]

His son, Baron Lionel de Rothschild, inherited no small share of his business acumen, and something more

[1] It is not without its significance that one of the few planters in the West Indies who anticipated Government action by doing something for the manumission of slaves was Isaac Simon, grandfather of the late Serjeant Sir John Simon, the eminent lawyer and philanthropist. This was not unnatural; for the slave legislation of the Bible, itself remarkable for its humanity (cf. Exodus XXI. 26f; Deuteronomy XXIII. 16) had been yet further developed by tradition. Thus the precedent of the English "Somerset Case" was anticipated at least fifteen centuries earlier by a Rabbinical decision, that an escaped slave, whether Jew or Gentile, automatically regained his freedom on touching Palestinian soil.

than his public spirit. He achieved a "particularly honoured position" in the financial life of Great Britain when in March, 1847, he offered the Government his financial assistance for dealing with the miserable condition of Ireland—then at the lowest point of its misfortunes. The Irish Famine Loan of £8,000,000 was subsequently raised without any view to profit through his agency, in collaboration with his greatest competitors, the house of Baring. Baron Lionel (who in 1858 became the first Jewish Member of Parliament) will be permanently remembered in the history of the British Empire for the public-spirited manner in which he came to the assistance of Lord Beaconsfield in 1875, when he advanced the money for the purchase of the Suez Canal shares, and took all risks pending the approval of Parliament. But for this action, it is doubtful whether Beaconsfield's *coup* could have succeeded.

§VII

The most important economic function of the Jews in our day has been in a field very far removed from that of finance. In various branches of industry, they have played an important share in that process—bound up with mass-production and improved distribution—which has wrought in our day a profound sociological change. Time was—and not so very long ago—when the rift between the rich and poor was more profound by far than it is at present, and when even the lower middle classes had to content themselves with the ugliest, coarsest, and barest necessities of life. The environment of the labouring classes was even more drab. Luxuries were completely out of the poor man's reach: his amusements were primitive: his clothing was coarse and shapeless, and could seldom be replaced: the division between the "classes" and "masses" was deep and unbridgeable.

In the course of the last generation, this has altered fundamentally. The poor man—and to an even greater extent the poor woman—dresses in the same manner as the rich, even though the cut and the materials may be inferior. His household amenities are not dissimilar. His diversions are much the same, even though he may have to wait a little longer until his local place of resort brings within his reach, for a few pence, what has been available elsewhere at high prices some weeks before. The radio provides the same entertainment for all. Even the methods of transport which were once a sign of distinction, are now within the reach of the humblest purse.

In this profound social revolution Jews have played an intimate part. It is the Jewish tailor, for example, who has broken down the sartorial gap between rich and poor. The persecutions in Russia at the close of the last century first reduced to beggary, and then drove into exile, large numbers of Jews, without resources and for the most part without a trade. In the Anglo-Saxon countries, a very high proportion of the refugees sought a livelihood in the tailoring industry—one for which they had a certain amount of proclivity, and in which Jews were already engaged to some extent. The influx of cheap labour, coupled with an intensive organisation (the so-called "Boston System") made a complete revolution in the tailoring industry. The sewing-machine became in their hands a scientific instrument of production: minute subdivision of labour was organised: the cost of manufacture was immensely reduced: and in consequence, the price of clothing was brought down to a fraction of its previous level, coming for the first time within the reach of every artisan's pocket. The Old

Clothes dealer (mainly Jewish heretofore, incidentally—there was no question of ejecting non-Jews from their employment) lost his importance. No longer was it necessary for the working-man to make use of the reconditioned garments of his social superiors: for the same amount, or less, he could periodically purchase a new suit. The reduction in the cost of women's clothing was even more striking. The process was repeated, and mainly by the same agency, in the boot-making and furniture-making industries. What had previously been the greatest distinguishing mark between the various social strata disappeared, and the beneficial effect on the morale of the labouring classes was incalculable. This epoch-making change was assisted by the great development in the distributive trades, and the growth of the single-price store, in which also the Jews played a considerable part (though not perhaps so considerable as is often alleged). By this means, prices in all commodities were vastly reduced, and one-time extravagancies came to be considered indispensable necessities of existence in every class.

In other respects too, Jews collaborated solidly in this far-reaching change. A generation ago, their participation in the catering industry in England brought the "restaurant" within the reach of the modest pocket, and was a remarkable boon to city workers of that generation. More important was the part which they played in what is termed the "entertainment industry". The function which Jews have filled in the development of the Cinema—as actors, inventors, technicians, producers and exhibitors—is enormous. They realised its implications when it was generally regarded as no more than an amusing novelty: and it was to a large extent under Jewish guidance that it became the great institution, and the universal amenity of life, that it is to-day[1]. Of the great levelling agencies of our time, it is only in the automobile industry and its popularisation that the part of Jews has been of negligible importance.

The implications of this change are enormous, though hardly appreciated as yet. The "sansculotte" has disappeared. It is no longer possible to regard the upper classes and the lower as divided by an insurmountable rift, in quite the same sense as in the past. The social life of the two, at least, is now conceived on very much the same lines, differing in scale rather than in nature. Through these recent developments, in short, the last generation has witnessed a sociological change unexampled in history. It is the great peaceful revolution of our time, and among the greatest stabilising forces in the modern world. In assisting to bring this about, rather than in a fictitious financial predominance, lies the real importance of the role of the Jew in modern economic life, and one of his most significant contributions to civilisation in recent times.

Appendix to Chapter X

THE JEWS IN AGRICULTURE

THE rapidity of the Jewish economic readjustment, once external pressure was removed, has been remarkable. True, the effect of fifteen centuries of repression cannot be shaken off in one or two generations.

---

[1] In this connexion, it is worth while to bear in mind the fact that, on the technical side, the modern cinema is indebted to Jewish genius fully as much as on the administrative. It is sufficient to recall that Levi ben Gershom was a pioneer in the development of the camera (*supra*, p. 171); the younger Herschel in the evolution of photography (p. 172); Berliner was the inventor of the microphone (p. 184); Lieben of the amplifier (p. 185); Lippman of colour photography (*ibid*).

But a beginning has been made, and its progress has been striking.

In the Hanoverian period, the majority of the Jews in England (as on the Continent) were probably engaged in petty trading, peddling, and old-clothes dealing. The testimony of scores of caricatures, engravings, popular songs, is sufficient to prove this fact. On the other hand, they were excluded almost completely from the professions : and it was generally urged by the opponents of Jewish emancipation that, until they shewed a greater interest in these more polite and useful callings, they would not make good their claim to be considered good and useful citizens.

A couple of generations were sufficient to wipe away this reproach. Nowadays, the positions are reversed. The Jewish pedlar is to-day non-existent, or almost so, in the areas in which he was previously best known. The itinerant Jewish old-clothes dealer, formerly a characteristic figure in the London streets, is completely extinct. The Jewish pawnbroker, a figure of the music-hall not so long ago, is now said to have disappeared entirely in the city of London. At the same time, the range of Jewish economic activity has immensely broadened; and the influx into the professions has grown to such proportions that great-grandchildren of those critics referred to above are now complaining of an over-great tendency in this direction. One point, however, is overlooked in this criticism : a man employs a doctor, a lawyer, or a dentist, not because of his race or his creed, but because it is anticipated that he will bring to bear the best qualifications and the most conscientious service.

The case of agriculture illustrates even more strikingly the progress which has been made in the economic re-adjustment of Jewish life. An urge to the soil has invariably manifested itself in Jewish history, immediately external pressure has been removed. There were Jewish agriculturalists in Russia under the Old Regime, though under the May Laws of 1882 they were uprooted from their holdings. There were old-established Jewish farmers established in South Germany, indistinguishable from their neighbours excepting by their religion: but the Nazi regime has made life impossible for them. In free lands, however, the process continues.

Jewish agricultural settlements exist to-day all over the world—in Russia, Poland, Roumania, even Siberia. In Canada, for example, there are a number of settlements, under the guidance of the Jewish Colonial Association: and 500,000 bushels of wheat are produced each year by the Canadian Jewish farmers. In the Argentine, there are whole areas covered by Jewish agricultural settlements, with their own vigorous community life. In the United States, at least 100,000 Jews look to agriculture for their livelihood and "more Jews are thinking to-day in terms of the farm than in any other period in the whole of American history". Above all, the return to Palestine, under the inspiration of the Zionist movement, is coupled with the ideal of the return to the land. Lack of funds and local obstructionism are responsible for the fact that the process has not been so complete as was at one time hoped: but, even so, some 15% of Palestinian Jewry is rooted on the soil. (In England, it may be mentioned for the purpose of comparison, only 7% of the general population is thus engaged.) The total number of Jews throughout the world who look to agriculture for their livelihood is now nearly 700,000; and the number is increasing almost daily. The phenomenon is unique in the world to-day, where the general tendency is not towards, but away from, the land.

It is nevertheless curious, in view of the long Jewish exclusion from the soil and his comparatively recent re-association with it, that services so outstanding have been made by Jewish agricultural experts. One may start at the commencement of the alphabet with Aaron Aaronson, one of a devoted family who rendered conspicuous service to Great Britain during the conquest of Palestine in 1917–18. (His sister, Sarah Aaronson, was killed for that reason by the Turks.) Aaronson, who founded the Agricultural Experimental Station near the ruins of the Crusading castle at Athlit, discovered in Palestine "wild wheat", which has been used extensively in the United States and elsewhere to strengthen the cultivated plant. More sensational were the discoveries of Fritz Haber, the chemical genius whose investigations (as has been seen above, p. 177) notably assisted Germany between 1914 and 1918, but whom an ungrateful Fatherland compelled to die in exile after the advent of the National-Socialist Regime. His greatest service to mankind was his discovery of the method of the fixation of nitrogen—the production, that is, of synthetic ammonia from the nitrogen in the atmosphere. From this, nitrates for fertilisation could be extracted, and were hence made available to the world in unlimited quantity. Thus was obviated the risk which serious thinkers, such as Sir William Brookes, once voiced, that when the deposits of natural fertilisers were exhausted, the world would be faced with starvation.

It must be added that the use of potash for agricultural purposes was due in the first instance to the activity of the German Jew Adolf Frank. He collaborated in his later years with the young Nicodem Caro, whose discovery of cyanamide, the first synthetic nitrogenous fertiliser, and new methods for the production of hydrogen are similarly of considerable importance for the development of scientific agriculture.

These discoveries were carried a stage further by Jacob G. Lipman, Dean of the Faculty of Agriculture at the Rutgers University in the U.S.A., whose principal work has been centred upon the determination of the nature of the chemical action produced by bacteria in making both organic and inorganic components of soils available for food. The bacteria which he has turned loose on the farms of the world, it is said, have more

s

than made up for the Jews' failure (not of their own making) to work on the land.

Finally, mention should be made of that idealistic Polish-American business-man, David Lubin, who, after various adventures and travels, gained a competence by inventing a device for the extremely prosaic purpose of rivetting buttons on overalls. He was thus enabled to fulfil his ambition of engaging in fruit-farming. But he found a complete absence of organisation in agriculture in all its branches. Every man worked for his own hand; experience was never pooled; and as a result there was a shocking degree of wastage in every department. After studying and comparing agricultural methods in Europe, Lubin published in 1900 his work, *Let there be Light* (confessedly based upon Maimonides' *Guide to the Perplexed*), in which moral and practical idealism were curiously mixed.

From now on, he set himself to work out the solution of the agricultural problem from the standpoint of the farmer as well as of the producer. He laid his views before the Agricultural Department in his own country, but received no encouragement; he travelled about Europe trying to interest official circles, but met with opposition and indifference at every turn. But at last he obtained an interview with Luigi Luzzatti, the Italian Jewish statesman, at that time a member of the Cabinet. The latter realised the practical importance of the suggestions implied in Lubin's idealistic approach, and secured him an audience with the King of Italy. In an hour's conference, Vittorio Emmanuele was won over to Lubin's theories and called an international conference to consider his plans. In 1905, the representatives of forty governments (characteristically excluding that of the U.S.A.) met in Rome, and the International Agricultural Institute, which has since done untold good, and without which the state of agriculture in the world to-day would be even more chaotic than it is, was established. In October, 1934, fifteen years after Lubin's death, a tribute to his memory was paid by the delegates from the sixty-three nations then represented in the institute: and the name of this Polish Jewish immigrant is commemorated, not only by a tablet in the institute which he founded, but also by a street in Rome.

Future enquirers may attach importance not only to the fact of the reconstitution of Jewish agricultural life in Palestine, but also to the type of the life that is emerging. The self-sacrificing devotion of the pioneers; the influence of the ideas of A. D. Gordon, that national regeneration can come only from personal labour and physical contact with the soil; the enthusiasm for social justice which inspires the new type of settlement, such as the co-operative colony, the *Moshav*, and the communal settlement, the *Kvutzah*, which have realised such outstanding triumphs; are all developments the significance of which is by no means restricted to Palestine. Above all, the new settlers have demonstrated for the first time in history that a peasantry can attain as high a level of cultural life and expression as the most sophisticated urban dweller. It is possible to discern in all this the kernel of a future contribution to rural perhaps even more important than the past contribution to urban civilisation.[1]

[1] It should perhaps be pointed out that a consideration for physical activities is by no means a new thing among Jews. Even in the Ghetto period, there was a definite proclivity, and sometimes even a superiority, in various fields of sport. A Rabbi of the third century maintained that it is a religious duty for a man to teach his son to swim. Later, fencing-masters were commonly Jews. Modern students are becoming interested in a mediaeval Rabbi's account of tennis as it was played by his coreligionists in Mantua. Jews took part in athletic contests at Rosenau in the fifteenth century, in the foot-races, jumps, putting the weight and so on. A particularly notable figure was the Jew Ott, champion wrestler in Germany under Frederick III (1440–1493), who even wrote a handbook on the art—as also did one Andreas Jud Liegnitzer. It is clear from all this that (even before the days of the great Anglo-Jewish boxers of the 18th century, Mendoza and the rest, and the champions in tennis etc. in our own day) the intellectualisation of the Jew was not exclusive of other interests.

CHAPTER XI

PUBLIC LIFE

§1

EXTERNAL circumstances are responsible for the fact that the Jews' participation in public life began only at a comparatively recent date. For centuries, Church and State had combined to inveigh against the occupation by Jews of any position of authority, and the exclusion remained effective until a hundred and fifty years ago. The first breach in the theory was made by the American Declaration of Independence, in 1775; it was introduced into Europe with the Declaration of the Rights of Man in 1789, followed by the formal emancipation of the French Jews in 1790. The following eighty years saw the gradual imitation of this example in Western Europe. Thus, in England, municipal rights were conceded in 1831–1835, and Jews were first admitted to the House of Commons in 1858, and to the Lords in 1886. After 1870, Emancipation was established, in name at least, in all the so-called "civilised" world. The only exception was Russia, where persecution continued in an exaggerated form, accompanied by frequent outbreaks of violence, as long as the authority of the Czars was maintained.

For this reason, any examination of the part played by Jews in public life after 70 A.D. must necessarily be restricted almost entirely to very recent times. In the Roman Empire, of course, exclusion was by no means complete: and we find Jews participating amply in municipal life, and the late Judaean rulers honoured as benefactors by Athens and other centres of Greek culture. In Moslem Spain, Jews occasionally rose to the rank of Vizier, directing the affairs of state: and even under Christian rulers, Jewish physicians, scientists, or fiscal experts sometimes enjoyed considerable influence. The same was the case in Turkey at the height of its power, in the middle of the sixteenth century. Converted Jews, too, occasionally rose to positions of authority. But, broadly speaking, it was not until the nineteenth century that the Jew had any opportunity for political self-expression.[1]

This fact should be taken in mind in any consideration of the irresponsible theory which has been summed up in the phrase "The Jews as Revolutionary Leaven": that is, that every upheaval in the history of modern Europe may be traced to the action of this one section of the population. The prototype of the modern Revolution was the "Great Rebellion" in England: but when

---

[1] There was indeed in France, at the close of the sixteenth century, a little group of men of Jewish origin who profoundly influenced the course of political thought. Best remembered to-day is Michel de Montaigne, whose mother, as has been indicated elsewhere, belonged to a crypto-Jewish family settled in France. His contemporary Jean Bodin, one of the most remarkable of French political thinkers, was reproached in his lifetime for his Jewish affinities and associates, and his mother, too, apparently belonged to a Marrano family. His great work, *Six livres de la République*, written as a reply to Machiavelli's *Principe*, champions the idea of a monarchy tempered by the States General, and is the outstanding vindication of the Constitutional Monarchy of its day. (Noteworthy, too, is the generous toleration in matters of religion, which he expresses in his *Heptaplomeres*.) More in the public eye than either of these was Michel de l'Hôpital, who, as Chancellor of France, exerted himself to the utmost to bring about a more generous spirit in questions of faith and to stop the bloodshed which had so long been the scourge of the country. He, too, is said to have been of Jewish origin. Thus the three chief intellectual voices of the party known as the "politiques", who opposed religious fanaticism, wished to suppress party faction and endeavoured to set up a strong monarchy to save France from further tribulations, were in part of Jewish blood.

this took place there was in this country only the merest handful of Marrano merchants, unable to profess Judaism and too timid to meddle in public affairs. One of the few Jewish comments upon the situation that has survived is that of a Marrano of Rouen, who expressed the conviction that "none of his Religion would ever adventure themselves among such bloody traitors as had murdered their own King".

The myth of the Jew as Revolutionary Leaven takes as its serious point of departure the French Revolution. Whether Jews would need to apologise for any share which they might have taken in it is a question upon which there is no need to express an opinion, in view of the fact that their role was almost entirely passive. In Paris, always the nerve-centre of the Revolution, no Jewish community was yet tolerated, and none of the few individuals living there played a part worth mentioning in Revolutionary activities. Indeed, the only French Jew who enjoyed the slightest prominence at the period was a moderate—Abraham Furtado, of Bordeaux, a close friend of the Girondin leaders, who narrowly escaped the guillotine. Others of his co-religionists were less fortunate, nine of them being executed during the Reign of Terror. Meanwhile, during the supremacy of the Goddess of Reason, synagogues were pillaged, Jewish observances were forbidden, the Sabbath had to be publicly desecrated, and Jewish ministers of religion were dragged to the Temple of the new state Deity to do homage.

There was one place, indeed, where the Jews enjoyed considerable influence during the Terror—St. Esprit, the Ghetto suburb of Bayonne, renamed Jean-Jacques Rousseau by the extremists. Here, Jews were so numerous on the Comité de Surveillance as to be almost in control. It is significant that, while heads were rolling across the river at Bayonne in an intermittent blood-bath, not a single capital sentence was passed in the suburb, where there were tokens of a humanity and moderation hardly to be found elsewhere in France.

That the Jew traditionally nourishes a feeling for equalitarianism admits neither argument no apology. An observer who cannot be charged with pro-Jewish sympathy, Hilaire Belloc, has indicated what he considers to be the foundation of this Jewish democratic instinct (*The Battlefield*, p. 134): "The Jew to-day in the slums of our great cities has kept intact this sense of equality which is coincident with the feeling of human dignity— for human dignity is a product of religion where religion binds the individual to a supreme god; and the Jewish millionaire does not, like *our* rich men, mistake his wealth for excellence, nor do his fellow Jews think him the greater for it, but only more fortunate."

If there exists a Jewish point of view in politics, it cannot be better illustrated than from the views of Don Isaac Abrabanel, the Spanish scholar-statesman of the fifteenth century who assisted in financing Columbus' first expedition, and was perhaps the only Jewish author of the Middle Ages to deal explicitly with political problems. In his commentaries on Deuteronomy and Judges, he formulates a well-rounded political theory. Monarchy, is, according to him, a human (not a divine) institution. His personal leanings were in favour of the constitutional form of government, such as he saw and admired in Venice, Florence, and so on. Yet he denied the right of subjects to rebel even against the most obvious grievances: and (as he informs us) he maintained this position on more than one occasion at Court, in conversation with Christian thinkers who held the opposite. "The Law of the land is our Law," taught a Talmudic authority sixteen centuries ago; and this has ever since been a cardinal principle of Judaism.

A recent detailed and impartial review of the biographies included in the *Encyclopaedia Britannica*[1] emphasises the point. Among the statesmen of first importance who are accorded entries in that work, fifteen only are of Jewish origin. Of these, nine are reformers (including some revolutionaries) while six may be classed as conservative. This conclusion is all the more remarkable if one bears in mind the fact that this particular survey excluded the United States and England, in which the conservative element is noticeably greater.

For it is perhaps only in these and one or two other politically advanced countries that the Jewish political genius has been able to find its natural level and direction. Where the Jew has been oppressed, deprived of economic opportunity, and excluded from public life, it was inevitable for him to throw his weight on the side of those parties which were endeavouring to effect a modification in the existing regime. Hence the activity of Jews in all the national movements of the nineteenth century, in which they imagined that their salvation lay. Hence the fact that in pre-war Russia, Jews were active in all the parties of the Left; though less by far among the Bolsheviks than among the moderates, the Constitutional Democrats and Mensheviks. Similarly, in countries where the clerical movement is strong, Jews have inevitably thrown themselves into opposition to those parties the policies of which must necessarily, though not perhaps intentionally, add to the difficulties of the Jewish position.

§II

The political movements with which the Jews have been associated out of proportion to their numbers

---

[1] "The Distribution of European Genius" in *The Nineteenth Century*, July 1936.

have hence not been (in general) Revolutionary but
National. Thus, they were particularly prominent
among the fighters for German unity, for Italian independence, for Hungarian self-government, in the middle
years of the nineteenth century.

It was in the great National movement of 1848, when
throughout Europe the forces of democracy shook off
the shackles of absolutism, and the peoples insisted on
their natural right 'of self-government, that the Jews
first had the opportunity to prove that they were
prepared to shoulder the responsibilities of the citizen-
ship of which they claimed the rights. Everywhere,
they took a leading share in the struggle and in the
sacrifice. In France, where the movement began,
Adolphe Crémieux was a member of the Provisional
Government. In Germany Johann Jacoby (who was
subsequently to raise an almost solitary voice in opposition to the annexation of Alsace Lorraine) had dared to
ask the King of Prussia for a constitution as early as
1841, and now, after a term of imprisonment, was once
more to the fore. Several Jews were killed in the street
fighting in Berlin. They were prominent, too, in the
Vorparlament of Frankfort, which anticipated German
unity. Here, the convert Eduard von Simson (later to
be President of the Reichstag and Reichsgericht) was
President ; the Austrian poet, Moritz Hartmann, was one
of the most striking figures ; and one of the Vice-presi-
dents, Gabriel Riesser, a stalwart champion of Jewish
emancipation, was with Simson among the delegation
which offered the crown of a united Germany to Frederick
William IV.

In the March Days in Vienna, Jews were similarly
active. The dare-devil Adolf Fischof was at the head of
the popular movement, which was inspired by Moritz
Hartmann, the poet and the famous journalist Ignaz

Kuranda: and several more were among the martyrs to the cause of liberty. (It was noteworthy, however, that the detested Prime Minister, Baron Doblhoff, owed his life to another Jewish leader of the popular party, who smuggled him away, at considerable personal risk, to a private house.) In Hungary, a Jewish regiment fought under Kossuth, and many Jews followed their leader into exile (such as Solomon Schiller-Szinessy, subsequently Reader in Rabbinic in Cambridge). From every part of Central Europe, indeed, Jewish refugees emigrated when the popular movement was suppressed, and it became evident that 1848 had brought no more than a false dawn. The United States benefited in particular; it is hardly an exaggeration to say that the great Jewish community of that country is a monument to the liberty-loving enthusiasm of Central European Jewry during those years of reaction.

In Italy, in particular, the part of the Jews in the *Risorgimento* was remarkable. In every part of the Peninsula, they took the lead in the movement to shake off the hated Austrian yoke. There were at least eight Jews among Garibaldi's *Thousand* (nine, if we include one romantic English co-religionist, Charles Alexander Scott). For many years, Cavour's closest collaborator was Isaac Artom, of whom he wrote, "He has a remarkable, mature mind, indefatigable zeal, golden character" (he was subsequently to take a prominent share in the public life of the united Italy for which he had worked). In exile, Mazzini had no friends more devoted than the Nathan family of London.

For a time the dramatic centre of the whole movement was Venice, where for a few months in 1848–9 the pale ghost of the Serenissima was revived in Victorian costume. *The Times*—an unfriendly critic at that period —paid eloquent testimony to the spirit which infused the leaders. From February, 1848, to the present hour, it wrote, on September 1st, 1849, "there has been no popular movement conducted with so much dignity and maintained with such unswerving decision as that of Venice".

Nor, even in that year of patriotic fervour, was there one in which the Jewish element was more prominent. The leader of the movement was Daniel Manin, one of the purest of Italian patriots, who bore the same surname as the last Doge. The coincidence was, however, purely accidental: he did not belong to an old patrician family, but was the grandson of a converted Veronese couple, Samuel and Allegra Medina, who had assumed the name of Manin in honour of their sponsor at baptism. There are few figures in the whole of nineteenth-century history so pure and noble as that of this last Venetian hero. Declared Jews seconded him eagerly—including several who were subsequently to play an illustrious part in the history of United Italy. In the National Guard, which fought bravely for the defence of the city, there were a dozen Jewish officers, and privates in proportion, one of whom was among the first to fall. Among the members of the National Assembly were three Jews, the number subsequently rising to seven; and they included two Rabbis, one of whom introduced into it one of the most dramatic motions in favour of Liberty. Leone Pincherle, who had played a prominent part in the events of the past heroic days, was Minister of Agriculture and Commerce in the Provisional Government; while Isaac Pesaro Maurogonato was Minister of Finance, his meticulous administration calling forth the grudging admiration of the Austrians themselves after the recapture. (He was subsequently Vice-President of the Italian Chamber of Deputies, and in 1884, when the Government recognised the Venetian loans of 1848, turned over his claims to the municipality of Venice.) The "Forty" who were exiled from the city with Manin for their share in the Revolution included a number of members of the group to which he traced his origin. This one case is recounted here in detail; but the tale may be duplicated for every part of Italy, and indeed of Europe, during that heroic period.

Contrary to what might be imagined, the case was the same even among the hyper-orthodox, caftanned Jews of Poland. Here, as early as 1794, they had participated in Kosciusko's revolt. A certain Berek, who held the rank of Colonel, had raised among them a troop of light horse, which was almost wiped out by Suvarov's troops during the siege of Warsaw. During the revolt against Russian misgovernment in 1830, Berek's son, Joseph Berkovitz, took the lead, and summoned his co-religionists to arms; with the result that a special "bearded" section of the Metropolitan Guard was formed in Warsaw, comprising 850 Jews. So also in the revolution of 1860–1863, the Jews of every school of thought took their place by the side of their fellow-Poles: and two Rabbis were sent to prison for daring to march in the funeral procession, behind the coffins of the demonstrators who had been cut down by the Cossacks. The artificial demarcation between Jewish and Catholic Poles had not yet been crystallised.

Adolphe Crémieux (who has been mentioned above) was perhaps the most typical, as he was the most brilliant Jewish statesman of the Age of Emancipation. From the days of the First Empire to the reign of Louis Philippe, he was one of France's great orators and advocates. In 1848, he became Minister of Justice, and it was due to his assiduity that the Royal Family left Paris unscathed. From that date almost to his death, 32 years later, he was one of the outstanding figures in

French public life. An old man of over seventy on the fall of the Second Empire, he was nevertheless forced by public opinion to take a part in the Government of National Defence,[1] and at this time offered a great part of his property to pay the War Indemnity imposed (and ruthlessly exacted) by the Germans. But his name is associated above all with humanitarian achievement. On writing to congratulate the American people on the emancipation of the slaves, he prided himself on the fact that he had been a member of the government of 1848 which had proclaimed the abolition of slavery in the French dominions: and perhaps the most important measure for which he was himself responsible, as Minister of Justice, was the abolition of the capital penalty for political offences.

The instances which have been assembled in the foregoing pages are by no means exhaustive. Illustrations of the sort may be multiplied to an almost wearisome degree. (They may indeed be carried back for half a century more, to the struggle for American Independence, in which the 2,000 Jews then resident in North America played a disproportionate role.) What has been said is, however, sufficient to demonstrate the participation of the Jews in the National—as distinct from Nationalistic—movements of the last century. Much the same was true in the popular governments which were set up all over Central Europe at the close of 1918, as indeed in Governments of National Emergency generally (such as those of 1870 in France, of 1931 in England, and so on). In settled periods, Jews have found a more catholic outlet for their political sympathies, which have under no other circumstances been confined to one party.

[1] He was a colleague in this of his former Secretary, Gambetta. There is no ground whatever for believing that the latter was a Jew, as is so often said; but there would be no reason for apologising were this indeed the case.

§III

One of the most prominent figures in German public
life, in the middle of the last century, was Ferdinand
Lassalle, whose influence is traceable not only in the
political conceptions of all Western countries, but also
(paradoxical though it may seem) in the ideology of the
Nazi party. He began his public life in the battle for
liberty in 1848: but in prison he came to the conclusion
that the wrongs of the masses lay more in the economic
than in the political sphere. From 1861 to his premature
death, in a duel, in 1864, he swept Germany with his
campaign of Economic Democracy. In 1863, he founded
the first Workers' Party—the General German Working-
man's Association—out of which grew the party of the
Social Democrats, or Socialists. In return for the
franchise and social welfare legislation, he was prepared
to support even Bismarck. On the Continent, his was
perhaps the first authoritative voice of the nineteenth
century to assert, notwithstanding the angry resentment
which his views aroused, the right of the masses to a
voice in the government. He was barely forty years
old at the time of his death: but he had prepared the
ground for a new attitude in Europe.

Lassalle's views seemed extreme in his day. After
him, the political interests of German Jews, if generally
inclining to the left, were predominantly moderate.
When in 1890 the ban on Socialism was removed and it
came once more into the open, it had lost its revolutionary
character—mainly owing to Eduard Bernstein, the
theoretician of the movement as a reformist doctrine.
The revolutionary ardour had clearly disappeared.[1]

[1] Elsewhere Jews contributed during this period a few important
names, but not many leaders, to the Left wing in politics. In France,

Thereafter, the tendency of the emancipated Jew in public life throughout Europe was predominantly liberal. In Germany, the mass of the Jewish population, now that its rights were (as it thought) won, inclined to the National Liberal Party. The founder of this, indeed (in the teeth of Bismarck's frenzied opposition) was the Jew, Eduard Lasker, who was ably assisted by Ludwig Bamberger and some others. This tendency in politics continued to attract the sympathies of the average German Jew. Lasker's greatest title to fame was achieved in a non-partisan role, on that memorable occasion in 1873 when, from the tribune of the Reichstag, he thundered against the "promotion swindle" and the misleading of the public by printing great names on the prospectuses of new ventures. This speech, one of the strongest ever delivered in the German Parliament, became historical and had wide repercussions.

In England, Jewish emancipation had been opposed by the Conservatives and supported by the Liberals. It was therefore inevitable that the earliest Jewish members of Parliament were all adherents of the latter party. But at the time of the Liberal Unionist split, Jewish public opinion veered round, and some of the

---

Olinde and Eugène Rodrigues, with their banker cousins Péreire, were among the earliest and most fervent supporters of Saint-Simon, and a few others (such as Gaston Crémieux and Alfred Joseph Naquet) were prominent in the troubled period which succeeded the Franco-Prussian war. (Later, the aristocratic Léon Blum was to be France's first Socialist premier.) In Holland, there was Henri Pollack, one of the organisers of the Trade Union movement in that country: in Austria the Adlers, father and son: in the United States, Morris Hillquit, one of the organisers of American Socialism, and Samuel Gompers, creator of the American Federation of Labour, who was for nearly half a century the dominant and moderating influence in the working-class movement. England can furnish the names of several Liberal leaders during this period, but none of real prominence belonging to the Left wing in politics. To the German names mentioned above should, of course, be added that of Moses Hess, who was unusual in that, like Lassalle, he retained his fidelity to Judaism.

outstanding representatives of English Jewry accompanied Chamberlain into the Conservative camp. From that period, the distribution between the opposing wings in politics reflected more evenly the general political tendency of the country. Thus, while in 1906 the Liberal members of Parliament who were Jews outnumbered the Conservatives by three to one (12 : 4) the numbers four years later were approximately equal (8 : 7).

Jewish ministers of the Crown have been appointed by Prime Ministers of all political complexions. If the Conservative party can point to no great public servants who belonged to the Jewish community of the calibre of the Marquess of Reading or Viscount Samuel, this does no more than accentuate the natural tendency pointed out above; while on the other hand the Liberal party can provide no parallel to Benjamin Disraeli.[1]

[1] A list of the British statesmen of Jewish descent of the last century embraces both of the great political parties impartially. Hugh Culling Eardley Childers (one of the fathers of Australian education) who was Secretary for War and Chancellor of the Exchequer under Gladstone, was a descendant of the eighteenth-century capitalist, Sampson Gideon. Ralph Bernal, the famous collector, who was Chairman of Committees in the House of Commons from about 1830 to 1850, was the scion of a family which had been prominent in the Spanish and Portuguese community in London: his son, Ralph Bernal Osborne, the famous wit, was Secretary of the Admiralty from 1852 to 1858, during the Crimean War. A more vigorous figure was Sir Henry Drummond Wolff, who with Churchill, Gorst and Balfour formed the "fourth party" from 1880 to 1885, and was founder of the Primrose League. His father was Joseph Wolff, the famous missionary, and his daughter was "Lucas Cleeve", the novelist. He was counterbalanced on the other side of the House by Farrer Herschell, also the son of a missionary, who was Lord Chancellor under Gladstone and Rosebery.

Sir Lopes Massey Lopes (head of an old Spanish family converted at the beginning of the nineteenth century, and brother of the famous Judge, Lord Ludlow) was a Civil Lord of the Admiralty in the Conservative administration of 1874–1880, though his main interests were in agriculture. Of professing Jews, there were Sir George Jessel, Solicitor-General under Gladstone in 1871–73 and subsequently Master of the Rolls (an office later filled by Sir Archibald Levin Smith, whose mother had been a Jewess): Baron de Worms, the Admirable Crichton of the Conservative Party, who filled various under-secretaryships under Salisbury: and Sir Julian Goldsmid, a very successful Deputy

So completely impartial a distribution was perhaps confined to the English-speaking world, in which effective emancipation has gone furthest and where for a long time past no reactionary party in the Continental sense has existed. Elsewhere, the Liberal and Left tendency is perhaps stronger; yet nowhere has it been exclusive. Indeed, it is everywhere possible to point to Conservative leaders of great influence, who were of Jewish extraction.

In the opinion of some competent observers, the most influential statesman of Jewish birth in the nineteenth century was Disraeli's German contemporary, Friedrich Julius Stahl. His was a fairly commonplace career in the Germany of those days. Brought up as a Jew, he found the inevitable difficulties in his path and was baptized at the age of seventeen. He became one of the best-known German jurists of his day, devoting himself especially to the philosophy of law; his great *Die Philosophie des Rechts nach geschichtlicher Ansicht* running into several editions. When in 1845 the Revolutionary agitation broke out in Germany, Stahl (unlike the majority of Jews) threw himself wholeheartedly into politics on the conservative (perhaps it is more correct to say, reactionary) side. In the Year of Revolutions, 1848, his was the most active, most biting and most effective pen on the side of the Government, and he was rewarded by appointment as a life member of the Upper House.

Throughout the following decade, he was recognised as the leader of the reactionary party, and he lost his power only with the fall of the Manteuffel ministry. An authority no less than Lord Acton regarded his influence in German conservatism as more dominant than that of Beaconsfield in England. He is described in the *Cambridge Modern*

Chairman of Committees, who had he lived a little longer might have become Speaker. These somewhat unimpressive but essentially respectable names practically conclude the roll.

T

History as "the intellectual leader of the conservative aristocratic party and the most remarkable brain in the Upper Chamber. . . . He largely supplied the ruling party with the learning and wealth of ideas on which to found their claims". Bluntschli describes him as being "after Hegel, the most important representative of the philosophical theory of the state". His influence on Bismarck, in the latter's formative period, was very strong. So, incidentally, was that of Professor Emil von Friedberg (brother of that Heinrich von Friedberg who was Minister of Justice in Prussia from 1879 to 1889), the great authority on ecclesiastical history, who was the Chancellor's principal adviser during the Kulturkampf, and was also of Jewish birth.

One of the heirs to Stahl's spirit, in the days when the Prussian *junker* had taken up a slightly more liberal attitude, was Karl Rudolph Friedenthal, nephew of a well-known Hebrew writer. Converted like Stahl in youth, he was a member of the Reichstag from 1867, and one of the founders of the Free Conservative Party. He it was whom Bismarck invited in 1870 to formulate the constitution of the German Empire, in collaboration with Blankenburg and Bennigsen; subsequently, he became Minister of Agriculture. The constitution which Friedenthal framed continued to function until the Revolution of 1918. It was then overthrown in favour of the Weimar Constitution, one of the principal architects of which was the Berlin jurist, Hugo Preuss. Hence the Weimar Constitution was no more Jewish than the Versailles Constitution had been. Both were the work of patriotic Germans, who happened to comprise in their number persons who were, by birth, Jews.

Austria provides a further illustration of the participation of Jews in formulating the ideology of the conservative element in Central European politics, in Heinrich

Friedjung (who has received mention in another connexion as perhaps the greatest of Austrian historians).
Born in Moravia, of Jewish parentage, he was by conviction a passionate German Austrian, equally proud of
the great traditions both of Germany and of Austria.
In 1880, in collaboration with George von Schönerer
(later the leader of the extreme Pan-Germans in Austria)
and the Jew Victor Adler (subsequently founder of the
Austrian Social Democratic Party, and Foreign Secretary
in the first Republican Cabinet of October, 1918), he
produced the Linz programme as a basis for the future
policy of the German Austrians. Two years later, this
programme was adopted by the new German Nationalist
party, with the addition of a single clause: "No Jew can
be a member of the German Nationalist party." Thus
the programme of the movement which is now menacing
the existence of German and Austrian Jewry, was in the
first instance drawn up by Jews!

In post-war Liberal Germany, contrary to what is
generally believed, the participation of Jews in public
life was not particularly marked. Thus in the twenty
cabinets which ruled the country from the downfall
of the monarchy to the Nazi Revolution, there were
some 200 different ministers in all. Of these, only
seven were of Jewish descent—Preuss, Rathenau, Lands-
berg, Schiffer, Gradnauer, Hilferding, and Dernburg
(who was, however, only half-Jewish). In the German
federal states, there were still fewer Jewish ministers.
Between 1920 and 1932 neither Prussia, the largest state,
nor Bavaria, the second in size, had a single Jewish
minister. The same was the case in most of the smaller
states. In the Reichstag of 1930, there was only one Jew
among about 600 members, and 20 members of known
Jewish descent; the Socialist party comprised 143
members, of whom none were Jews and only 14 of Jewish

blood. In fact, the only outstanding Jewish statesman in Germany in recent years was Walther Rathenau, whose essential work lay in his courageous effort to rehabilitate Germany, both morally and economically, after her shattering defeat in 1918. Nor can he, a capitalist by birth and training, be regarded by any stretch of the imagination as an exponent of extreme political principles. He was, however, quick to realise that Class had left the era of privilege and entered that of responsibility, and wisely endeavoured to bridge over the gap which divided the proletariat from the bourgeoisie.

§IV

"His German extraction gave him an objective view of the British Empire not always obtainable by an Englishman," wrote a contemporary historian, with reference to the late Lord Milner.[1] A similar fact perhaps explains the enduring influence of Disraeli in English politics. His exuberant imagination made it possible for him to realise not only the romance, but also the potentialities of the Empire. At a time when the majority of political Englishmen regarded the "colonies" as a potential home for younger sons (where the English language was providentially spoken, but which were predestined to fall away like ripe fruit), he had more than a glimmering of what has subsequently come to be termed the "Commonwealth of Nations", composed of equal partners who might perform an important function in maintaining a balance among nations.

More important still, perhaps, was his conception of Conservatism—not as the party of privilege (and hence of a perpetual minority) but as the representative of

[1] Chapman-Huston, *The Lost Historian*, London, 1936. [A life of Sir Sidney Low, Editor of the *Dictionary of English History*, etc., and a Jew by origin.]

historic instead of radical development. The very fact that the Conservative party, under his auspices, could introduce the Second Reform Act (in the same year that Marx published *Das Kapital!*) was astounding to contemporaries. Looking back upon it, after the lapse of an entire generation, it is possible to see that it gave a new turn to English politics, shewed the labouring classes that their salvation lay in the ballot-box rather than in the exercise of force, and, by increasing a sense of balance in England, added to the stability of the world. It is remarkable but (in view of all this) not astonishing that, of the statesmen of the last century, this "superlative Hebrew conjuror" is alone a living force and a source of political inspiration.

There are many persons who consider Luigi Luzzatti, Prime Minister of Italy in 1909–11, the greatest Italian of modern times. His work was, of course, greater in the economic than in the political sphere. From early manhood, he devoted himself to the task of raising the economic status of the people. His ideal was to abolish the monopoly of wealth through other means than those advocated by the socialists, the remedies proposed by whom were, in his opinion, ridiculously inadequate to the unhealthy state of affairs which they criticised. Long before the union of Italy was an accomplished fact, he toured the country advocating the foundation of people's banks and co-operative societies. In pursuance of this he founded the Banco Popolare of Milan, and started the first co-operative store in Italy. His influence is stamped upon the co-operative movement in Italy as strongly as is that of Schulze-Delitzch in Germany, or that of the Rochdale pioneers in England. As Cabinet Minister, even before he became Premier, he forwarded this same policy. It was Luzzatti, in D'Annunzio's happy phrase, who spiritualised the power of gold.

§v

The instances adduced above are sufficient to shew that the identification of the Jews with extreme opinions in politics rests upon slender evidence, and that even their dominant Liberal sympathies are by no means exclusive. They have been identified with every party; and it is as easy (so far at least as Western Europe is concerned) to quote instances of Conservatives, or even reactionaries, as it is to cite exponents of extreme Left principles. It is certainly significant that the paladins of Conservatism both in England and in Germany were of Jewish birth.

Karl Marx was to be sure (like them) of Jewish extraction. His affiliations are, however, absurdly exaggerated, both by his admirers and by his detractors. His father, Hirschel Marx, a typical Rhenish lawyer of the assimilationist period, was baptised some time between the midsummer of 1816 and the spring of 1817—some while, therefore, before his famous son was conceived. Karl himself was received into the Evangelical church at the age of seven, and was brought up as a Christian. Not only was he ignorant of Judaism; he was—unlike Disraeli—bitterly antagonistic to it. (The story of his association with Zunz and Heine in the *Verein für Cultur und Wissenschaft der Juden* is an absurd fable, as that institution was founded when he was less than three years old, and decayed before he was ten!) "The Hebrew faith is repellent to me", he wrote, at the age of twenty-five; or again, a few years later: "What is the worldly foundation of Jewry? Self-interest. . . . What is the worldly worship of the Jews? Huckstering. What is their worldly God? Money!" Nor was there anything Jewish about his teaching—an intellectual product of the essentially Gentile, and characteristically Teutonic, doctrines of Hegel and Feuerbach.

In point of fact, the whole of the Marxian theory, far from being essentially Jewish, is a reaction against the decorous conclusions drawn by another theorist who happened (like Marx) to be a Jew by birth. Orthodox economics are to a large extent the creation of David Ricardo, the most illustrious English economist of the nineteenth century and founder of the science of political economy. He was, indeed, rather more Jewish than Marx, as he had been born and bred in the faith of his fathers, which he left only after attaining manhood. Unlike Marx, moreover, his attitude towards Jews and Judaism was friendly to the end. (It may be remarked that Nassau Senior, the most distinguished English economist of the ensuing age, was similarly of Jewish descent, his ancestor, Aaron Senior, having emigrated from the West Indies at the beginning of the eighteenth century.)[1]

Ricardo's Theory of Value dominated English, and in fact European, thought in the sphere of political economy until the end of the nineteenth century, and still constitutes the core of accepted economic theory. But his conclusions ran counter to the whole of the social and humanitarian preconceptions of Karl Marx, who could think only in terms of human suffering and upheaval. The two attitudes are clearly expressions of the temperaments of the two theorists: but the one is just as much, or as little, Jewish as the other. It is therefore highly unfortunate that the Jews should be ascribed sole responsibility for one whose connexion

---

[1] For some other outstanding Jewish economists, see above, p. 237. Among the pioneers in this sphere was the Jewish astronomer Mashaala (*supra*, pp. 46, 97), who composed in the eighth century one of the earliest works on the subject, a dissertation on Prices, as well as a remarkable political treatise on Communities, Faiths, and Nations.

with them was so slender, and whose attitude so unfriendly : all the more so in view of the fact that Engels
(to whom Marxism owes hardly less than to Marx himself)
had no Jewish connexions or affiliations whatsoever.
But perhaps time has dealt no less unkindly with Marx
himself, whose name has been associated in Russia, and
hence in the world, with the Bolshevik form of autocracy.

In fact, the persons responsible for the translation of
Marx's theories into the amalgam which is associated
with the term "Bolshevism" were mainly Russians—
men like Herzen and Bakunin. Russian Bolshevism
lies deep down in the root of the Russian nature and
in the politico-economic structure of the Empire of the
Czars. To conceive it merely as a variant of the prole-
tarian socialism of the Marxist school would be to
disregard its distinctively national character. The Russian
Jew of the period before 1917 was essentially a bourgeois.
In 1918, the Lenin Government issued a manifesto
violently attacking the Jewish workers for their anti-
Bolshevik attitude. That same year, in the Jewish
National Assembly of the Ukraine, no less than 63%
of the representatives were affiliated to bourgeois groups :
while among the fiercest opponents of the Bolsheviks
was the General League of Jewish Workers, known as
the Bund—subsequently suppressed by the new regime.
It is hence as absurd to ascribe the triumph of Bolshevism
in Russia to the Jews as it is to ascribe it to the Germans,
who sent Lenin in a sealed carriage across Germany
in 1917 with the express purpose of inculcating com-
munist ideas into the Russian masses.

On the other hand, since the Jews were the only
portion of the Russian proletariat who were as a rule
highly educated, it was inevitable that the Bolshevik
government drew a considerable number of its instruments
from their ranks. The proportions involved, however,

have been absurdly exaggerated. Out of 48 persons who constituted Lenin's administration in 1919, only eleven, or some 20% (not 90%, as is sometimes alleged) were of Jewish birth. The attitude of this group to Judaism, moreover, may be gauged from the reply of Trotsky to a representative Jewish delegation which begged him to resign: "Go home to your Jews. I am not a Jew, and I care nothing for the Jews or their fate."

§vi

Is it possible, nevertheless, to find any common factor in those Jews who were active in public life and some of whose names have been mentioned above? There is the instinctive anti-Semitic reply: that all were a disruptive influence in the State. This, in the face of the names of the Reactionaries, the Conservatives, and the very moderate Liberals which may be marshalled on the other side, is palpably absurd. Nor among the members of this group, so far removed from one another in background, in object, in character and in policy, is there discernible any community of purpose.

One bond of union, only, may perhaps be observed. There seems to have been among them all what may be termed a broad sympathy with the under-dog. The people which had suffered for two thousand years could not fail to feel sympathy with those who suffered in their own day. The children of those to whom the prophets had addressed their message could not but retain some inkling of the ideal of social justice. And so the Jewish statesmen, whether elaborating plans for Young England like Disraeli, or endeavouring to institute a new order on earth like Karl Marx, all appear to have been actuated by that wide sympathy with suffering humanity which is, one may hope, part of the Jewish heritage.

The foregoing pages are essential to an objective consideration of the part played by Jews in European political life. They imply no criticism of the systems involved. There are circles in every country in which the fancied responsibility of the Jews for the triumph of Bolshevism in Russia is even now considered a high compliment; the name of Disraeli is nearly as unpopular in some groups as is that of Karl Marx in others. In the interest of veracity, however, it is necessary to remove the current misunderstanding. Individual Jews have played some part in politics at all times; "the Jews", never—save perhaps (and there were exceptions even then) in the heyday of the national revivals in the middle of the last century. And, though it is possible to discern a certain propensity on the part of Jews to that side in politics which was formerly termed "liberal", that tendency has never been exclusive. All parties and outlooks have found their response in the Jewish community: and in nothing does its essentially representative character shew up more clearly. Western civilisation has however been permanently enriched by their devoted, and sometimes heroic, leadership in the cause of self-government, of humanitarianism, and of social reform.

Appendix to Chapter XI

JEWS AND EUROPEAN LAW

ANY evaluation of the part of the Jews in the legal development of modern Europe must necessarily take account of the Bible. For, while European law harks back in the main to Rome, the influence of Hebrew ethics on the mind of legislators and on the growth of customary law cannot be overlooked. Moreover, the mediaeval Canon Law, based to a considerable extent on the Old Testament, could not but exercise a profound influence upon the Civil Law contemporaneously with which it was studied.

According to a theory which has now been put forward, the Jewish influence on European law was far more profound and far-reaching than this would imply. It has been maintained in a recent study, with a wealth of learning and great force of argument, that Talmudic law deeply affected Syrian law, which in turn (it will be recalled that Berytus, now Beyrout, was the seat of one of the most famous Imperial schools of jurisprudence) had a great influence on the Byzantine codes and the Roman Law as it was formulated by the great legalists of the Eastern Empire. If this theory is correct, the exclusive claims of the Roman jurists and the German folk-ways to the paternity of the European codes must be modified.

It is indisputable that the parallels (it is unwise to use a stronger term) between European and Talmudic law go beyond a few vague general principles. There is Rabbinic, but not Roman, precedent for the principle *qui facit per alium facit per se* ('He who acts through another acts through himself'). The mediaeval Rabbis evolved a law of copyright which is probably anterior to the practice among their neighbours. The Jewish system of tenant-right, or right of possession, became familiar in general circles through the *Jus Gazaga*, miserably evolved through force of circumstances in the Italian Ghetto, and may not have been a barren example. The suggestion has even been made that one or two institutions and formulae of English law (such as the Writ *Eligit*, the mortgage, and the phrase *cuius est solum eius usque ad coelum usque ad inferos*) are derived from Jewish deeds, current among, and familiar to, mediaeval lawyers in these islands. The 'universal code' based on the Bible (termed by the Rabbis the Laws of the Sons of Noah) is paralleled (to say the least) by the *jus naturale et gentium*, or Natural Law, recognised by mediaeval jurists : this in turn was the formative principle at the basis of the English Equity Law, and of the

Continental legal philosophies upon which the nineteenth-century codifications depended. The great jurists of the seventeenth century—Grotius on the Continent, Selden in England—were positively soaked in Hebraic lore—Biblical, Rabbinic and contemporary—traces of which may be discerned throughout their writings.

The God of Israel is the God of Justice: and it is not remarkable that, since the age of emancipation began, the profession of law has exercised a powerful attraction on the Jewish mind. There can be no doubt as to the importance of the part played by Jewish lawyers in modern jurisprudence. Even before the period of emancipation, a few eminent legalists of Jewish extraction emerged, such as the Austrian humanitarian, Joseph von Sonnenfels, who was responsible for the abolition of torture in Austria (infra, p. 298). The nineteenth century saw the beginning of a series of notable Jewish jurists and advocates in every country. Pre-eminent in England, above all, was Sir George Jessel, one of the great law-making judges of his time, and generally recognised to be the founder of the Court of Chancery as it exists to-day. His judgements were models of clarity and learning, and were seldom reversed on appeal. Jessel was in his prime when Judah Philip Benjamin, the eminent Southern statesman ("the Brains of the Confederacy", he was called), found refuge in England on the conclusion of the American Civil War. The latter was admitted to the Bar and for some years enjoyed a practice which even to-day has seldom been surpassed. While waiting to be called, he wrote his Law of the Sale of Personal Property, which has remained a classic to the present day. It is believed that his elevation to the Bench —an honour for which he was more than qualified—was prevented only by deference to American public opinion.

Among the other eminent English lawyers who were of Jewish extraction may be mentioned Lord Justice Ludlow during the last century and Lord Justice Slesser to-day, both of Jewish descent; and Sir Archibald Levin

Smith, a great Master of the Rolls (and, incidentally, one of the great cricketers of his generation), who had a Jewish mother. Lord Chancellor Herschell, on the other hand, was the son of a converted Missionary among the Jews. England has had, too, one Jewish Lord Chief Justice in Lord Reading, whose greatest eminence was however, in a different sphere. Arthur Cohen, Junior Counsel to His Majesty's Government in the famous Alabama Arbitration, and standing Counsel to the India Office, was pre-eminent in his day as a barrister, and is known to have refused a Judgeship. Solicitors included Sir George Lewis, sponsor of the Prisoners' Evidence Act of 1898 and of the Court of Criminal Appeal ten years later—both great steps in humanitarian progress.

In France, among many Jewish lawyers of high repute, the outstanding name is undoubtedly that of Adolphe Crémieux (*supra*, pp. 265, 268), one of the most brilliant of advocates and a great Minister of Justice, who did much to abolish the many cruel penal punishments which still persisted even in his day. Holland owes its code of judicial procedure to an equally great lawyer and friend of his co-religionists, Michael H. Godefroi, Minister of Justice in that country in 1866. J. L. Simonsen was for many years the outstanding lawyer in Denmark. Germany, in the course of a single generation, has produced a host of Jewish jurists of high distinction—Eugen Fuchs, Herman Staub, Max Hachenburg, Eduard von Simson (*supra*, pp. 115, 265), Heinrich Dernburg, Eduard Gans, Joseph Unger, Georg Jellinek, Heinrich von Friedberg (at one time the Minister of Justice), Hugo Preuss (*supra*, p. 274) and a vast number of others. They were virtually the creators of the science of the Philosophy of Law, in which Germany was pre-eminent: and Friedrich Julius Stahl's great *Die Philosophie des Rechts nach geschichtlicher Ansicht* is still a classic. So also is Levin Goldschmidt's great history of commercial law, one of the triumphs of German scholarship of the 19th century.

In Italy, one of the earliest Jewish lawyers to achieve

a high reputation was Gioacchino Basevi, who had the courage to defend the German-Austrian hero, Andreas Hofer, during the Napoleonic domination. Later, the contribution of Cesare Vivante, the founder of the new school of Italian commercial law (with Leone Bolaffi and David Supino): of Vittorio Polacco, one of the most important Italian legalists; and of Ludovico Mortara, the great systematiser of the procedure of Italian civil law; was of the utmost importance. Federico Cammeo, a recognised expert in Administrative Law, played a part of some importance in negotiating the recent Treaty with the Vatican.

While Jews are largely represented in the legal profession in America, two in our own day have achieved a peculiarly high reputation, both members of the Supreme Court: Louis Brandeis for the liberal spirit which won him, before his elevation to the Bench, the title 'the People's attorney'; and Benjamin Nathan Cardozo, the philosopher of American jurisprudence. Both are conspicuously liberal in their sympathies; but it is significant that they were elevated to their present position by Presidents of opposite tendencies in politics. Another outstanding contemporary American is Professor Felix Frankfurter, one of the most eminent legal theorists in the country, author of a number of standard works on political and constitutional problems and Professor of Law at Harvard University.

That Jews have been exceptionally active in the field of International Law is only what might be anticipated. A great part in the development of the modern system was taken by the Dutch jurist, Tobias Michael Carel Asser. The name of Albrecht Mendelssohn-Bartholdy was particularly prominent in the same field in Germany. In England, Leone Levi, primarily an economist, was largely responsible for the codification of international commercial law. He was the author of several important works on this subject, in one of which he anticipated the modern view as to the disastrous consequences of any war, victorious or otherwise.

CHAPTER XII

"THE GREATEST OF THESE IS CHARITY"

§1

It is natural, in a work which deals with the Jewish contribution to civilisation, to devote a section to beneficent activities; for, if there was any quality which the Jew was able to maintain and to enhance even during the age of persecution, it was the spirit of charity.

Research upon this subject is still necessary in order to bring out to the full the distinctive quality of this Jewish contribution. For it had certain specific characteristics which were all its own. The degree of destitution among the Jews was enormous, at the time when Ghetto deprivation was at its height; it is computed, for example, that in the eighteenth century one in three of the Jewish population in Germany, England and Italy, was dependent upon his co-religionists for relief, and as many more were living upon the border-line of penury. Yet the cry for assistance was never made in vain; and relief was given in such a manner as to facilitate the maximum of self-reliance, and to avoid pauperisation. It is significant that the most bulky work on charity ever published (with the exception of Lallemand's four-volume *Histoire de la Charité*) is the *Meil Zedaka* by an eighteenth-century Jewish author of Smyrna, Elijah Cohen.

Some of the outstanding characteristics of post-Biblical and mediaeval Jewish philanthropy deserve cursory mention. It was realised from the beginning that the poor have rights, and the rich have duties: and this, explicitly laid down in the Mosaic code, was extended and crystallised in Talmudic practice. From the period of the fall of the Jewish state, the charity overseer was part of the recognised institutional system of every community. It was expected of the mediaeval Jew that he should devote a tithe of his income, at the very least, to philanthropic objects: and this ideal has been preserved to our own day. Even the pauper, who lived on the charity of others, was expected to contribute his mite to the relief of those more needy than himself.

A series of voluntary associations took care of the indigent at every stage, from birth to death. The mother could expect assistance in child-birth, the ailing on their sick-bed, the mourners in their hour of affliction, the prisoner in his dungeon, the slave in captivity. Another charitable activity which was particularly highly esteemed was the dowering of poor brides. In Rome, in the Ghetto period, not less than thirty of these benevolent associations existed, in a population which did not exceed five thousand souls.

Every Ghetto had its Lodging House for indigent strangers, which was also used as hospital (the institution is found at Cologne as early as the eleventh century); every community had its salaried physician, so that medical attendance was available for all. There was, too, (*supra*, pp. 35-7) a free educational system, supported by voluntary subscriptions, and open to every child. A town without its proper charity organisations, it was laid down in the codes, was no proper residence for a self-respecting Jew, any more than if it lacked its place of worship. Yet at the same time, it was established as a cardinal principle, that the poor should not be put to shame by the method of administering relief. As early as the fourth century, the Emperor Julian, when he ordered the institution of inns for strangers in every city, referred with admiration to the example of the Jews, "the enemies of the Gods", in whose midst no beggars were to be found.

It should be noted though, in this connexion, how catholic was the Jewish conception of charity. It is a man's duty, we are informed in the Talmud, to relieve the Gentile poor, and to visit their sick, and to bury their dead, just as though a co-religionist were in question. This principle was not inculcated for the sake of appearances or of policy, but on a purely ethical basis, being deduced from the verse of Psalm cxlv, which tells how the tender mercy of the Lord is over *all* His creatures. Moreover, the principle was taken over in the Ghetto period, and reiterated in such intimate ethical treatises as the *Mesillat Yesharim* of Moses Hayim Luzzatto. It is illuminating to compare this with the spectacle which horrified the world at the time of the expulsion from Spain in 1492, when zealous friars wandered among the groups of starving Jewish refugees on the quay-side in Genoa, loaves of bread in one hand and a crucifix in the other, offering food in return for a recognition of the spiritual pre-eminence of Christianity.

§II

With this tradition in the background, it was natural that Jews should have played a conspicuous part, once they were given the opportunity, in every modern humanitarian movement. It is impossible to give a detailed account in these pages of their record in this sphere; but an attempt will be made to outline some of the more significant achievements.

It has been pointed out above that the Jewish ideal in charitable relief was to avoid pauperisation and do all

U

that was possible to render the beneficiary self-supporting. Scientific charity, in a word, took the place of indiscriminate giving. This ideal was adopted by the Jews in their general philanthropic work, as soon as the breach in the walls of the Ghetto enabled them to assume their natural place in such activity.

The wealthy Jews who took the lead in this process, at the beginning of the last century, made it a rule to employ their almoners, to investigate the cases which they were called upon to assist. This simple beginning developed into the rudiments of a scientific and constructive system of charity administration, which replaced the haphazard alms-giving which had previously been the general rule. In the present state of knowledge upon this point, it is impossible to say that the Jews took the lead in this : but they were certainly among the pioneers, and they continued to develop the new ideal.

One of the most remarkable illustrations of this comes from across the Atlantic. It was perhaps the fact that he himself belonged to a misunderstood and persecuted group which directed the attention of Julius Rosenwald to the amelioration of the condition of the American Negro. The total of his benefactions has been estimated at some 62,000,000 dollars : and a good part of this sum was devoted to Negro welfare. Eighteen Negro Y.M.C.A.s and no less than 3,433 Negro rural school buildings were the result of his interest. The method of his giving, above all, marked an epoch in philanthropy. It was not only scientific : it was also impersonal. He organised a staff of experts and consultants to advise him, and to ensure that his benefactions were expended to the utmost advantage. He made it a rule, moreover, to give conditionally—that is, provided that certain further amounts were raised, or certain local conditions fulfilled. He had a rooted objection on the other hand to having his name associated with his donations. So little did he look for eleemosynary immortality, indeed, that he took steps to ensure that his benefactions should be expended within a comparatively short period of years. The spirit of his charities was thus even more important than their extent. It was a contribution not to one cause or another, but to the common store of humanity.

The Rothschild family is to-day taken as the out-standing example of the Jew in high finance. It is less generally realised how unselfishly they have made use of the riches which they amassed: for, if any family has regarded its accumulated wealth as a public trust, it is this one. For a period of several generations, the name is repeated with impressive regularity in every beneficent enterprise and endeavour over half of Europe; and, up to the war of 1914-18, their firm figured at the head of the subscription list of almost every charitable fund raised in the City of London. To recount their benefactions in detail would be a wearisome task; but it is impossible to touch upon this subject without making specific mention of their liberality in some directions.

It is perhaps legitimate to say that they were among the foremost to recognise that housing conditions are the key to many other social problems, and that they led in the attempt to cope with the abuse. Betty de Roth-schild, of Paris (widow of Baron James de Rothschild, founder of the French house), shewed her interest in the timid spirit of unscientific benefaction when, on her death in 1886, she left 600,000 francs to the public charities, to assist poor labourers in paying their rents. Her three sons, advancing beyond this elementary conception, subscribed 10,000,000 francs in 1904, to be employed in the erection of inexpensive dwelling-houses, and for the general furtherance of plans for ameliorating the condition of the working classes. Their cousin, Ferdinand de Roth-schild, made Waddesdon, in Buckinghamshire, one of the first "model villages" in England. And one of the most remarkable achievements of practical philanthropy, before the time when the Government had begun to interest itself in the Housing Question on the enormous scale of to-day, was the first Lord Rothschild's organisation of the Four Per Cent. Industrial Dwellings, which replaced some of the most notorious East End slums with model tenements, new additions being built year after year without any fresh call on capital. It is not without significance that, at the time when Jews played a really considerable part in the municipal life of Frankfort-on-Main, that city's housing policy was a model for the whole of Europe.

No account has hitherto been taken in these pages of benefactions for specifically Jewish purposes. Yet there are certain instances of this, the significance of which is more than denominational. In his day there was no greater or more objective philanthropist than Baron de Hirsch, who, in addition to his multifarious other activities, endeavoured to solve the problem of Russian Jewry single-handed, by diverting it to the agricultural colonies which he founded in the New World. He maintained a regiment of supervisors and almoners, in the hope of achieving a scientific approach to the questions that engaged his attention. The total of his charities, at the time of his death, was estimated at more than twice the fortune which he left. In the event, he was unable to do more than touch the fringes of the problem which he had endeavoured to solve; but his work is a land-mark in the history of scientific beneficence.

The founders of two of the greatest English philanthropic agencies happen to have been of Jewish blood, though in neither case were they Jews by religion.

One was Thomas John Barnardo, who established in
1867 the first modest nucleus of Dr. Barnardo's Homes,
which by the time of his death, forty years later, had
rescued 250,000 children from the gutter, and has continued the work since on an expanding scale. According
to his official biographer, J. M. Bready, the "Father of
the Fatherless" was the son of John Michaelis Barnardo,
a Hamburg *Sephardi* who, settling in Dublin, had lost
all connexion with his co-religionists. Even greater than
this institution in the extent of its work for the relief of
human misery is the Salvation Army—which, in addition,
introduced a new spirit into religious life in England in
the middle of last century and awakened Church circles
to a sense of their wider social responsibilities. The
founder of this organisation, "General" William Booth,
was the son of a Nottingham woman named Moss: and
it is generally assumed, rightly or wrongly, that he owed
to her his Rabbinical appearance, his prophetic enthusiasm, and his burning sympathy for the poor.

§III

The people who originated the adage that the whole
universe is poised on the breath of school-children, and
whose family life was a model for the world, naturally
shewed a particular interest in children's welfare. A
curious illustration of this comes from Leghorn. Here, in
the eighteenth century, when the death of children
through "overlaying" was shamefully common, the
community passed a regulation, enforced by the severest
religious sanctions, forbidding mothers to take their
infant children to sleep with them in the same bed.
Such devoted regard for infant welfare, coupled with
the hygienic regulation of the traditional Jewish life, had
its consequence in a greatly reduced death-rate among

Jewish children. In Czarist Russia, that for infants under one year among Jews was 13·21 per cent: among non·Jews, 25·96 per cent. In Vienna at one period the rate for infants under one month was, among Jews, 8·3 per cent: among non-Jews, 16·1 per cent. These figures are reflected in other parts of Europe, though the contrast is not always quite so striking. Even in New York, Jewish infant mortality in 1915 was 78 for each 1,000 births, while that for the remainder of the population was 105; and the infant death rate among Palestinian Jewry to-day is almost the lowest in the world.

It was natural, therefore, that Jews took a prominent part in infant welfare work on a larger scale, immediately they were allowed to become part of the general community. In another connexion (*supra*, p. 212) something has been said regarding the Jewish contribution to the science of pediatry. Here, a few details will be added which illustrate that same interest from a different angle.

Perhaps the greatest of the world's orphanages is the nexus which goes by the name of the Barnardo Homes, founded (as has been seen) by Dr. Thomas John Barnardo. Similarly, the Wandsworth Orphanages were founded under the will of Lord Wandsworth, a member of the Stern family, with a bequest of one million pounds sterling. In London, the Evelina Hospital for Children was founded by Baron Ferdinand de Rothschild in memory of his wife, who had died in child-bed, and the Children's Hospital in Westminster by Robert Mond. In Paris, the first organised attempt to provide warm clothing for school children in winter (a recognised concomitant of the old Jewish educational system) was made at the close of the last century by Baron Edmond de Rothschild. (It was characteristic of the anti-Semitic mentality that this act of benevolence was decried as "Jewish propaganda".)

One of the most remarkable philanthropic endeavours of our day was that of the American philanthropist, Nathan Straus, who, appalled at the wastage of child-life through the inroads of tuberculosis, devoted his whole energies to an attempt to grapple with the problem at its source. In 1890 he installed a system for the distribution of sterilised milk to the poor of New York. A greatly reduced infant mortality shewed that the experiment was more than justified. He then set about installing this same system and providing pasteurised milk in various other cities of the United States and abroad, maintaining his own laboratory for this object. It was through his efforts that the relationship of bovine tuberculosis to the spread of the disease was finally demonstrated at the Eighth International Tuberculosis Conference at Stockholm in 1909. Immediately afterwards, developing this idea, he established the first Tuberculosis Preventorium for children. During one period of his life, he gave away more than his income to charity: he sold his yacht, and his wife sold her jewels, so that the proceeds could be devoted to more useful purposes. But the aged philanthropist retained his greatest treasure—a slip of paper which he carried about in his pocket to his last day, on which were shewn the numbers of infant deaths in New York before and after he introduced his scheme.

Another American philanthropist who did work in this direction, though not on so large a scale, was the inventor, Emile Berliner, who was a foremost advocate of milk pasteurisation, besides doing much to popularise preventive medicine. It is noteworthy that a similar system was set up in France by another Jew, Henri de Rothschild—a rare instance of the heir to wealth who has devoted his whole energy to science and philanthropy— who founded the first Infant Consultations in Paris and was instrumental in establishing milk-depots for the poor in that city. Emile Deutsch de la Meurthe, during the war of 1914-18, organised the Franco-American Brotherhood, which ultimately took care of 286,000 orphans.

In England, Ernest Abraham Hart, founder of the *British Medical Journal*, was responsible for the Infant Life Protection Act, which reformed the hideous old type of Baby Farm out of existence, as well as for the Act which established the Metropolitan Asylums Board. In the following generation, Herbert Samuel, as Home Secretary, was to pilot the Children's Bill, a notable step in social reform, through the House of Commons. In the United States, the Federal Children's Bureau was originated in 1908 by Lilian D. Wald, who six years before had organised the municipalisation of school nursing in New York. She is better remembered, however, by the famous Henry Street Settlement which she founded in 1893 in the teeth of considerable opposition, but which originated a new era in welfare work in America. (Later, she was to be responsible for the beginning of the district nursing system throughout the United States.) In Germany, Lina Morgenstern (who later convened the first International Women's Congress) was the most sedulous advocate of the Kindergarten system, her *Childhood's Paradise* of 1860 being one of the epoch-making publications in this sphere; and the earliest effective kindergarten in Italy was established by Adolph Pick, the pioneer of Froebelian methods in that country. Similarly, it was Albert Neisser who founded the first Society in the world to combat venereal disease and safeguard maternity.

By a coincidence, Jews have played an important role in removing the calamities of another common affliction of infancy. At one time, a child born deaf was necessarily considered dumb, and generally semi-idiot also; for, unable to hear what was said to it, it could not understand any language or express its thoughts. It was only in the eighteenth century that this horror was averted. The pioneer was a certain Jacob Rodrigues Pereira, an ex-Marrano returned to Judaism, and grandfather of the famous bankers of the Second Empire. After long study of anatomy and physiology, and numerous experiments on congenital deaf-mutes, Pereira perfected a system for teaching them, which received official recognition from the Académie des Belles Lettres of Caen in 1747. Unfortunately, his religion and origin told against him, and the Abbé de l'Epée's method, not greatly dissimilar from his own and to some extent based upon it, was officially adopted. Nevertheless, Pereira's work, as first teacher of deaf-mutes in France, remains a perpetual title to the gratitude of posterity. A subsequent worker in the same field was Sir Henry Isaacs, Lord Mayor of London in 1889, and uncle of the first Lord Reading; while a pioneer in lip-reading for the deaf was Lionel van Praagh.

§IV

The Hebraic abhorrence of capital punishment is to be traced throughout the centuries. In the Second Jewish Commonwealth, it was virtually abolished: so much so, that a court which passed a capital sentence once in seventy years was stigmatised as one of murderers. (This, incidentally, is one of the many indications that the execution of Jesus of Nazareth was the outcome of the sentence of a Roman, not a Jewish, court.) What more natural than that in England Sir Moses Montefiore, the Jewish philanthropist, was among those who led the opposition to capital punishment, and was overjoyed when he secured the remission of the sentence of the only person sentenced to death during his shrievalty in the

City of London? It was symptomatic of the times that Lord John Russell, when approached, took no interest in the subject, while Marshal Soult (then on a visit to London) showed nothing but astonishment at these humanitarian views. Indeed, Montefiore received his main encouragement from another Jew, Sir David Salamons, who was whole-heartedly opposed to the savage penalties which had survived Peel's reforms.

Similarly, in France, Adolphe Crémieux procured the abolition of capital punishment for political offences. In the previous century, it had been a baptised Jew, the jurist Joseph von Sonnenfels, who was responsible for the abolition of torture in Austria in 1776—a revolutionary step, as it then appeared, though in accordance with the Jewish tradition, which had never admitted this perversion into the judicial system. It was Uriah Phillips Levy, the first Jew to rise to high rank in the American navy, who brought about the discontinuation in that service of the flogging which had previously been one of its disgraces.

The record may be continued. In the field of prison reform, John Howard was preceded by Antonio Ribeiro Sanches, a Portuguese Marrano physician, who spent part of his time as a professing Jew in London. Elizabeth Fry, who continued Howard's work, had no stauncher supporter in England than Sir Isaac Lyon Goldsmid, the first Anglo-Jewish baronet. Similarly, in all the other humanitarian endeavours of the great age of reform which we call the nineteenth century, Jews stood by the side of their fellow-citizens in every country, always seconding and sometimes directing them.

The origin of the movement for the humane treatment of animals is particularly significant: for in this a Jew was working in the oldest Jewish tradition. It is a matter in which (as it appears to the Jewish mind) the

Old Testament is in advance of the New. The simple humanitarianism of the Biblical precept, "Thou shalt not muzzle the ox when he treadeth out the corn" (Deuteronomy xxv. 4), contrasts strangely with Paul's comment, "Doth God take care for oxen?" (I Corinthians ix. 9). That all this is not a matter of twentieth century apologetics is made plain from Josephus (*Contra Apionem* II. 29), "So thorough a lesson has he (Moses) given us in gentleness and humanity that he does not overlook even the brute beasts"—a sentiment which Philo also echoes. Cattle and oxen and asses were enjoined to share in the Sabbatical repose (Exodus xx. 10; Deuteronomy v. 14): Nineveh was spared on account of its four-footed inhabitants, as well as the human beings (Jonah, last verse): the Psalmist praised God for preserving beast as well as man (Psalm xxxvi. 7).

This strain continues in the Talmud. Thus, from the verse, "And I will send grass in thy fields for thy cattle, and thou mayest eat and be full" (Deuteronomy xi. 15), it was deduced that a man should not sit down to table until he had fed his domestic animals: and, in a legend paraphrased by Coleridge, it was told how God marked out Moses as a fitting pastor for his people by reason of his devoted treatment of a lamb which had strayed. Even the much-decried law of *Shehita*, or the ritual slaughter of animals, seems to have been dictated to a large extent by humane considerations.[1] This was in keeping with the Rabbinical conception, that cruelty to animals was a breach of the Divine law and of the Mosaic code. It has been pointed out that, until the nineteenth century, cruelty to animals was nowhere illegal—excepting under Jewish law.

[1] "I should be happy to think that my own end were likely to be as swift and painless as the end of these cattle killed in this [the Jewish] way undoubtedly is." (Lovat Evans, Professor of Physiology in the University of London.)

Who was responsible for the change in attitude? More almost than any other man, it was a Jew, following the Prophetical and Rabbinical teaching. Lewis Gompertz belonged to a Jewish family established in London since the beginning of the eighteenth century, one of whose brothers was a famous mathematician and another a much-admired poet. Lewis, on the other hand, an active and successful inventor, devoted his best energies to the cause of kindness to animals. In 1824, he set out his views in a work entitled *Moral Enquiries on the Situation of Men and Brutes*. This attracted considerable attention and powerfully contributed to the movement as a result of which the Society (subsequently Royal Society) for the Prevention of Cruelty to Animals was founded. Gompertz was associated with the institution from the first, revived it when it was in difficulties, acted for years in an honorary capacity as its Secretary and nursed it back to life. Religious prejudice was not as yet dead in England. A dispute arose between the Secretary and the Executive Committee: and the former's *Moral Enquiries* were denounced as hostile to Christianity. In consequence, he was compelled to sever his connexion with the Society. He then formed the "Animals' Friend Society", which speedily outstripped the parent body. However, in 1846 he was obliged by ill-health to retire from public life: his society was disbanded: and the Royal Society for Prevention of Cruelty to Animals henceforth held undisputed sway, ultimately being the parent-body of a net-work spread all over the civilised world. It has long since forgotten that it owes its very existence, as well as its inspiration, to a professing Jew, working in the Talmudic and Biblical tradition.

§v

The visitation and relief of the sick was regarded as one of the cardinal Jewish virtues: and Jews have naturally taken their share in the endowment and support of hospitals. In England, the tradition goes back to the eighteenth century, when the names of prominent members of the London community are found among the earliest subscribers to, and governors of, the London Hospital, the Foundling Hospital, and most of the other institutions established at that period. Towards the end of the century, it was Benjamin Goldsmid who was primarily responsible for the foundation of the Naval Asylum, which first cared for the orphans of sailors fallen in England's wars. His nephew, Sir Isaac Lyon Goldsmid, in an age of greater freedom, was drawn by his interest in University College, London, to an interest in the University College Hospital, of which he was one of the founders: subsequently, he took a similar part in the establishment of the North London Hospital.

A number of other English hospitals owe their existence to Jews. The great Edward VII Sanatorium at Midhurst for the cure of consumption—one of the finest of its kind in the world—derived the money for its upkeep from Sir Edward Cassel. In Liverpool stands the Great Northern Hospital, refounded by David Lewis, who left a sum of £400,000 in trust for charitable purposes and is responsible for the existence of some other similar institutions. The Albert Levy Ward at the Royal Free Hospital is a tribute to the generosity of its Treasurer, Sir Albert Levy, who in 1929 created a benevolent fund which will eventually amount to £400,000 for the purpose of assisting hospitals and other charitable causes. The second founder of the Middlesex Hospital is Edward Meyerstein, whose recent benefactions towards the relief of sickness have attained astronomical figures. At the Middlesex Hospital, too, the Cancer Wing was endowed by the Barnato and Joel families with a gift of £250,000. The German Hospital in London was founded by Jonas Freund. Sir Edward Stern, himself a sufferer from deafness, devoted a large fortune to the relief of those in humble circumstances who suffer from the same affliction. Mention has been made already of the Evelina Hospital for Children, and of the Children's Hospital in Vincent Square, founded by members of the Rothschild and Mond families respectively.

Other benefactions have been spread more widely. Almost every London hospital has its "Zunz Ward", provided by R. S. Zunz in memory of his wife. The wide-spread donations of the late Bernhard Baron, unique both in scale and in method, are fresh in the public memory: among the charitable institutions which owe their existence to him being the new dispensary at Guy's Hospital. Baron de Hirsch, it is said, contributed to the London hospitals the entire winnings of his racing stable.

Apart from their natural and proper interest in general foundations, Jews have made it a point of pride to maintain institutions for the support of their own sick and poor. These, besides caring for a great many non-Jews, varying from 15 to 33 per cent of the total (for there is no denominational restriction on admissions) sometimes fulfil a public service in the wider sense. Thus the Victoria Memorial Jewish Hospital in Manchester was one of the first in England to institute a later waking-hour for patients (7 a.m., instead of the conventional, and sometimes harsh, 5 a.m.). It was the first hospital in the country, too, to introduce a scheme whereby out-patients were given tickets to see their doctors at a definite time, thus obviating the long, distressing, and needless hours of waiting. Finally, it was the first English institution to introduce a 48-hour week for nurses. So also the Jewish Board of Guardians in London instituted the earliest English tuberculosis service, blazing the trail which was followed in time by the stately march of national effort; while the Infant Welfare movement in London was similarly initiated by Jewish institutions. The influence of these reforms is not of communal significance only.

If these instances are derived from England only, it is merely because of the difficulty of drawing up, and wearisomeness of studying, a detailed list in which every country of the world would require mention. It is sufficient to say that illustrations, certainly no less striking, could be assembled for France, for Germany, for the United States, and for every other land in which Jews are resident.

§VI

The Jew of the Ghetto period was brought up to realise the supreme importance of Rabbinic learning. Admitted to the general world, he translated this conception into general terms, and became a munificent patron of scholarship and pioneer in the establishment of educational institutions. Sir Isaac Lyon Goldsmid, for example, collaborated whole-heartedly with Joseph Lancaster in his great work of spreading enlightenment among the masses and arousing public interest in education. It was he too who headed the group of Jews who worked fervently for the establishment of University College, London—the first non-sectarian British University—the site of which he purchased; and he was thus one of the fathers of the University of London. The Library of the University of Liverpool is a monument to the munificence of Harold Cohen, just as a great Public Library in Frankfort commemorates the generosity of the House of Rothschild and long bore its name. Baron Edmond de Rothschild, of Paris, in addition to his multifarious other benefactions, endowed a foundation for scientific research with a gift of 40,000,000 francs—at that time reckoned among the most princely endowments of its generation. Emile Deutsch de la Meurthe, in 1922, established a group of buildings on the outskirts of Paris, where 350 destitute students could live while receiving their university training. These illustrations, too, could be extended almost indefinitely.

The case of the University of Frankfort-on-Main is an outstanding one. William Merton, a member of a Jewish family which had emigrated to England and anglicised its name, was a real prince of charity, and a scientific benefactor as well. He established out of his own means the Academy for Social and Commercial Sciences ("Akademie für Sozial- und Handelswissenschaften"), which flourished exceedingly and in 1914 was transformed into the University of Frankfort. This University had a special charter and a more liberal constitution than the other German seats of learning. It was a communal affair, the State making no contribution to its upkeep; and the significance of this, in a city which contained many wealthy and open-handed Jews, is obvious. George Speyer contributed the "Institut für experimentell-chemotherapeutische Forschung" (Georg Speyer Haus), and so made it possible for Paul Ehrlich to discover Salvarsan. Mathilde von Rothschild, the Sterns and others made large bequests to it. Even Jacob Schiff, in far-away New York, remembered it. And to-day, no Jews are permitted to enter its lecture-halls.

More specialised benefactions include the Beit Foundation at Oxford, for the study of Colonial History: the Institute of Physical Chemistry at Cambridge, which owes its existence to Sir Robert Waley Cohen: and the characteristic foundation by Sir Montagu Burton at more than one University of Chairs for Industrial and International Peace. The thirty Beit Fellowships for Medical Research have already done an enormous amount for the relief of human suffering, and, it is to be hoped, will do much more. In the United States, the John Simon Guggenheim foundation, established with a capital of 3,000,000 dollars for aiding scientists and artists in their education, without distinction of race, creed, or colour, is one of the most munificent agencies for the encouragement of post-graduate research. To another member of the same family is due a princely endowment for the study of aeronautics. Lucius Littauer is one of the most liberal supporters of the Harvard University. The Institute for Advanced Study at Princeton was the creation of Louis Bamberger and his sister.[1] The first American Planetarium was a gift to the city of Chicago from Max Adler; but it was run closely by that added by Samuel Fels to the Franklin Institute in Philadelphia. James Loeb, another Harvard benefactor and formerly a partner in the famous American banking firm, established the Institute of Musical Art in New York, as well as founding the famous Loeb Classics, which have placed the masterpieces of Latin and Greek literature within the grasp even of the ill-equipped reader. On his demise, after the beginning of the Nazi regime, his residuary estate, amounting to over $1,000,000, was left to the

[1] It may be added that as far back as the middle of the eighteenth century, when the Brown University was founded at Newport, Rhode Island, contributions were forthcoming from Jewish magnates of the Southern cities, while the timber was provided by Aaron Lopez, a local merchant-prince.

Institute for Experimental Psychiatry in his beloved Munich. In 1927, Baron Edmond de Rothschild (mentioned so often in these pages) gave the princely sum of 30,000,000 francs for the establishment in Paris of a Biological Institute to continue the research work of Claud Bernard, the digestive specialist. Similarly, one of the greatest benefactors of the Pasteur Institute, where so many Jews have done useful work, was the Jewish philanthropist Osiris Iffler. In the East, David and Albert Sassoon, father and son, did an enormous amount to further education among all races and creeds in India, China, Turkey, Persia and even Japan; while the Kadoorie bequests are applied for the benefit not only of the Jews, but also the Arabs, in Palestine.

The wide-spread connexions of the Jew prevent his purview from being confined to a single country. The "international" outlook, however, has consistently been exercised on behalf of a peaceful understanding between peoples. It is only characteristic that Sir Ernest Cassel could think of no more fitting manner of commemorating his beloved friend, King Edward VII, than by his gift of £200,000 to found the Anglo-German Institute, for the promotion of English studies in Germany and German studies in England. It was in this tradition that the first public speech delivered by a German in England after the war of 1914–18, which did so much to clear away international misunderstanding, was that of Albert Einstein: and that Rufus Isaacs, Marquess of Reading, became first President of the Anglo-German Fellowship, when it was organised at the same period.

The same spirit is shewn with regard to other countries. Many seats of learning, both in England and in Italy, have reason to be grateful to the memory of Arthur Serena, who devoted the whole of his fortune to fostering improved cultural relations between the two countries,

ALBERT EINSTEIN
From a portrait by John Philipp

and whose name is associated with Chairs of Italian Studies in all the more important English universities and with parallel foundations in the land of his birth. Similarly, the London centre of the *Institut de France* was established by Baron Edmond de Rothschild; while the Casa Velasquez in the University City at Madrid, which performs a similar function, owes its existence to the same noble philanthropist. The same ideal inspired the establishment of the Kahn Travelling Fellowships and the Henry Travelling Fellowships, the latter being intended to foster closer relationships between this country and the United States. In all this we have the justification in its widest sense of the acute comment made by Joseph Addison in the *Spectator*, over two two hundred years ago:—"They (the Jews) are, indeed, so disseminated through all the trading parts of the world, that they are become the instruments by which the most distant nations converse with one another, and by which mankind are knit together in a general correspondence."

§VII

A chapter of this study has already been devoted to a consideration of some Jewish contributions to art. But the function of the patron and collector in this field should not be neglected. Their work is indeed imperfectly appreciated: yet it is through them that the artist exists, that works of art are preserved, and that collections are brought together.

The circumstances of their history made it impossible for Jews to figure conspicuously in this capacity in the Ghetto period. Nevertheless, there is evidence that they patronised Giotto, Bonifazio il Giovane, and other eminent painters, for illuminating their liturgical and scientific manuscripts. The Roman community possesses ritual appurtenances ascribed to Cellini: the Florentine Jews appreciated the iron-work of Niccolo Grosso, "Il Caparra"; and it is certain that Rembrandt was supported by those Jewish neighbours of his, in whom he shewed such great interest.

It was only with the nineteenth century that Jews had the opportunity to shew their artistic appreciation freely. At once they stepped into the front rank of artistic patrons. Once more, it is inevitable that a beginning must be made with the Rothschild family, who patronised artists of every sort with a magnificence which recalled the Italian merchant-princes of the Renaissance. In volume after volume of recent reminiscences it is possible to read enthusiastic appreciation of their munificence and taste. But there were many more—the Bischoffsheims and the Sterns and the Wertheimers and the rest. Among the great English collectors of an earlier date may be mentioned Ralph Bernal, son of a pillar of the Spanish and Portuguese synagogue in London, who was without doubt the outstanding connoisseur of early Victorian times, and assembled a noble collection of works of art, which even to-day is spoken of by experts with respect. More recent in their memories is Henry Oppenheimer, whose collection of Old Master Drawings was perhaps the most comprehensive ever brought together by a private individual. His business associate, Marten Erdmann, of New York, built up a collection of mezzotints unequalled for range of examples and discrimination of choice.

The collector is of greater significance when he becomes a benefactor: and many are the Jews who have taken measures to ensure that the treasures in which they took delight during their lives should be accessible to a larger circle after their deaths. Most of the great art-centres of the world exemplify this fact. The Cà d'Oro— that magnificent, treasure-filled Renaissance palace on the Grand Canal at Venice—was bequeathed to the city by the Baron Franchetti. The Hertz collection of paintings was left to the Italian Government and is now in the Palazzo Venezia at Rome. In Paris, there was inaugurated in 1936 the Nissim Camondo Museum, of decorative art of the eighteenth century, founded in memory of a young French Jew who died on the field of honour. This is not the only memorial of the family in Paris: for another member, Isaac de Camondo, left his remarkable collection of nineteenth-century art to the Louvre in 1911. At the Louvre too, as at the Bibliothèque Nationale, are many other monuments to Jewish taste, including the wonderful collection of French engravings formed by Baron Edmond de Rothschild, whose munificence is commemorated on a marble tablet in the former institution; here too is the Salle Rothschild, containing masterpieces of gold-work and enamel of the Middle Ages and Renaissance, presented by Baron Edmond's kinsman Adolphe. And it was Daniel Osiris who presented to the French nation the Empress Josephine's home, Malmaison.

In Germany, among a host of important donations, may be mentioned those lavishly made by James Simon to the Kaiser Friedrich Museum in Berlin, and the famous collection of antiquities given by Fritz von Gans to the Altes Museum. The collection of pictures which Jules Bache presented to the City of New York in 1937, valued at some £2,000,000, is among the most munificent gifts ever made to any city.

In England, Jews supported the British Museum almost from its inception: and perhaps the most remarkable accession that the institution has ever received was the great Waddesdon Bequest—in itself almost a complete museum of mediaeval and renaissance art—left to it by Baron Ferdinand de Rothschild in 1898. Some of the greatest treasures of the National Gallery are included in the collection of Ludwig Mond, maintained as a separate entity. Mention must be made also of the great Duveen endowments, at the British Museum, Tate Gallery, and National Portrait Gallery, which transformed that institution from a species of artistic mausoleum of patriotic interest into the palace of delight which it is to-day. All these institutions owe much to the National Arts Collections Fund, one of the founders and greatest supporters of which was the well-known connoisseur, Henry Oppenheimer, whose collections have been mentioned above, and in the support of which Jewish benefactors, such as Lord Bearsted, have been prominent throughout. Somewhat different was the function of Blanche Lindsay, a grand-daughter of Nathan Meyer Rothschild, who (with her husband, Sir Coutts Lindsay) established in the 1870's the Grosvenor Galleries, long the centre of the Pre-Raphaelite school.[1]

§VIII

From the point of view of the conforming Jew, it is perhaps regrettable that persons who were Jews by birth have taken so prominent a share in forwarding the interests of other religions. On the other hand, it is a remarkable commentary upon the religious genius of the Jewish people, and a standing refutation of the preposterous idea (all the more preposterous in view of the notorious aversion of the Jews to proselytisation), that a deliberate attempt is being made by persons of Jewish origin to establish the supremacy of Judaism in the world. One may for the moment overlook the fact that the founders

---

[1] One of the most remarkable acquisitions which the Berlin Museums owe to James Simon (who has been mentioned above) is the famous bust of the Egyptian Queen Nephretiti. Simon was also founder of the German Oriental Society and the most munificent supporter of the German archaeological expeditions to the Near East. Similarly, the collection of modern paintings at the Berlin Gallery was presented by Robert von Mendelssohn, and the German Academy at Rome founded by Edward Arnhold.

of Christianity, many of the Church Fathers (including the first three Popes), and a goodly proportion of the Catholic saints, were of Jewish birth. Coming down to a date when all suspicion of legend disappears one may mention Saint Isidor of Seville, one of the most commanding and devout figures in Spanish Church History of the Visigothic period: or the family of Santa Maria, (descended from Rabbi Solomon Levi of Burgos) who contributed to the Spanish Church in the fifteenth century several prelates and ecclesiastical writers, as well as one of the most active spirits in the Council of Basle.

The tradition has continued to the present time, without interruption. Not many persons of our day have influenced the Catholic Church to a greater extent than the brothers Ratisbonne—Jews by birth—who founded the Order of Notre Dame de Sion in 1842. This was given canonical existence by Pope Pius IX, and consists of Societies of both Priests and Sisters, who maintain schools, orphanages and workrooms for the poorer classes as well as secondary schools for the well-to-do. Under the auspices of the Congregation there has been established the Archiconfraternity of Christian Mothers, which numbers nearly 2,500 branches in different parts of the world. Similarly, the Catholic Church cherishes the memory of the Venerable Francis Mary Paul Libermann, an Alsatian Jew baptised at the age of 22. By his foundation of the Congregation of the Immaculate Conception (since merged in the Congregation of the Holy Ghost) he initiated the modern movement for the evangelisation of the negroes, through which the influence of the Catholic Church has been firmly established in Africa. The movement for the beatification of this convert from Judaism has already made very considerable progress, and it is anticipated that he will shortly be added to the list of officially-recognised Catholic saints.

To take another instance: the Society of St. Vincent de Paul—an international association of Catholic laymen engaging systematically in personal service of the poor —was founded in the middle of the last century by Antoine Frédéric Ozanam, a distinguished jurist and historian, who desired (as he put it) "to insure my faith by works of charity". He belonged, according to the accepted account, to an old French Jewish family: being great-grand-nephew of Jacques Ozanam, the most eminent French mathematician of the age of Louis XIV, whose *Recréations Mathématiques et Scientifiques* continued to enjoy a vogue and to be translated into foreign tongues 150 years after they first appeared. It is asserted, too, that St. Francesco of Paola, who founded the order of the Minims in 1436, was the son of a Jewess.

Turning to the Protestant Church, Sir Culling Eardley, a descendant of the Jewish financier, Sampson Gideon, was founder of the Evangelical Alliance, which secured the independence of the Bulgarian Church and the abolition of the penal laws against the Catholics in Sweden. Michael Solomon Alexander, formerly minister to the Plymouth Synagogue, was responsible for the Anglican missionary activity which established the influence of the Church of England in the Holy Land, and for the foundation of the Anglican Bishopric of Jerusalem, of which he was the first incumbent. Again, Dr. Isaac Capadose was associated with the disciples of Irving in launching the Catholic Apostolic Church; Felix Adler was the founder of the Ethical Culture movement; and Maximilian Low (father of Sir Sidney and Sir Maurice Low) collaborated with Charles Annesley Voysey in the foundation of the Theistic Church.

Finally, the father of Church history in the modern sense is Johann August Wilhelm Neander, originally named David Mendel, who embraced Christianity only at the age of seventeen. His impressive *Allgemeine Geschichte der christlichen Religion und Kirche*, the composition of which occupied over quarter of century, has established his position as one of the greatest Church historians of all time. Yet perhaps his Jewish upbringing was responsible for the spirit which inspired his classical reply to the Prussian government, which had asked his opinion as to whether Strauss's *Life of Jesus* should be prohibited: "Scholarly works are to be fought with the weapons of science, not by the power of the State."[1]

§IX

"God knoweth no vessel so full of blessing for Israel as Peace", runs a well-known Rabbinic dictum. It is not remarkable that a group, brought up under the influence of such an ideal, and aware that the Jewish masses must necessarily suffer to a disproportionate extent in time of war (as they have done throughout history) should have made a practical contribution to the realisation of this hope.[2] After Medicine, the greatest proportion of Jewish Nobel prizewinners received the award for services to Peace. They include Tobias Michael Carel Asser, the famous Dutch jurist and one of the great figures in the development of International Law: and Alfred Hermann Fried, who worked passionately for the ideal of

---

[1] It may be pointed out, incidentally, that not all the Jewish benefactions to Christian objects have emanated from non-professing Jews: for the traditional tolerance has often been sufficiently strong to overlook the difference of faith. Thus the Marrano magnate of the seventeenth century, Abraham Senior Texeira, supplied the copper roofing for the Church of St. Michael at Hamburg: several Jews subscribed to the completion of the Trinity Church in New York in the eighteenth century: while the English Church was first erected at Rio de Janeiro through the exertions of Denis Samuel.

[2] It is not perhaps without its significance that Florence Nightingale's Swiss collaborator, Jean Henri Dunant, founder of the Red Cross, was also one of the great Gentile forerunners of Zionism.

international peace for several decades. The latter, among
his other achievements, founded the German Peace
Society in 1892, and published a series of works dealing
with the subject to which he had devoted his heart.

Lazar (Ludwig) Zamenhof laboured for international
understanding through a different medium. He felt that
a universal language was the one certain means of removing
the conflicts and misunderstandings and differences which
separate nation from nation and create national rivalries.
In the midst of his professional work as a physician, he
worked hard to propagate this ideal, signing his first
essays by the nom-de-plume "Dr. Esperanto". The plan
which he suggested achieved a remarkable success. Within a few years, the new international language had been
created, an international Esperanto Congress had been
held, an Esperanto literature had come into being.
Though the high hopes which the movement once aroused
have not been realised, it has achieved something at least
in that direction, and its utility as an international instrument is incontestable.

Slightly anterior to him, and more important by far,
was Jean (Ivan Stanislavovich) Bloch. He was the
author of a weighty work, published in 1898, in which he
maintained a thesis, now familiar, which was then
strikingly novel. Technical progress, he declared, had
made such strides that future war would mean the
suicide of humanity, and it was vitally necessary to
devise some other means for settling international dis-
putes. This work attracted the attention of the Czar
Nicholas II. Notwithstanding his anti-Semitic bent, the
latter was so impressed that he took the steps which led
to the convening of the Peace Conference at The Hague
in 1899, and ultimately to the establishment of the
Hague Tribunal. A prominent member of this body for
some years was the American representative, Oscar

Straus—subsequently Chairman of the League of Nations Peace Committee. And it was a Chicago Jewish lawyer, Salmon Levinson, who in 1927 first published the plan for the Outlawry of War, which was the basis for the significant, though abortive Kellogg Pact.

Thus, in the present generation, Jews have endeavoured to act up to the noble sentiment expressed by Azariah de' Rossi, nearly four centuries ago (*Meor Enayim*, Mantua 1573, p. 169b):

> All the peoples of the earth should know that while we, the remnant of Israel, live in dispersion, we are obliged, according to the words of the Prophets and the tradition of the Fathers, to pray for the peace and welfare of the state that rules over us. At the present time above all, when for our sins we are scattered to the four winds, it is our duty to supplicate Almighty God for the peace of all the inhabitants of the world, that no people may lift up the sword against another . . . and that He may remove from their hearts all strife and hatred, implanting instead peace in the world: for in their peace we too have peace.

EPILOGUE

As this survey reaches its close, a final word seems needed to ensure that there shall be no misunderstanding as to the object or the conclusion. The names of a large number of Jews have been adduced, whose contribution to European culture, and to human civilisation as a whole, has been of considerable importance. Yet it is not desired to exaggerate the share that these persons of Jewish birth have had in the evolution of the modern world. Of the great names of human history, the Jews have not produced a remarkable proportion, save in the religious sphere with Moses and Isaiah, Jesus and Paul. In modern times, there have been no towering figures, standing head and shoulders above their generation, excepting perhaps Spinoza in the seventeenth century, Disraeli in the nineteenth, Einstein in the twentieth (I leave out of account, of course, those whose essential work was performed within the bounds of their own religious community). The proportion may be respectable; it is not abnormally large.

But it is not by the giants alone that civilisation can be assessed. Great advances in human progress are the work, not of a single genius, but of scores of less-known pioneers, from whose work, experiences, and failures the genius profits. Civilisation is a complex affair. There is constant action and reaction. The more startling results would be in most cases impossible without the painstaking research of scores of humble, unrecorded workers of a previous generation. The battles may be won by the general; they are fought by the private soldiers, and victory is prepared by the laborious plans of the staff. It is accordingly a more solid contribution to progress on the part of any one of the subsections of the human race if it has performed its duty consistently in the lesser functions than if it has contributed one of the giants of discovery, whose intuition and good fortune enable him to sum up the work and the tendencies of his generation.

The Jews have provided both the one and the other. For centuries past, they have formed an integral part of the culture of Europe, and have contributed to it incessantly—as scientists, as men of letters, as translators, as explorers, as pioneers, as physicians. Had Haber or Reiss or Ehrlich not made his discoveries, it may well be that someone else would have done so—a little later, perhaps—for those discoveries were in the air. It is of even greater significance, then, to recall that in the more remarkable achievement, the evolution of that vibrant intellectual atmosphere in which these discoveries were made, the Jews also collaborated effectively—and not in the last century only. Western civilisation would not stand where it does to-day without that collaboration. The world could not afford to dispense with it any more than with that of England, of France, or of Germany.

There is a corollary, however. These Jewish investigators and discoverers had in almost every case non-Jewish teachers on the one hand, non-Jewish pupils on the other; just as many (or most) of the other great scientists and discoverers of modern times received their training partially from, and transmitted it to, Jewish experts. The resultant discoveries cannot be logically qualified as "Jewish" or "non-Jewish". The distinction is, from this point of view, arbitrary and ridiculous. (If the term has been used in the foregoing pages it is simply as a convenient ellipsis, without any exclusive implication.) Such contributions are human; it is absurd to say less, as it is impossible to say more.

The Jew, in fact, is heir to a double tradition. There is the religious history of three and a half millennia, which fructified above all on the soil of Palestine, and with God's help may fructify there again. And there is the political history of the past twenty centuries, which has been associated principally with Europe, in the civilisation of which persons of Jewish birth have taken, not indeed a dominant, nor yet perhaps disproportionate share, but a share which is worthy of study and respect.

The point gains in force from a glance at the map. Palestine, the cradle of the Jewish people, is a narrow, fertile strip on the eastern seaboard of the Mediterranean, between the Arabian Desert and the sea. Let us imagine for the moment that the geological upheaval which is responsible for the present configuration of that area had happened otherwise; that the desert had come down to the sea on the west of the Arabian Peninsula, as it now does on the east: but that instead, on the shores of the Indian Ocean, there were a tiny fertile area capable of human habitation, to which the Israelites had migrated from Babylonia and Egypt. Palestine would thus have faced East instead of West—towards Asia instead of towards Europe.

It is difficult to imagine any slight geological change which would have influenced the history of mankind to quite the same extent. One may imagine that Europe would have remained Pagan, divided between the immoral deities of Rome and Greece and the blood-thirsty gods of the Teutonic Valhalla. The Latin and Greek genius would not have been fertilised by Christian religious thought. It would have lacked the unity and the force which is based in the last instance upon Semitic monotheism. It would have lacked, too, the invigorating influence of the Jewish mind. Notwithstanding its fertility, its favoured geographical position, its temperate situation, Europe might have remained in the condition in which it was left by the Dark Ages.

The Hebraic influence, on the other hand, would have radiated Eastward. India and China, rather than Rome, would have received the Jewish message through Christianity. The Unchanging East would have known those influences which set European thought, discovery and progress in motion. The ingenious inventions of the Orient would have received just that impetus which they lacked. America might have been colonised from Asia instead of from Europe. One may sum the matter up thus: Palestine, though situated on the Asiatic seaboard, is to a large extent cut off from Asia because of the sea of desert which nearly surrounds it; and, facing west as it does, has always had a more important influence on Europe than on Asia (and, reciprocally, has received more important influences from Europe than from Asia), ever since it first came into the orbit of the Greek world in the fourth century before the beginning of the Christian era.

"There is," writes H. A. L. Fisher, in his *History of Europe*, "a European civilisation. . . . It is distinct; it is also all-pervading and preponderant. In superficial area Europe is surpassed by Asia, Africa and America, in population, by the vast stable peasantry of Asia. Yet, if a comprehensive survey of the globe were to be made, it would be found that in almost every quarter of it there were settlements of European men, or traces of the operation of the European mind. . . . The political influences of Europe are apparent even where they are not embodied in direct European control. The ideas of nationality and responsible government, of freedom and progress, of democracy and democratic education, have passed from the west to the east with revolutionary and far-reaching consequences. It is, moreover, to European man that the world owes the incomparable gifts of modern science. It is hardly excessive to say that the material fabric of modern civilised life is the result of the intellectual daring and tenacity of the European peoples."

It is absurd to contest the essential truth of this passage. But one modification is necessary. The term "Europe" is an arbitrary one. To the ancient world, the differentiation would have been meaningless excepting as a mythological exercise. Hellenic culture flourished nearly as much on the shores of Asia—and, at a later date, of Africa—as it did in Greece proper. Lasting contributions to the Roman heritage, whether in literature or in law or in religion, were made by persons living on the southern and eastern seaboards of the Mediterranean. It is hence invidious and inaccurate to place too rigid an interpretation on the terms "Europe" and "European Culture". That civilisation to which Mr. Fisher refers had its birth in the Eastern Mediterranean —not in the irregular peninsula and archipelago which we now term "Greece": it subsequently moved westward: and finally, after the Renaissance, it moved northward and became Oceanic.

The centre of gravity of the Jewish people moved with it: starting in the East, moving gradually to Greece, Italy, France and Spain, finally to northern Europe and the Atlantic seaboard. Each stage of Western culture has affected them profoundly: they, on their side, have (so far as they have been allowed) exercised a considerable influence upon it, at every stage and in every land. There is in this nothing to boast or to parade. Contemporary events have, however, shewn that, even in the twentieth century, it is necessary to emphasise the fact that in the tradition of Western Culture, in all its branches and centres, the share of the Jew has been—as it was proper that it should be—solid, continuous, and integral.

For two thousand years, then, the Jews have formed part of Europe. They have throughout that period—though more intensively during the past century, since the gates of the Ghetto were broken down—made their contribution to the common heritage: sometimes as intermediaries, sometimes as pioneers, more often (so far as their activities were not curtailed) as participants. In the long run, their contribution has become interwoven inextricably with the common stock by a thousand different strands. Disintegrate these, and the tree of western culture would be mutilated. Allow them unobstructed growth, and it may bear in the future through this means fruit yet more splendid than in the past.

Y

BIBLIOGRAPHY

THE nature of this work renders it impossible to give a detailed bibliography illustrating every statement made. The works listed below will give guidance for the reader who desires to study the question more thoroughly. The utility of the volumes is not of course necessarily confined to those chapters in connexion with which they are mentioned. A preference has been given to works in the English language. Those listed in the first group have proved particularly useful throughout.

CECIL ROTH, *A Short History of the Jewish People*. London, 1936.
  (The Bibliography to this mentions most of the more dependable English works on the subject.)
*JOSEPH JACOBS, *Jewish Contributions to Civilisation: an Estimate*. New York, 1919.
The Legacy of Israel. Planned by the late I. Abrahams and edited by Edwyn R. Bevan and Charles Singer. Oxford, 1927.
*ABRAHAM MYERSON and ISAAC GOLDBERG, *The German Jew: his share in modern culture*. London, 1933.
LAURIE MAGNUS, *The Jews in the Christian era from the first to the eighteenth century, and their contribution to its civilisation*. London, 1929.
ELIEZER BEN DAVID, *Gli Ebrei nella vita culturale italiana*. Città di Castello, 1931.
SALO WITTMAYER BARON, *A Social and Religious History of the Jews*. 3 vols. New York, 1937.
The Jewish Encyclopaedia. New York, 1901–1906. 12 vols.
Encyclopaedia Judaica. 10 vols. Berlin, 1928–1934 (incomplete.)
L'apport des Juifs d'Allemagne à la civilisation allemande (ed. Cahiers Juifs). Paris, 1933.

CHAPTER I

THE HEBRAIC HERITAGE

ISRAEL ABRAHAMS, *Permanent Values in Judaism*. Oxford, 1924.
RICHARD G. MOULTON, *Literary Study of the Bible*. London, 1895.

* (It is the author's duty to acknowledge particularly the assistance which he has derived from these three admirable works.)

J. Trénel, *L' Ancien Testament et la langue française*. Paris, 1904.

P. C. Sandys, *Literary Genius of the Old Testament*. Oxford, 1926.

Mayer Sulzberger, *The Am Ha-Aretz : the Ancient Hebrew Parliament*. Philadelphia, 1910.

J. H. Hertz, *A Jewish Book of Thoughts* (latest edition). London, 1937.

Idem. The Pentateuch. Five vols. London, 1929–1936.

(The excursus to this commentary illustrate many instances of Hebraic influences in the modern world.)

William Fairweather, *The Background of the Gospels*. Edinburgh, 1908.

F. J. Foakes Jackson (ed.), *The Parting of the Roads. Studies in the Development of Judaism and early Christianity*. London, 1912.

Nicolas Berdyaev, *The Meaning of History*. London, 1936.

CHAPTER II

THE PROCESS OF DEGRADATION

Marvin Lowenthal, *The Jews of Germany*. Philadelphia, 1936.

Cecil Roth, *History of the Jews in Venice*. Philadelphia, 1930.

Oreste Dito, *La storia calabrese e la dimora degli ebrei in Calabria*. Rocca S. Casciano, 1916.

Israel Abrahams, *Jewish Life in the Middle Ages* (2nd edition). London, 1932.

James Parkes, *The Conflict of the Church and the Synagogue*. London, 1934.

Georg Caro, *Sozial und Wirtschaftsgeschichte der Juden*. 2 vols. Frankfort-on-Main, 1924, 1920.

Joseph Sessa, *Tractatus de Judaeis*. Turin, 1717.

Nathan Morris, *The Jewish School*. London, 1937.

CHAPTER III

THE REVIVAL OF LEARNING

Ernest Renan, *Averroës et l'Averroïsme*. Paris, 1866.

Moritz Steinschneider, *Hebräische Übersetzung des Mittelalters*. Berlin, 1893.

Martin Hume, "Some debts the world owes to Spanish Jews" in *Transactions of the Jewish Historical Society of England*, vi. 138ff.

King Manoel of Portugal, *Catalogue of Early Portuguese Books*. London, 1929–1935.

Umberto Cassuto, *Gli Ebrei a Firenze nell' età del Rinascimento*. Florence, 1918.

L. I. NEWMAN, *Jewish Influence on Christian Reform Movements.* New York, 1925.

MORITZ GÜDEMANN, *Geschichte des Erziehungswesens und der Kultur der abendländischen Juden während des Mittelalters und der neueren Zeit.* 3 vols. Vienna, 1880–1888.

CHAPTER IV

THE GREAT VOYAGES OF DISCOVERY

MORITZ KAYSERLING, *Christopher Columbus and the participation of the Jews in the Spanish and Portuguese Discoveries.* New York, 1894.

A. LIONEL ISAACS, *The Jews of Majorca.* London, 1936.

CHARLES DE LA RONCIÈRE, *La Découverte de l'Afrique au moyen âge.* Vol. I. Cairo, 1925.

CHARLES DUFF, *The Truth about Columbus.* London, 1936.

F. CANTERA BURGOS, *El judio salmantino Abraham Zacut.* Madrid, 1931.

MANUEL SERRANO Y SANZ, *Origenes de la dominación española en América.* Vol. I. Madrid, 1918.

ERNST HEPPNER, *Juden als Erfinder und Entdecker.* Berlin, 1913.

A. SCHÜCK, *Der Jakobstab.* Munich 1896.

CHAPTER V

THE JEW IN LETTERS

D. S. BLONDHEIM, *Les parlers judéo-romains et la Vetus Latina.* Paris, 1925.

LEOPOLD STEIN, *Untersuchungen über die Proverbios Morales von Santob de Carrion.* Berlin, 1900.

E. COTARELO Y MORI, *Cancionero de Anton de Montoro.* Madrid, 1900.

UMBERTO CASSUTO, *Dante e Manoello.* Florence, 1921.

MIGUEL ASIN, *La Escatologia musulmana en la Divina Comedia.* Madrid, 1919.

RICHMON NOBLE, *Shakespear's Biblical Knowledge.* London, 1935.

H. F. FLETCHER, *Milton's Semitic Studies.* Chicago, 1926.

—— *Milton's Rabbinic Reading.* Urbana, 1930.

LUDWIG GEIGER, *Die deutsche Literatur und die Juden.* Berlin, 1910.

GUSTAV KROJANKER, *Juden in der deutschen Literatur.* Berlin, 1922.

J. LICHTENSTEIN, *Racine, Poète Biblique.* Paris, 1934.

M. DEBRÉ, *Der Jude in der französischen Literatur.* Ansbach, 1909.

CHAPTER VI

ART, MUSIC, STAGE

KARL SCHWARTZ, *Die Juden in der Kunst*. Vienna, 1936.

ERNST COHN-WIENER, *Die jüdische Kunst*. Berlin, 1929.

MARTIN BUBER, *Jüdische Künstler*. Berlin, 1903.

A. I. COHON, *An Introduction to Jewish Music*. New York, 1923.

HEINRICH BERL, *Das Judenthum in der Musik*. Stuttgart, 1926.

GDAL SALESKI, *Famous Musicians of a wandering race*. New York, 1929.

LAZAR SAMINSKI, *Musicians of the Ghetto and the Bible*.

A. Z. IDELSOHN, *Jewish Music*. New York, 1929.

M. J. LANDA, *The Jew in Drama*. London, 1926.

EDWARD D. COLEMAN, *The Bible in English Drama*. New York, 1931.

ARNOLD ZWEIG, *Juden auf der deutschen Bühne*. Berlin, 1928.

CHAPTER VII

THE JEW IN EUROPEAN THOUGHT

A. A. ROBACK, *Jewish Influence in Modern Thought*. Cambridge, Mass., 1929.

ARIEL BENSION, *The Zohar in Moslem and Christian Spain*. London, 1932.

ISRAEL EPHROS, *The Problem of Space in Mediaeval Jewish Philosophy*. New York, 1917.

LEON ROTH, *Spinosa, Descartes and Maimonides*. Oxford, 1924.

HARRY AUSTRYN WOLFSON, *Crescas' Critique of Aristotle*. Cambridge, Mass., 1929.

JACOB GUTTMANN, *Moses ben Maimon*. 2 vols. Frankfort, 1908–1914.

DAVID KAUFMANN, *Studien über Ibn Gabirol*. Budapest, 1899.

CHAPTER VIII

SCIENTIFIC PROGRESS

LOUIS GERSHENFELD, *The Jew in Science*. Philadelphia, 1934. (This work must be used with the utmost caution.)

JOSEPH CARLEBACH, *Lewi ben Gerson als Mathematiker*. Berlin, 1910.

CHAPTER IX

MEDICINE

MAX GRÜNWALD (ed.), *Die Hygiene der Juden*. Dresden, 1911.

S. R. KAGAN, *Jewish Contributions to Medicine in America*. Boston, 1934.

I. MÜNZ, *Die jüdischen Ärzte im Mittelalter*. Frankfort, 1922.

HARRY FRIEDENWALD, *The Bibliography of Ancient Hebrew Medicine* (n.d.), and various other writings by the same authority.

MAX NEUBERGER, *Die Stellung der jüdischen Aerzte in der Geschichte der medizinischen Wissenschaften.* Mitteilungsblatt der vereinigung jüdischer Ärzte, April, 1936, Vienna.

I. EPSTEIN (ed.), *Moses Maimonides : Eighth Centenary Memorial Volume.* London, 1935.

I. SIMON, *Asaph Ha-Iehoudi.* Paris, 1933.

SAMUEL KRAUSS, *Geschichte der jüdischen Ärzte.* Vienna, 1930.

DAVID CASTELLI, *Il Commento di Sabbatai Donnolo sul libro della creazione.* Florence, 1880.

AUGUSTO DA SILVA CARVALHO, *Garcia D'Orta.* Coimbra, 1934.

CHAPTER X

THE ECONOMIC SPHERE

COUNT CORTI, *The Rise of the House of Rothschild.* London, 1928.
—— *The Reign of the House of Rothschild.* London, 1928.

WERNER SOMBART, *The Jews and Modern Capitalism.* Trs. by M. Epstein. London, 1913.

LOUIS HERRMAN, *A History of the Jews in South Africa.* Johannesburg, 1935.

H. WAETJEN, *Das Judentum und die Anfäenge der modernen Kolonisation.* Berlin, 1914.

M. STECKELMACHER, *Randbemerkungen zu Werner Sombart.* Berlin, 1912.

M. HOFFMANN, *Judentum und Kapitalismus.* Berlin, 1912.

A. M. VAZ DIAS, *Over den vermogenstoestand der Amsterdamsche Joden in de 17e en de 18e eeuw,* in Tijdschrift voor Geschiedenis, vol. 51, 165–176 (and other studies by the same writer).

RICHARD LEWINSOHN, *Jüdische Weltfinanz.* Berlin, 1925.

HERBERT I. BLOOM, *The Economic Activities of the Jews of Amsterdam in the seventeenth and eighteenth centuries.* Williamsport, 1937.

LUCIEN WOLF, *Essays in Jewish History.* London, 1934.

PAUL EMDEN, *Money Powers of Europe.* London, 1937.

KURT ZIELENZIGER, *Juden in der deutschen Wirtschaft.* Berlin, 1930.

CHAPTER XI

PUBLIC LIFE

ERNEST GINSBURGER, *Le comité de surveillance de Jean-Jacques Rousseau.* Paris, 1934.

RUDOLF SCHAY, *Juden in der deutschen Politik.* Berlin, 1929.

CHAPTER XII

"THE GREATEST OF THESE IS CHARITY"

EPHRAIM FRISCH, *An Historical Survey of Jewish Philanthropy.* New York, 1924.

MAURICE FLEUGEL. *The Humanity, Benevolence and Charity legislation of the Pentateuch and Talmud.* Baltimore, 1908.

WILLIAM MOSES FELDMAN, *The Jewish Child.* London, 1917.

INDEX

(Vital Dates are given—excepting for some contemporaries—only in the case of Jews and persons of Jewish origin).

PRINTED BY PURNELL AND SONS, LTD.
PAULTON (SOMERSET) AND LONDON

A SHORT HISTORY

OF

THE JEWISH PEOPLE

1600 B.C.—A.D. 1935

By CECIL ROTH

With Maps.   18*s. net*

"At last a book has appeared which is in accord with the needs of the time . . . All those who have felt the stirring of their Jewish soul will find what they require in Dr. Roth's very competent volume. . . . Dr. Roth has been eminently successful not merely as an historian but also as an artist."—*The Jewish Chronicle.*

"A triumph of balanced scholarship and lucid statement, in which the author is nowhere overcome by his learning or his loyalties.—*Philip Guedalla in The Sunday Times.*

"Great learning, handled with great discretion, has made it possible for a record covering more than 3,000 crowded years to be contained within a single volume."—*The Times Literary Supplement.*

"Dr. Roth has given us a learned history that is as brilliant as it is comprehensive; nor is it likely to be superseded for many years to come."—*The Church Times.*

MACMILLAN AND CO. LTD., LONDON